D1460496

The Essence of Human Resource Management

PUBLISHED TITLES

The Essence of Human Resource Management

EUGENE MCKENNA AND NIC BEECH

Prentice Hall

London   New York   Toronto   Sydney   Tokyo   Singapore
Madrid   Mexico City   Munich

First published 1995 by
Prentice Hall International (UK) Limited
Campus 400, Maylands Avenue
Hemel Hempstead
Hertfordshire, HP2 7EZ
A division of
Simon & Schuster International Group

Typeset in 10/12pt Palatino
by Keyset Composition, Colchester, Essex

Printed and bound in Great Britain by
T J Press, Padstow, Cornwall

Library of Congress Cataloging-in-Publication Data

McKenna, Eugene F.
    The essence of human resource management/by Eugene McKenna
and Nic Beech.
        p.   cm. – (The Essence of management)
    Includes bibliographical references and index.
    ISBN 0-13-076357-8
    1. Personnel management. I. Beech, Nic. II. Title.
III. Series.
HF5549. M3397 1995
658.3–dc20   95–10434
                                                                    CIP

British Library Cataloguing in Publication Data

A catalogue record for this book is available from
the British Library

ISBN 0-13-076357-8

---

1 2 3 4 5   99 98 97 96 95

To Alison and Linda

Contents

Contents

vii

Preface

Our major aim in writing this book was to introduce the reader to the established topics and critical issues in the broad field of Human Resource Management (HRM) in a succinct way. The student, the HRM specialist and the line manager grappling with people problems will derive benefit from this text which is comprehensive, accessible and up-to-date.

Throughout there is analysis and reflection on both practical and theoretical issues in this developing area of study. In addition, a large number of case studies and vignettes are used to help the reader see the connection between the relevant body of knowledge and its application. By introducing the essence of key current debates in HRM, a balanced view is taken of the present standing and development of this important subject.

1

Introduction and overview

Human resource management (HRM) can be viewed as a comparatively new approach to personnel management which considers people as the key resource. It subscribes to the notion that it is important to communicate well with employees, to involve them in what is going on and to foster their commitment and identification with the organization. In addition, a strategic approach to the acquisition, management and motivation of people is heavily emphasized.

If HRM gets some of its basic sustenance from the practice of personnel management, this begs the question: what do we know about the origins of personnel management and its current standing? Before answering this question, a definition of personnel management would be useful. Personnel management assists with the management of people in an organization. It is concerned with establishing, maintaining and developing systems which provide the framework of employment. These systems operate throughout an employee's membership of the company, starting with the system for entry (recruitment and selection) through the management of the employment relationship (reward, appraisal, development, industrial relations, grievance and discipline), finishing with the termination of the relationship (retirement, resignation, redundancy and dismissal). This management process is underscored by the drive for efficiency and equality of opportunity.

Historical development

In the latter part of the 1800s the concept of welfare personnel developed. This was prompted by the humane concerns of certain families involved

1

in business (e.g. Cadbury and Rowntree), and could be referred to as the Quaker tradition. Welfare personnel was concerned with the provision of schemes, considered progressive at that time, dealing with unemployment, sick pay and subsidized housing for employees. The introduction of these schemes could be viewed as a reaction to the harshness of capitalism at that period of British history. The motives of some industrialists adopting welfare schemes were questioned because there was a belief that some practices were intended as an alternative for realistic wages, and as a ploy to keep trade unions at bay.

Welfare personnel continued as a force until the Second World War, and later manifestations of it were the provision of canteens and company outings for workers. Even today it can be recognized that the welfare tradition has some significance in the practice of personnel management, for example, health schemes and crèches for the children of employees.

The next phase in the development was the emphasis on personnel administration. This amounted to support for management and was basically concerned with recruitment, discipline, time keeping, payment systems, training and keeping personnel records. It came into its own in the period between the First and Second World Wars. The growth in the size of organizations is a factor to consider in connection with this development.

After the Second World War and up to the 1950s personnel management incorporated a wider range of services, including salary administration, basic training and advice on industrial relations, but the main focus was at the tactical rather than the strategic level. Again, increasing organizational size was notable in activating certain changes in industrial relations practices. For example, the movement from collective bargaining at industry level to the level of the company was apparent, resulting in the advent of the industrial relations specialist within personnel management.

The 1960s and 1970s saw a significant increase in the number of staff engaged in personnel work. This could be attributable in part to an increase in the amount of employment legislation. However, the state of the economy had a part to play as well. In conditions of full employment, up to the early 1970s, there was evidence of much recruitment, selection, training and payment system activities in the practice of personnel management. This was prompted to some extent by labour shortages, and was reflected in actions to retain skilled labour and increase the skill levels of the work-force.

The approach to training was systematic and planned, heavily influenced by the establishment of the Training Boards, which exacted a training levy from industry and offered grants to companies that conducted training to acceptable standards. In turn this spawned a rapid growth in the number of training specialists within the personnel function. Related activities, such as performance appraisal (e.g. management by objectives) and management development, also assumed importance, as did forecasting manpower needs (manpower planning).

The prevalence of ideas and insights derived from behavioural science ought to be acknowledged as having a part to play as well. Also during this period the strength of the bargaining power of the trade unions at the work-place was conspicuous. The consequence of greater union influence was a substantial increase in the work load of the personnel specialists. The involvement of the personnel function in matters connected with industrial relations issues, and with productivity deals as well, elevated its concern to some extent to matters of strategic significance to the organization, at a time when most of its activities could be considered as tactical in nature. The emphasis on industrial relations heralded a delicate role for the personnel specialist interacting with both management and workers. This signalled a need to develop negotiation skills and to learn more about various systems of remuneration, and there was a tendency to identify the personnel function with management.

The 1980s saw personnel management entering the entrepreneurial phase, adapting itself to the market economy and enterprise culture. It was not uncommon to find senior personnel executives contributing to the debate within the company about future direction, the relevance of existing business objectives, and improved ways of achieving revised objectives. This era heralded a preoccupation with the management of change, the development of appropriate corporate culture, the acceptance of Japanese industrial relations practices, such as single unions to represent a company's work-force, and Japanese management practices in the form of quality circles and total quality management. A noticeable feature in the practice of industrial relations, in some but not all cases, was the shift in emphasis from work-force collective bargaining to centralized bargaining, and in the process a reduction in the involvement of personnel managers in negotiations at local level.

As the recession in the economy began to bite, the role of the trade unions began to change. The threat of strike action became less effective as organizations could replace workers relatively easily. This resulted not only from the recession and high unemployment, but also from new legislation introduced at this time. The power of trade unions was reduced with the ending of closed shops, and changes in the rules about industrial action, including balloting and picketing.

The relative weakness in the power of trade unions signalled the need for less elaborate processes in collective bargaining and conflict management. It also culminated in swifter negotiated wage settlements. Also, organizations were better placed to make changes in work practices which resulted in increased productivity and a reduction in the numbers employed. There were changes in personnel practices due to the large pool of available labour. For example, the emphasis switched from recruitment (attracting candidates) to selection.

The reduced volume of negotiations based on collective bargaining between unions and personnel specialists, together with the reduction in time devoted to recruitment and selection, provided personnel management with opportunities to manage redundancy programmes and enter negotiations to set lower wage settlements in a relatively calm industrial relations climate.

Then the first signs of fundamental change to the nature of personnel management appeared on the horizon. Hunt (1984) speculated about the personnel function shifting in its emphasis. It was during the 1980s that the rise in HRM began to attract the attention of personnel practitioners. There was a move away from the traditionally adversarial industrial relations of the 1970s towards an approach which sought to achieve excellence in the organization through a committed work-force. The reasons for this will be offered later.

The post-entrepreneurial phase for personnel management in the 1990s is likely to embrace HRM as the standard bearer, though some would argue that HRM will subsume personnel management. The early 1990s witnessed a change in emphasis. The reaction to individualism and unjustifiable greed of the 1980s is likely to make way for the spirit of consent and the value of teamwork. There is concern for core workers who are essential to the operation of the organization since high commitment is required from these workers. They are expected to be flexible about the hours they work and to work above and beyond their job descriptions. Wages tend to reflect the market rate rather than the rate determined by agreements with trade unions. The number of part-time and fixed-term contract workers as a proportion of the total work-force is increasing.

There is likely to be a continuing preoccupation with the value of a strategic approach to human resource management in the context of organizational success. Of course the challenges of the single European market will have to be faced and the significance of the Social Chapter in the practice of human resource management will have to be considered, particularly by companies with European operations. Amongst the issues covered by the Social Chapter are improved working conditions, equitable remuneration, equal opportunities, labour mobility, union representation, access to information and workers' involvement, and health and safety provisions.

Personnel management activities

In organizations of reasonable size one can expect to find a personnel function, just as one would expect to find a finance or marketing function.

However, in the smaller organization this level of specialization may not prevail, and the personnel function is performed by a manager who handles personnel matters in conjunction with other duties. In very small organizations personnel activities could be carried out by all managers. Even where personnel management is normally seen as a specialist function, it could be carried out by other managers where the amount of work did not warrant employing a specialist. Part of the concept of human resource management, by contrast, is that whatever the size of the organization, all managers should be involved.

A number of activities can be identified with the personnel function, though not all the activities listed below may be carried out in some organizations.

Human resource planning

This process has developed from what was previously called manpower planning. Human resource planning is concerned with matching the organizational demand for quantity and quality of employees with the available supply. The demand is derived from current and forecasted levels of company operations. The supply side consists of human resources available both internally and externally. The internal supply, which has been the target for rationalization in recent years, consists of the existing work-force and its potential to contribute. The external supply resides in the population outside the organization and is influenced by demographic trends, developments in education and competitive forces in the labour market within the European Union (EU).The planning exercise outlines the manpower needs of the organization and provides useful information for a number of activities listed below, e.g. selection, training and rewards.

Recruitment

Prior to recruitment, job analysis is undertaken. This is a process whereby the work to be undertaken by an employee is closely examined, and results in the preparation of a job description. Then a specification is produced of the attributes a suitable candidate will need in order to perform the job. The most appropriate means of recruitment, e.g. newspaper advertisement, employment agency or job centre, is specified with the intention of attracting suitable applications.

Selection

A variety of techniques, e.g. application form, interviews, tests and assessment centres, is available to select the best candidate from a pool of applicants. It is likely that a shortlist of applicants will be produced as a first step in the selection process. This may be unnecessary where there are only a small number of job applicants. Some measure, i.e. criteria relating to the ideal candidate, is used to assist in making a selection decision.

Performance appraisal

This is a technique, not universally accepted, of assessing the performance of employees against agreed targets. The personnel practitioners would be most likely to be involved in designing the procedures, leaving the line managers normally to administer the process. This commonly takes the form of an interview following the completion of forms which facilitate assessment of achievement in the period since the last interview (often one year). Performance can be measured against criteria set previously. The outcome could signal the need for training, or in some cases remuneration.

Training

This is a process concerned with establishing what type of training is required and who should receive it. Training ranges from simple on-the-job instruction to educational and training courses offered by providers external to the organization. Training, coupled with development, is apparent when organizations plan the progression of key employees through the company, in which case an attempt is made to reconcile organizational needs with individual career development.

Rewards

This covers a wide area incorporating rates of pay, trade union involvement where appropriate, and other factors such as the use of job evaluation in the determination of rates of pay, methods for calculating pay (e.g. flat rate, piece rate or performance-related pay) and fringe benefits.

Industrial relations

Under this heading could be considered collective bargaining, grievance procedures and employment legislation. In collective bargaining the personnel/industrial relations specialist normally prepares and presents the employer's case in the negotiations with the employees' representative (trade union official). A responsibility of the personnel manager is to monitor the outcome of collective agreements.

With respect to grievance procedures, the personnel manager could be involved in preparing and implementing those procedures and be actively involved in trying to settle disputes that fall outside the collective bargaining process. Disputes within the gambit of collective bargaining could be considered to be group- rather than individual-based matters. The personnel specialist is normally involved in discipline cases, and has the function of gathering evidence and preparing the case, and also ensuring the employee is treated fairly.

The personnel specialist is likely to be called on to give advice on matters connected with employment legislation, and is expected to be conversant with the practical issues relating to the applicability of relevant legal provisions.

Employee communications and participation

This could amount to taking on board activities in connection with communicating relevant information to employees, and arranging for ways in which employees can participate in the processes of the company (e.g. suggestion schemes). In certain circumstances counselling could become part of the service under this heading. Increasingly, participation also incorporates aspects of Japanese management practices, such as quality circles and teamwork, in which operators take over certain aspects of production control such as quality control. In this way employees are involved in decision making which affects their work.

Personnel records

A record of the employee is likely to be kept centrally by the personnel department. This could contain information provided in the original application, with subsequent additions to reflect qualifications and experience gained, achievements and potential. The employee record could provide a useful input to personnel decisions. Records are normally computerized and can be used as part of the human resource planning process.

The personnel activities described above, which are expanded in subsequent chapters, can be executed in diverse ways (Needle, 1994):

☐ The personnel specialist or senior manager with responsibility for personnel matters can be involved at a strategic level at which policies are formulated.

☐ The personnel specialist or senior manager with responsibility for personnel matters provides an advisory service for line managers. For example, he or she could set up a performance appraisal system and advise managers on its use.

☐ The personnel specialist or senior manager with responsibility for personnel matters could join forces with a line manager in order to perform a specific function. For example, the line manager and personnel specialist could sit on the same interview panel when interviewing candidates for a job vacancy.

☐ The personnel specialist or senior manager with responsibility for personnel matters may engage in a specified number of activities, leaving line managers with a high level of autonomy for personnel matters close to their area of responsibility, e.g. selecting their own staff.

In practice, particularly in large organizations, personnel activities will often consist of several of the above roles. For example, if a production manager has a vacancy for a chargehand or team leader, there will be a planning exercise to consider the need for the job, the internal supply of labour and the cost of filling the vacancy. If there is a decision to appoint somebody, the personnel specialist may support the production manager by provision of particular expertise, for instance by drawing up the job specification, preparing the advertisement and advising on the interview process. The employment contract will normally be issued by the personnel specialist. This example indicates a high level of involvement on the part of the personnel function. In some organizations, and often for jobs which are lower in the organization, the involvement of the personnel specialist is less, and may be confined merely to preparing the advertisement and employment contract.

Personnel management versus HRM

Although personnel management shares a platform with human resource management on some key issues – a natural concern for people and their needs, together with finding efficient means to select, train, appraise, develop and reward them – there are some points of dissimilarity. Traditional personnel management tended to be parochial, striving to influence line managers, whereas HRM is integrated into the role of line managers, with a strong proactive stance and a bias towards business. Personnel management has a history of placing emphasis on bureaucratic control often in a reactive sense, i.e. control of manpower and personnel systems. To be fair it has had to respond to various bouts of employment legislation over the years and has been forced to develop adeptness in the design and use of administrative systems catering for statutory and non-statutory matters.

Some of this process was positive in a societal sense; for example, the efforts against unfair discrimination based on sex or ethnic origin. Other acts also had an effect on practice. For example, the Equal Pay Act (1970) (amended 1983) led to a growth in job evaluation in order to establish that people doing the same type of job would be uniformly rewarded. However, some would argue that personnel management represented a highly compartmentalized system, with thinking to match.

By contrast, as the commentary on HRM in the next section will show, HRM makes a determined effort to be a more integrative mechanism in bringing people issues into line with business issues, with a pronounced problem-seeking and problem-solving orientation, and a determination to build collaborative organizational systems where employee development features prominently. The role of top management in setting the agenda for change and development is very much in evidence in HRM. The typical concern here is offering good leadership and vision, with a commitment to creating and sustaining strong cultures which are compatible with evolving business needs. A strong culture is one in which there are clear organizational values and approaches which are held by all the members of the organization.

Some personnel managers will no doubt see the growing influence of HRM as a threat, fearing that they may just become custodians of personnel systems. But the future for the personnel manager, referred to in the literature as the 'deviant innovator' (Legge, 1978), certainly does not look bleak. This type of personnel specialist, though unorthodox in some of his or her ideas, is a thinker, displays impressive professionalism and commands the respect of the line managers with whom he or she interacts (Torrington, 1989). These creative thinking skills are what is required if organizations are to be flexible and adaptive in the context of frequent and ongoing changes in the business environment.

We have already characterized personnel management as a series of activities related to various aspects of an employee's relationship with the organization. Human resource management is also concerned with these issues, but in addition stresses the primacy of business needs. Other points of departure are that HRM embraces individual flexibility and congruency between individual and organizational goals, whereas personnel management is concerned with systems applied to individuals and collectivism.

Distinctive features of HRM

Before looking at the distinctive features of HRM it seems appropriate to identify some of the factors that have led to the creation and popularity of HRM. Forces in the environment have influenced organizations to be responsive. This could be reflected in increased competitiveness, an emphasis on quality in staff and products/services, flexible modes of operation and a willingness to adapt to change. In such circumstances it would not be surprising to find organization and management structures and systems responding to the new business conditions in the changed environment.

Examples of management and organizational responses would be increased decentralization to facilitate a better reaction to market conditions, and greater autonomy and accountability for the efficient use of resources. Also, there could be a striving to inject flexibility in the roles employees play in teams (e.g. autonomous groups) and in getting people to adopt a wider range of skills (multi-skilling). A key point here is that these developments allow an increased speed of reaction which is vital if the organization is to adapt to the changing environmental and market conditions which characterize the current situation. An example of this is the difference between IBM and Apple in their reactions to conditions in the personal computer market (Box 1.1).

Box 1.1

IBM's ORGANIZATIONAL RESPONSE

IBM had become a very large and successful company which dominated the large computer market. It was slow to meet the challenge of smaller organizations such as Apple which operated a team approach to creative thinking and product development aimed at the personal computer market. The teams at Apple were not subject to bureaucratic control and were flexible in the way they explored and exploited ideas. They were small, and responded promptly to events and displayed a high level of individual commitment and flexibility. The result of competition of this nature was that IBM fell behind some competitors in the changing market and profitability was adversely affected. Now IBM is restructuring its organization to decentralize and create business units which are closer to their markets and better equipped to react more quickly.

A major theme running through HRM is the acknowledgement that employees are valued assets of the company, that there should be an interplay between a strategy for human resource and the main strategy for the business, that corporate culture should be managed so as to make it compatible with the requirements of corporate strategy (Beer and Spector, 1985), and that seeking the commitment of employees to the organization is of far greater value than forcing compliance to the demands of the organization. The value of commitment is that it binds employees to the organization. But one has to recognize that commitment to an organization is not something that springs out of thin air with little prodding. Individuals have attitudes and attachments to their own values as well as values connected with membership of the family, the trade union or professional body, and these could clash with commitment to the organizational values. Therefore changes in attitudes and behaviours have to be contemplated.

One can view employee commitment as part of the 'psychological contract'. This is an unwritten contract between management and employees whereby management offers challenging and meaningful tasks and employees reciprocate with loyalty and commitment (Tichy *et al.*, 1982). One should add that commitment on its own, without competence, may be an empty shell.

To elicit commitment, reference is often made to mutuality. This stands for HRM policies that provide mutual goals, mutual influence, mutual respect, mutual rewards and mutual responsibility (Walton, 1985). But mutuality may be a tender creature, as it is not uncommon to find a situation where the employee is short-changed by the employers. In a climate of mutuality the cause of commitment is advanced, with the consequence of both improved productivity and the development of people.

A method used to foster mutuality is the 'development appraisal' discussed in chapter 6. The aim of this approach is not to control the employee by judging past behaviour alone, but to offer encouragement by examining how the employee can contribute to organizational goals, and to specify the nature of the individual's development needs in order to achieve these goals.

Another feature of HRM which is often emphasized is the existence of the 'common interests' of management and employees in the profitability of the enterprise, which can lead to the tapping of a substantial reservoir of initiative and commitment within the work-force. The objection raised to this view is that while it sounds good in principle, in practice there will be divergent interests. For example, the organization could damage goodwill when the wages bill is curtailed following a cost-minimization exercise.

The interaction between the HRM system and the corporate planning process is something which receives special attention. Proactive intervention on the part of the HRM system is advocated here. The guiding light comes from the strategic direction enumerated in the corporate plan. It is expected that the HRM policies and practices that develop as a result of identifying the human resource needs of corporate strategy can prove useful to managers (Guest, 1989; Legge, 1989). The following are examples of questions that might be asked with a view to establishing whether key facets of HRM are underpinning business strategy. Has the organization the right calibre of employee to meet the demands of business strategy? Are the techniques for selection, appraisal and promotion of people supportive of business strategy? Are managers as committed to human resource issues as they are to issues related to their primary specialism and function? Are the employment systems flexible enough to allow speedy adaption to change? (There is further discussion of strategic HRM in chapter 2.)

Other key considerations are as follows (Beer and Spector, 1985):

☐ People ought to be considered as social capital capable of development.

☐ Participation in decision making is of value, and people's choice of options or alternatives ought to be based on informed judgement.

☐ Power should be distributed throughout the organization, rather than centralized, in order to foster trust and collaboration between people who are credited with a realistic sense of purpose.

☐ The interests of all parties with a stake in the organization (e.g. employees, shareholders, suppliers and customers) should be harmonized.

There are two models of HRM: one is called 'hard' and the other 'soft' (Storey, 1992), but this does not mean one is difficult and the other easy. The models are used in the context of problem solving and decision making. A hard problem is one that has a clear definition and an agreed method for working it out, and it will have a definite solution. For example, $2 + 2 = 4$ is a hard problem and solution. Soft problems are less clearly defined, and there are alternative problem-solving methods and potential solutions. An example of a soft problem is how to motivate your subordinates or to suggest the best way to manage people.

In HRM the hard approach is concerned with costs and head counts, and tends to be associated with a unitarist view; that is that the goals of individuals and the organization converge. (This is akin to the 'Michigan School' of HRM (Fombrun et al., 1984), introduced in chapter 2 in connection with strategy.) The following is an illustration of one aspect of the hard approach. In human resource planning the organization will need to know its turnover rate. This gives the number of leavers in a given period as a proportion of the number of employees and is calculated by the formula

$$\frac{\text{Leavers in year}}{\text{Average no. staff in post during year}} \times 100$$

This statistical approach exemplifies the hard approach and naturally is less compatible with ideas derived from behavioural science which are ingrained in the soft approach. The soft approach will be concerned with the complexities behind this simple formula – for example, if there is a high turnover, is this because people are demotivated? If so, what can be done about this situation? The soft model, which is similar to the 'Harvard School' of HRM (Beer *et al.*, 1984), includes the following features:

☐ There is a view that individual needs and organizational needs will not always be the same (i.e. a pluralist view), but the organization will endeavour to balance the different types of needs.

☐ The uniqueness of the human resource must be recognized, and cannot be treated like any other resource. After all, people have feelings and emotions.

☐ People are creative and responsible and can benefit from involement in the participative management process.

☐ A climate of consent features prominently.

☐ There is a belief that commitment by employees to the organization is nurtured when the organization informs them of important matters, such as the mission statement, the values it cherishes and trading prospects. In addition, it is considered wise to involve employees in decisions related to organizational and job design, and allow them to function in self-managing groups.

☐ There is a recognition of the role of trade unions in representing the collective interests of employees, but at the same time it is important to respect the rights of management to liaise directly with individuals and groups within the organization.

Objectives of an HRM system

The following list reflects the major items you would expect to find in a set of objectives relating to an HRM system (Armstrong, 1992):

1. The company's objectives are to be achieved through its most valued resource – its work-force.

2. In order to enhance both individual and organizational performance, people are expected to commit themselves to the success of the organization.

3. A coherent set of personnel policies and practices geared towards effective organizational performance is a necessary prerequisite for the company to make the optimum use of resources when striving to meet business objectives.

4. An integration of HRM policies and business objectives should be sought.

5. HRM policies should support the corporate culture, where appropriate, or change the culture for the better where it is deemed inappropriate.

6. An organizational climate which is supportive of individual creativity and in which energetic endeavours should be nurtured. It will provide a fertile terrain for the promotion of teamwork, innovation and total quality management.

7. The creation of a flexible organizational system that is responsive and adaptive, and helps the company to meet exacting objectives in a competitive environment.

8. A determination to increase individuals' flexibility in terms of the hours that they work and the functions they carry out.

9. The provision of task and organizational conditions which are supportive of people trying to realize their potential at work.

10. The maintenance and enhancement of both the work-force and the product/service.

Implementation issues

Some time is now given to an examination of selective issues associated with the implementation of a human resource management policy. Because of the selective nature of the examination, certain topics are excluded. For example, although some of the concepts and issues (e.g. commitment, mutuality) discussed earlier have features which relate to the implementation process, it is felt that enough has been said about them in this introductory chapter. The issues which will now be discussed are: the role of management, the role of values and culture, the use of personnel management techniques and HRM–business strategy interaction.

Management

There seems to be the view that it is important for management to display a strong interest in the continuing profitability of the organization, with an appropriate vision for the future. The chief executive is said to be an important person when it comes to eliciting the commitment of employees. For example, it is he or she who sets the scene for change, takes responsibility for the change process, and by his or her actions reinforces the existing corporate culture, if appropriate, or reshapes it if not appropriate.

The responsibility for the implementation of HRM policy should rest with all managers who adapt it realistically to local circumstances. Although the personnel function may have been vocal in the setting of the guidelines contained in the HRM policy, it is the responsibility of all managers to implement the policy. The personnel function has the responsibility for monitoring and developing it. Robert Ayling, a previous Director of Human Resources for British Airways, stated that it was BA policy and culture that every manager should be a human resource manager. This emphasizes the importance of people management in all managerial roles.

An important feature is the management of human resources in a strategic way when managers are pursuing normal commercial and organizational   objectives. It seems as if HRM is a frame of mind determining a behavioural perspective on everything a manager does from policy making to normal everyday decision making (Armstrong, 1992).

Values and culture

The culture of an organization is the collection of values, beliefs, attitudes and behaviours commonly held by the members. The culture is learnt and reinforced through interaction. Culture and its management are explicit features of HRM. Values expounded by top management have significance in gluing together policies and practices with respect to human resources. In this context, respect for people is crucial because without respect how can the necessary commitment be created? Commitment is a reciprocal process (Beer and Spector, 1985). To this would be added trust, and its operationalization could be seen in the adoption of open management styles, particularly participative management.

Senior management is strategically placed to imprint its values on human resource policies and practices right across the spectrum of activities, ranging from selection practices to reward systems. In the process, considerable influence can be exerted in shaping corporate culture. Training is commonly used to shape cultures. When British Aerospace wanted to introduce autonomous teamworking at one of its production plants it undertook extensive training of all the work-force affected by the changes. The training was not just in the technical skills which would be needed but also in the culture and behaviour that needed to be developed. It necessitated a movement from a belief in hierarchical organization to an acceptance of organizational roles where greater responsibility and involvement feature prominently.

Commentators who have examined HRM values from an industrial relations perspective refer to the existence of a unitarist perspective (Guest, 1989) in the sense that management and workers share a common interest, and that there is not much need for communication or negotiations between these two camps to be conducted by a representative system associated with the role of trade unions. This can be contrasted with a pluralist system – a voluntary system reinforced by collective bargaining at the local level – where the interests of the employers on one side and employees on the other, including many trade union members, are not seen as identical.

The traditional industrial relations system in the United Kingdom and the rest of Europe is most likely to embrace a pluralist perspective unlike the situation in the United States (although, as stated earlier, union power in the United Kingdom has waned somewhat in recent years). Perhaps a control strategy studded with adversarial industrial relations practice where conflict of interests occupies a position high on the agenda is akin to a pluralist perspective, whilst the unitarist perspective is more compatible with a commitment strategy which in its ideal form reflects mutual interests and respect in interpersonal and management–worker relations, where flexibility exists with respect to the nature of organizational roles, and participative management pervades the area of decision making.

A strong culture underpinning key aspects of organization functioning (e.g. product quality, a climate of creativity, rapid response to environmental pressures) could be associated with an HRM system (Legge, 1989). To some, this could be construed as a control system reinforced by internal propaganda and persuasion to exact commitment from people, irrespective of whether or not it serves their interests. The natural consequence would be to label HRM as a manipulative process. Supporters of HRM might retort by maintaining that HRM is manipulative, but only in a benign way. They might ask what is wrong with a system that offers realistic personal benefits and job security to those who commit themselves to the company's objectives and values, which encapsulate efficiency, innovation, quality products, customer service, etc. – the hallmarks of a potentially successful organization. That is fine if the benefits, etc., are realistic and fairly dispensed!

Earlier in this chapter the virtue of flexibility was acknowledged as a key feature of an HRM system. But can the cause of flexibility be served by a potent, all-pervasive culture which requires employees to conform to specified values? Perhaps flexibility could be neutralized in such circumstances! Where a potent culture supports a prompt reaction to familiar events, because the prevailing ethos accommodates such an eventuality, it could be a different story when the organization faces unfamiliar events (Legge, 1989). In such circumstances the organization could benefit from flexibility to confront novelty and uncertainty but is denied it because of the strong culture. This was the situation in the IBM case described in Box 1.1. IBM had a strong culture and an established way of doing things. Apple was small, flexible and able to try out new ideas and innovate in a highly competitive market. Such a situation also raises the question of the tension between individualism, which flexibility supports, and collectivism, which is promoted by certain features of organizational life. Normally organizations try to tackle this tension, not always successfully, when on the one hand individual competence and achievement are recognized by a reward system, such as performance-related pay for individuals, and on the other the value of teamwork is advocated with reference to autonomous work groups. Further discussion of culture can be found in chapter 3.

Personnel management techniques

The question to ask about techniques is are they good enough to select the right calibre and mix of people, to develop them and to ensure that working relationships and incentives are of the required standard so that their services are retained in the implementation of a realistic corporate plan? Coherence in the application of personnel management techniques is something that is continually stressed. A set of techniques that do not fit neatly together is anathema to the serious HRM practitioner. What is not required is the application of isolated techniques which have more to do with practitioners displaying their technical prowess in their chosen field than tackling problems awaiting solution.

The preferred action is the purposeful interrelationship and reinforcement of the battery of techniques in the service of the organization's objectives (Hendry and Pettigrew, 1990). However, it must be acknowledged that it is no easy matter to develop a consistent and integrated set of personnel management techniques. It requires perseverance, managerial competence and a personnel function tuned into commercial thinking and sympathetic managerial attitudes and behaviour.

The internal coherence of HRM policies in practice could receive a fundamental challenge from the way the organization is structured. (There is a discussion of organization structure in chapter 2.) In well-developed divisional structures, authority can be delegated to business or divisional units with a high level of autonomy. The head office in such a structure might confine itself to overall financial control and setting broad guidelines, leaving the division to implement its own brand of personnel management. Some divisions may adopt a full-blooded HRM approach, but others may not because of an absence of firm guidance from top management at headquarters, in which case there is a lack of consistency in the use of HRM systems.

The role of reward systems is given pride of place in HRM. Reward systems are normally used as a change mechanism to create a more pronounced performance-oriented culture. Also, they can be used to encourage the development of new skills, and can be linked to performance-appraisal schemes. A discussion of reward management appears in chapter 7.

Another technique to consider is training and development because HRM embraces the notion of developing employees and enabling them to make the optimum use of their abilities for their own sake as well as in the interest of the organization. Given the pivotal role of managers in the implementation of HRM policies, they should be targeted for training in this context. Training and development are considered in chapter 8.

HRM–business strategy interaction

Earlier there was reference to the importance of successfully integrating the HRM strategy with the business strategy. It would be a positive advantage if the HRM director or personnel director is involved in decision making with respect to normal business issues at board level. In this way he or she is in a better position to orchestrate the development of HRM strategies that flow from business strategy and to put in place a coherent set of personnel strategies related to selection, training and development, rewards and employee relations.

As was stated above in connection with the difficulties of achieving coherency in the application of personnel management techniques, the successful integration of HRM strategy with business strategy may also be difficult to achieve for the following reasons. There may be a lack of determination to do so; the required managerial competence at all levels may not be available; the personnel function may be too traditional in its outlook and operation; entrenched traditional managerial attitudes and behaviour may still prevail; and if business strategy with its primary emphasis on considerations such as marketing, finance, etc. receives the bulk of attention, human resource issues may be neglected. There is further discussion of the interaction of HRM strategy with corporate strategy in chapter 2.

Conclusions

HRM can be seen as a development which originated from traditional personnel management and which has replaced it to some extent. Key managers and some professionals in the personnel function felt the old system was no longer functional and there was a need for a change in the status of personnel practitioners as well as for getting them more involved in business decisions. HRM also reflects changes in philosophies and practices with respect to the management of people in organizations.

In HRM there is a greater emphasis on strategic issues, and the way in which the human resource contributes to the achievement of corporate objectives. Among the natural concerns of the organization are sensitivity to the needs of stakeholders, the development of human resources to meet future challenges, and ensuring that people's energies are sufficiently focused in order to add value to organizational inputs. HRM underlines the importance of flexibility and the ability to react and adapt quickly to changes in the organization's environment. It is also concerned with quality management, where the requirements of the quality of both the operations of the organization and the product or service trigger a need for high calibre staff to secure competitive advantage.

Although HRM unashamedly embraces a cost-effective business approach, it values employees for perfectly understandable reasons. Being concerned with the well-being of people is seen as a powerful way to motivate and inspire the work-force. HRM takes a systems approach to the analysis and management of organizations. It likes to see the different parts of the organization functioning effectively and together moving cooperatively towards meeting the overall goals of the enterprise. This is facilitated through the management of systems such as human resource planning, recruitment and selection, appraisal, training and development, and rewards. These systems must be integrated and 'pull in the same direction'. In this way the HRM function assists the organization to be more effective and profitable.

References

Armstrong, M. (1992) *Human Resource Management: Strategy and action*. London: Kogan Page.

Beer, M. and Spector, B. (1985) 'Corporate transformations in human resource management', in Walton, R. E. and Lawrence, P. R. (eds.), *Human Resource Management Trends and Challenges*. Boston, MA: Harvard Business School Press.

Beer, M., Spector, B., Lawrence, P., Mills, Q. and Walton, R. (1984) *Managing Human Assets*. New York: Free Press.

Fombrun, C., Tichy, N. M. and Devanna, M. A. (1984) *Strategic Human Resource Management*. New York: John Wiley.

Guest, D. E. (1989) 'Human resource management: its implications for industrial relations', in Storey, J. (ed.), *New Perspectives on Human Resource Management*. London: Routledge.

Hendry, C. and Pettigrew, A. (1990) 'Human resource management: an agenda for the 1990s', *International Journal of Human Resource Management*, **June**, 17–43.

Hunt, J. W. (1984) 'The drifting focus of the personnel function', *Personnel Management*, **February**, 14–18.

Legge, K. (1978) *Power, Innovation and Problem-solving in Personnel Management*. Maidenhead, Berks: McGraw-Hill.

Legge, K. (1989) 'Human resource management: a critical analysis', in Storey, J. (ed.), *New Perspectives in Human Resource Management*. London: Routledge.

Needle, D. (1994) *Business in Context: An introduction to business and its environment*, 2nd edn. London: Chapman & Hall.

Storey, J. (1992) *Developments in the Management of Human Resources*. Oxford: Blackwell.

Tichy, N. M., Fombrun, C. J. and Devanna, M. A. (1982) 'Strategic human resource management', *Sloan Management Review*, **Winter**, 47–61.

Torrington, D. (1989) 'Human resource management and the personnel function', in Storey, J. (ed.), *New Perspectives on Human Resource Management*. London: Routledge.

Walton, R. E. (1985) 'Toward a strategy of eliciting employee commitment based on policies of mutuality', in Walton, R. E. and Lawrence, P. R. (eds.), *Human Resource Management Trends and Challenges*. Boston, MA: Harvard Business School Press.

2

Strategy and structure

This chapter consists of two major parts and deals with issues which interrelate and at times complement each other. The first part briefly examines the nature of corporate strategy and strategic human resource management, and the interaction between the two. The second part will explore the structure of organization, within which strategy unfolds, from a number of angles.

Corporate strategy and strategic HRM

Corporate strategy

Before entering into a discussion of strategic human resource management the concept of strategic planning in business should be examined. In its simplest form it amounts to setting organizational objectives, and then deciding on a comprehensive course of action (i.e. a strategy) to achieve those objectives.

The strategy used is concerned with the efficient use of resources, as well as ensuring that the mobilization of those resources achieves the maximum impact. In this context a company could, for example, focus on the following:

☐ To pursue markets with high growth potential.
☐ To improve channels of distribution.
☐ To reduce the cost structure of the organization through the application of modern technology.

At least five basic steps can be identified in the process of strategic planning (Walker, 1980):

1. *Definition of corporate philosophy and the preparation of a mission statement.* Nowadays it is fashionable to prepare a mission statement which deals with matters such as the values of the organization and the reasons for its existence. A mission statement of a business organization may make reference to the following points:

   (a) the customers to be served in a particular niche of the market; and

   (b) the actions necessary first to serve the needs of customers, stressing, for example, the need for skilled and motivated employees, the pursuit of long-range profits and a commitment to meaningful and comprehensive employee development, second to serve the business, social and cultural needs of the communities in the area where the organization is located, and third to achieve levels of profitability equivalent to the leading companies in the organization's industry.

   It is suggested in some quarters that an organization should be sensitive to threats to its profitability and seriously consider issues such as 'cost leadership' and 'differentiation' (Porter, 1985). Cost leadership could amount to using low cost as a means to enhance competitiveness, and differentiation is visible when a unique product attractive to consumers offers higher profit margins, and competitors find the market difficult to penetrate.

2. *Scan environmental conditions.* This amounts to a systematic analysis of the technological, economic, political and social forces affecting the organization's capability to pursue its mission. Questions that might be asked are as follows:

   (a) Are there advances in technology affecting the organization's production technology, office technology, or product design that should be seriously considered?

   (b) Are there changes in the economy likely to have an impact on the operation of the company?

   (c) Are political circumstances conducive to the exploitation of market opportunities (e.g. market deregulation)?

   (d) Are demographic trends relevant with respect to future availability of labour?

   Taking a particular view of commercial considerations with respect to environmental forces, Porter (1985) draws our attention to the following:

   □ immediate competitors in the industry;

□ the threat emanating from new entrants to the industry;
□ the threat posed by substitute products;
□ the power of buyers;
□ the power of suppliers.

3. *Evaluate the organization's strengths and weaknesses.* Here the focus of attention is the internal resource base of the organization, and a consideration of various facilitating or constraining influences. The following questions immediately spring to mind:

   (a) What distinctive strengths or advantages does the organization possess?
   (b) What critical limitations (e.g. lack of managerial talent to undertake an ambitious project) does the organization have?

4. *Develop objectives and goals.* Having assessed the internal and external factors affecting the capability of the organization (as in 2 and 3 above), and given special consideration to the competitive advantage of the organization in the market-place on the basis of cost structure and product distinctiveness, there is now a movement towards determining specific goals and objectives aimed at fulfilling the mission of the organization. Among the questions to pose at this stage are:

   (a) What are the company's objectives for sales volume, profit and return on capital?
   (b) How can performance be measured in areas such as customer service and employee development?

5. *Develop strategies.* Having gone through the four steps outlined above, the next step is to develop strategies. The types of question relevant at this stage are:

   (a) What specific changes of direction should the company take?
   (b) What new or changed organization structure and processes, technological development, financial arrangements and human resource policies should the company adopt?

   This is the stage where the organization begins to think strategically for human resources. It is acknowledged that unless decisions with respect to human resources are taken by top management, we cannot expect a strategic plan for human resources (Purcell, 1992). When careful attention is paid to matters connected with acquiring, assigning, developing and rewarding employees at the top of the organization, this sets the scene for harmonizing human resource planning with corporate strategic planning.

   Reflecting on the above five steps in the strategic planning process, the impression might be given that this type of activity is neat, rational and free from messiness. The reality could be something different, because of limitations in the information-processing capability of managers faced with conceiving and making sense of options open to them (Lindblom, 1969) and the inherent weakness in the notion of arriving at the outset with an all-embracing corporate strategy. The more likely scenario according to Quinn (1989) is that strategy unfolds from an experimental process in which the organization uses a series of partial steps (logical incrementalism). Although one recognizes that strategy formulation is not purely rational, nevertheless it is important for an organization to have a long-term view of the direction it is proposing to take, and at the same time to develop response flexibility so that it can adapt to significant internal and external events. (A sister text on the essence of strategic management expands on a number of the points raised above; Bowman, 1990.)

Strategic HRM

A school of thought in HRM, known as the Michigan School (Fombrun *et al.*, 1984), places a lot of emphasis on the importance of a strategic approach. This involves relating corporate strategy to strategic HRM issues in areas such as structure, discussed later in this chapter, culture, discussed in chapter 3, and employee resourcing and development discussed in chapters 4–8. The closeness of the connection between corporate strategy and strategic HRM is understandable if we recognize that a predominant concern with HRM is functional in terms of organizational success. For example, Hendry and Pettigrew (1986) emphasize the role of HRM in creating a competitive advantage for the organization. In essence this means that HRM techniques (e.g. selection, training and rewards) should complement each other and that corporate strategy and HRM should coalesce if we are to be realistic about a positive outcome.

However, it is argued that in some circumstances there is a certain incongruency between corporate strategy and strategic HRM (Legge, 1989). This could arise when, for example, the corporate plan dictates cost minimization through a reduction in labour costs. Putting such a plan into action could involve making staff redundant, and this could run counter to an HRM perspective that puts the accent on commitment to employees. In this illustration we see HRM as reactive to corporate strategy. The opposite, a proactive stance, would be a more preferable course of action according to some researchers (Tyson and Witcher, 1994). This could manifest itself as HRM having a proactive role in batting for the interests of the human resource (e.g. actively putting forward an expenditure plan for the long-term development of employees) in the corporate planning process.

Finally, there are those who argue against matching corporate strategy with strategic human resource management (Boxall, 1992; Kamoche, 1994). In particular, Kamoche does not like the idea that investment in the human resource can only be justified if it leads to a concrete improvement in organizational performance, because the latter is subject to a number of factors (e.g. market forces) quite independent of the specific contributions of employees. Boxall could envisage a situation whereby it would not be possible to pursue a particular business opportunity enshrined in the corporate plan because of the implications in terms of fundamental changes to the contract of employment which would be unacceptable to the employees concerned.

It has been suggested that the basic human resource techniques or activities (i.e. recruitment and selection, performance management, reward management, training and development) can be related to corporate strategy at three different levels of the organization as follows (Hall and Goodale, 1986):

1. *Strategic.* At this level attention is focused on the interface between the organization and the external environment and the primary interest is the organization as a total entity. There is a natural concern with long-term issues, although short-term performance considerations are not ignored. One would expect a director of personnel or human resources to play an influential role as a member of the top management team and the following activities are likely to feature prominently at this level:
   (a) succession planning – aimed at providing future generations of managers;
   (b) human resource planning – laying the foundation for forecasting the quantity and type of staff needed over, say, the next decade;
   (c) performance management – specifying the type of performance evaluation system likely to be most suited to the organization and capable of producing the best results;
   (d) reward management – deciding on the reward system most likely to be effective in the future, and identifying the type of rewards that ought to be linked to the attainment of long-term business objectives;
   (e) training and development – outlining a general development plan to nurture the future work-force.

2. *Managerial.* At this level, one step removed from the top, the emphasis is on refining human resource policies, practices and systems. Long-term plans and policies for human resources are translated into specific systems, such as the design of a recruitment and selection process, or a reward package. It is important that this takes place within the

boundaries set by the guidance and direction originating from the strategic level.

For example, a bank devised a clear business strategy to move into non-traditional financial services and consultancy. At the strategic level a decision was made to devise a reward system which would dispense higher rewards to staff working in the new area. As a result, the bank established a policy to have a differentiated reward system. At the managerial level it was the responsibility of line managers, aided by an HRM specialist with expertise in the area of rewards, to develop differentiated reward systems.

3. *Operational*. This is the level where supervisors and operatives are involved at the 'coalface' in the production of goods or the rendering of services. Here the appropriate human resource systems are operationalized. Using the banking example above, the final course of action would be the dispensing of rewards to employees.

Practice of HRM

Uniformity is unlikely to prevail in approaches to strategic planning; in fact distinctiveness within and between organizations is the more likely practice, and it should be acknowledged that lower levels of the organization can also exert influence in the determination of strategy (Tyson and Witcher, 1994). Although there is evidence to support a significant adoption of HRM practices in organizations, it appears that companies will not pursue all aspects of HRM practice at the same time and it is likely that priorities will be given to certain techniques over time (Storey and Sisson, 1993). For example, development with the accent on teamwork could receive substantial endorsement at a particular moment in time and other activities could be shelved for the time being.

Storey and Sisson noted that there was little evidence to substantiate the link between corporate strategy and HRM strategy. The lack of this link was also found in a sizeable number of organizations in a survey of HRM practices in the Republic of Ireland (Monks, 1992), but it was present in a survey of UK companies when the following practices were studied: employee and management development, employee relations and organizational development (Tyson and Witcher, 1994). However, there is some recent evidence indicating a less than satisfactory relationship between HRM strategy and corporate strategy. For example, surviving workers in some 'right-sized', 'right-skilled' organizations are showing disaffection. This can arise from job insecurity and increasing workloads, and is reflected in lack of pride in working for the company and low trust in the organization. The danger with this employee disposition is that it could undermine people's capacity to be innovative, adaptable and customer-oriented (all cherished HRM characteristics).

The Leading Edge Forum, a collaborative venture which includes the London Business School and organizations such as W. H. Smith, British Telecom and the National Health Service, suggested that personnel departments are failing to adopt a long-term view of their impact on business strategy because of organizational pressures to meet short-term goals, as well as their own natural predilection for short-termism. Personnel departments were, however, applauded by the Forum for developing close working relationships with line managers (Pemberton and Herriot, 1994). The practice of HRM is described in the case of Singapore Airlines (SIA) in Box 2.1, showing the integration of the different strands of HRM strategy and the link between corporate strategy and strategic HRM.

In this case SIA faced an uncertain environment, and a clear message was to control costs. The company pursued a strategy aimed at market differentiation through innovative approaches to the provision of quality services. To achieve these objectives the practice of HRM supported the drive for quality. This was evident in the way the selection and appraisal processes were operated, and career development plans and rewards were geared to fostering commitment and identification with the organization.

Organization structure

Organization structure is the infrastructure within which strategy is conceived and implemented. Since HRM has an overwhelming interest in providing people with space and opportunity to utilize their abilities and skills to an optimum level, it pays particular attention to the way organizations and jobs are designed. In this part of the chapter there will be an examination of theories and perspectives on organization structure and design. There is a specific reference in chapter 7 to job design as an outcome of the application of motivation theory.

Classical bureaucracy

A concept of bureaucracy was developed by Weber (1947), a German sociologist. In its ideal form it was known as the rational–legal framework. This type of organization is rational because it is specifically designed to perform certain functions, and it is legal because its operation is based on a set of rules and procedures for every position or job within it. Weber

Box 2.1

HRM AT SINGAPORE AIRLINES

Singapore Airlines (SIA) has experienced rapid growth over the past 22 years and currently employs approximately 23,000 people. The company has received high ratings in a number of market research surveys and has won a number of awards for quality service.

The business environment facing the company was challenging and volatile. Deregulation of the airline business in the United States and competition from carriers in the Asia Pacific region, whose costs were lower, led to increased competition and fare reductions. SIA has differentiated the service it offered from that of immediate competitors by projecting an image of high quality in many spheres of its operations, ranging from global in-flight telecommunications at the disposal of passengers to the ticket reservations service.

The two major categories of operational costs are fuel and staffing. Efficiency through savings in fuel consumption is achieved by having a young fleet of aircraft. The average aircraft age in the SIA fleet is five years, whereas the industry average is eleven years. There is a determination to control costs through productivity increases and to maximize quality through linked human resource strategies of recruitment and selection, performance appraisal, career development and rewards. These strategies are considered to be equally important and mutually interdependent.

The selection process is thorough and rigorous for all potential employees. Apart from the interview, there is a reliance on psychometric tests. The company places a lot of emphasis on selecting applicants who are likely to fit the corporate culture which is task-oriented. SIA sees training and development as a very important HRM technique to equip employees to do their jobs better, as well as contributing to career development. Line managers play a key role in the orchestration of training related to job skills (e.g. computing skills). Training directed at the development of more general skills (e.g. management skills) is coordinated centrally. On average each employee receives eleven days of training each year.

There are two systems of performance appraisal: one for senior staff and the other for staff generally. Assessment of an individual's potential and career planning is a distinguishing feature of the appraisal of senior staff. With regard to career development, there is a strong tendency to fill senior posts from the lower ranks. Therefore, those with good potential satisfy their needs for advancement by progressing within the organization, and many others are given the opportunity to move horizontally to broaden their experience. In practice, most employees have the chance to change jobs every four years. The staff turnover rate is rather low (between 3 and 6 per cent).

Rewards consist of a package of benefits. Apart from pay, the benefits include medical insurance, travel loans and share options. There are performance-related and profit-related components built into overall pay. Total benefits are thought to be attractive, but actual pay is not high by the standards of pay offered by other Singaporean employers.

(Chee, 1993).

distinguished the legal–rational model from other models he had in mind, namely charismatic (leader-driven) and traditional (influenced by custom and practice). The features of classical bureaucracy (legal–rational) are as follows:

- ☐ Clear definition of duties and responsibilities.
- ☐ Maximum specialization.
- ☐ Vertical pattern of authority.
- ☐ Obedience to authority.
- ☐ Post-holders rely on expertise derived from technical knowledge.
- ☐ Maximum use of rules.
- ☐ Impersonality in administration.
- ☐ Remuneration is determined by rank and job responsibility.
- ☐ Promotion is determined by seniority or achievement as judged by superiors.
- ☐ Clear separation between ownership of the organization and its control.

It is now apparent that bureaucratic organization in its ideal form is heavily dependent on rules, procedures, well-defined duties, relationships and responsibilities. It is allegedly a rational, impersonal system of organization, free from the whims and preferences of individuals who occupy roles within it.

Scholars who studied the blueprint of classical bureaucracy felt it had a number of shortcomings. For example, it was felt that the pressure placed on the individual to act methodically and cautiously, with strict adherence to rules and procedures, could create a situation where the preoccupation with the means to the end becomes far more important than the end itself. Also, there could be a ritualistic attachment to rules and procedures, with undue insistence on authority and status rights, which could have the effect of not advancing the interests of the organization. In such a setting, resistance to change could become a real issue. Finally, even if classical bureaucracy could be justified as functional, this is likely to happen only in conditions where tasks are simple and repetitive and are performed consistently over time. But where tasks become more complex and subject to change, the conditions likely to be compatible with classical bureaucracy cease to exist.

Classical principles

The classical principles of organization developed by theorists and practitioners many years ago still have some relevance when the structure of organization is studied. In this section the classical principles will be acknowledged in their original form, but at the same time interpretations will be forthcoming in order to put them in a present-day context. The following classical principles are examined:

1. *Division of labour.* Economic benefits can result from the breaking down of tasks and allowing the employee to specialize in a narrow area. Specialization makes it possible to apply technology to tasks, with potential for productivity gains, and facilitates ease of training. Although certain segments of the working population may be happy with routine jobs and repetitive tasks that flow from the division of labour and specialization, others may have a preference for enriched jobs and can be more productive in such conditions. In the final analysis the negative effects of repetitive work have to be offset against the alleged economic benefits.

2. *Unity of command.* The subordinate reports to only one superior from whom he or she obtains advice and guidance. Having access to only one official source of direction and assistance might be construed as restrictive, and could be a negative influence when coupled with the division of labour.

3. *Authority and responsibility.* Rights vested in the position occupied by the employee are referred to as authority. The obligations placed on employees to perform are referred to as responsibility. Authority and responsibility are co-equal. Authority can be delegated within the organizational 'chain of command', but responsibility probably cannot, though this requires clarification. It is accepted that ultimate responsibility cannot be delegated, but there can be delegation of operational responsibility.

   Authority can be referred to as line authority, that is the type of authority which each manager possesses, and it flows through the chain of command. This should not be confused with the authority of the staff specialist (e.g. HRM specialist) whose role is to help the line manager in executing his or her responsibilities.

   The concept of authority had greater validity in the days when superiors were knowledgeable about all the jobs within their area of influence. Today over-reliance on authority could be dysfunctional if subordinates are well trained and the superior is not fully conversant with everything within his or her section. Also, it would be unwise to place reliance on authority to the exclusion of other factors, such as the persuasive skills and power base of the manager.

   What is becoming more apparent in the age of HRM is the strengthening of the role of the line manager with the accent on its 'enabling' aspects in a climate of teamwork, participative management and availability of various specialisms, either internal or external to the organization. Currently, it is customary to refer to authority as part of a larger concept of power.

4. *Span of control.* The span of control refers to the number of subordinates reporting to one boss. It was originally suggested that the number should not be more than six. The span of control has an inverse relationship to the number of layers in the hierarchy (e.g. the narrower the span of control, the more layers there are in the hierarchy). When a conscious decision is made to widen the span of control it could be associated with a growth in the number of better qualified and more experienced employees. The flatter organizational structure which is created by the wider span of control is popular today.

The following factors are likely to influence the size of the span of control:

(a) job complexity (the more complex the job, the greater the justification for a narrower span of control so that the supervisor has the capacity to assist the subordinates);

(b) physical proximity of subordinates (a wider span of control is more manageable if subordinates are geographically closer to their boss);

(c) extent of formalization and standardization (it is easier to justify a wider span of control when the jobs of subordinates are governed by well-specified rules and procedures) – these will be examined again later;

(d) preferred managerial style. (Some managers could feel comfortable and confident supervising a large number of people, and because of the wide span of control they resort to delegation of authority in a pronounced way. Such a course of action could cramp the style of other managers who prefer a narrower span of control.) There is also reference to managerial style in chapter 9.

5. *Departmentalization.* In effect this is a form of division of labour, whereby certain cells of specialized activity are created which require overall coordination. This seems to be as far as classical theory goes in addressing the question of departmentalization. If we take departmentalization a stage further, the following groupings emerge:

(a) functional – there is a division of the organization by function, such as finance, manufacturing, HRM and so on;

(b) product or service – there is a division by product, e.g. ICI's Paints Division, with associated functions such as production, marketing, etc., while a division by service is evident when a firm of chartered accountants is organized in accordance with service to clients, e.g. auditing, taxation, insolvency;

(c) customer – the nature of the customer base determines the structure used; for example, in a particular company there could be a wholesale division as well as a retail division;

(d) process – in a manufacturing company production processes can be differentiated by section or department, e.g. a manager with responsibility for a particular production process would report to the manager of the plant;

(e) geographic – a part of the organization, e.g. sales/marketing function, is fragmented on a regional basis.

The types of departmentalization described can be combined to create a mixed structure. For example, one might find functional department-alization having within its boundaries process departmentalization and a sales function organized by region. Within the region there could be departmentalization by customer. (An important feature of HRM is giving pride of place to the customer.)

Matrix organization

This system of organization integrates two groupings. For example, a project department (e.g. a Vehicle Centre in the Ford case study in Box 2.2) is superimposed on the division by function described above. In practice this means that a particular employee belongs to a function (e.g. marketing) but also works on a project. Effectively he or she reports to two supervisors – one is the manager of the project and the other is the boss within the function. Matrix organization can be a complex system and if it is to be effective it has to be operated with a certain amount of skill.

Among the problems to anticipate are role conflict among subordinates because of the dual system of reporting and power struggles about the use of authority in particular situations (Larson and Gobeli, 1987). Reflecting on the proposed global matrix structure for the Ford Motor Company, which is examined in Box 2.2, Lorenz (1994a) had this to say about matrices in general:

the matrix organisation used by multinational companies in the 1960s and 1970s, especially by US companies, was, with a few notable exceptions, plagued by internal conflict, inefficiency, expense and delay, as divisional, geographic management debated and fought with each other. In many cases disputes were only resolved laboriously by powerful coordinators acting as matrix police.

You will notice in the case in Box 2.2 that HRM techniques are mobilized to sustain the new form of organization. The concept of the team (the project team) seems to be an important feature of matrix organization. As we shall see later, in the spirit of HRM teams are created to cut across departmental boundaries to promote flexibility and innovation, with the needs of the consumer high on the agenda.

Box 2.2

GLOBAL MATRIX AT FORD

In early 1995 the Ford Motor Company merged its North American and European operations into a single global structure. A justification for the change is that the old 'command and control' culture promoted the power of departmental barons at the expense of innovation, prompt decision making and cross-functional teamwork. The company created five transatlantic 'Vehicle Centres', four located in the United States and one in Europe. Each centre has responsibility for designing, developing and launching a particular size and type of vehicle for the North American and European markets. In addition, the centres have responsibility for the cash flow and profitability of each product throughout its life. Ford's Asia Pacific and Latin American operations remain separately organized for the time being.

The new structure consists of a matrix organization, and as a consequence a large number of managers will have more than one boss. They will report to a manager from the 'vehicle centre' to which they are attached, but they will also report to a boss in their 'functional' department (e.g. manufacturing or marketing). Within the company there seems to be a lot of enthusiasm for the new matrix structure. It is suggested that it will promote flexibility, considerable informality, allow for improvisation as situations change, and is vital to global teamwork and organizational effectiveness.

Ford hopes to prevent the matrix organization from being overcome by the problems stated earlier that have traditionally bedevilled this type of structure by proposing to take the following action:

- Take extra precautions to make sure that objectives are agreed precisely between the vehicle centres and the functional parts of the organization.
- State clearly the roles and responsibilities of individuals in both arms of the matrix.
- Only appoint people to senior executive positions who have proved they are capable of working with colleagues on a collaborative basis.
- Train all those involved in developing cooperative modes of working implicit in operating a matrix system, in order to avoid the need for policing mechanisms.
- Adjust the performance appraisal and reward management techniques in order to harmonize with the new system of organization.
- Introduce much more intensive and open communication than the organization has been accustomed to.

Apart from the adoption of matrix organization, the transformation of the company called 'Ford 2000' also includes measures such as delayering and business process re-engineering (a topic discussed in chapter 3).

(Lorenz, 1994a).

Organizational configuration

The configuration or mode of arrangement of the organization will be examined in the first instance from the angle of the five traditional features listed below. These features indicate the level of complexity within the organization. Subsequently, there will be a brief acknowledgement of the six types of configuration identified by Mintzberg (1983).

1. *Vertical differentiation.* This is concerned with the number of levels or layers within the hierarchy through which control and coordination are exercised. Because information has to flow through a number of layers, the potential for problems connected with the dissemination of information and the monitoring of operations is ever-present.

2. *Horizontal differentiation.* This is akin to the division of labour and specialization, whereby specialist activities are arranged in a lateral form and staffed by employees with specific orientations. For example, employees in the finance function could interpret commercial reality differently from those in the HRM function. This could give rise to communication difficulties which ultimately could affect modes of cooperation.

3. *Spatial differentiation.* If the organization is fragmented in a geographical sense we refer to spatial differentiation.

4. *Formalization.* The key characteristics of formalization are job descriptions and well-defined procedures. When formalization is rated highly, employees have little opportunity to exercise discretion and use initiative in the job. The reverse is the case in conditions where formalization receives a low rating.

   The position of a job within the hierarchy can determine the degree of formalization. For example, we expect employees occupying positions in the higher echelons of the organization to exercise more discretion in making decisions than employees located further down the organization. The particular type of function might also be a factor influencing the degree of formalization. For example, the production function may lend itself to a higher degree of formalization than the marketing function. Finally, where formalization is well established, the terrain is fertile for standardization to take root.

5. *Centralization/decentralization.* These occupy the opposite positions on a continuum and reflect the location of decision making within the organization. Factors likely to influence centralization or decentralization are as follows:

   (a) The organization is geographically dispersed (spatial differentiation) and this signals the need for decentralization. However, if an organization has sophisticated and comprehensive management information systems aided by information technology, it would appear that there is a strong drive to go in the opposite direction and resort to centralization.

(b) Where spatial differentiation is not an issue because the organization is located on one site, decentralization could be used for reasons connected with stated corporate policy or managerial preferences. A justification to adopt the opposite position and use centralization could be an attachment to the notion of bureaucratic control, or the existence of autocratic tendencies within the organization.

Mintzberg (1983) identified six types of structure, each appropriate to the dominant needs of the organization as follows:

1. *Simple structure.* This structure could apply to a recently created organization where authority is centralized in the hands of the owner manager or small group. The trappings of a bureaucratic organization are minimal.

2. *Machine bureaucracy.* This structure has a number of the features of bureaucratic organization referred to earlier and assumes the characteristics of the mechanistic system of organization discussed later in the chapter. The organization is large and long established and operates in a relatively stable environment.

3. *Professional bureaucracy.* This structure allows the exercise of professional expertise where autonomy and the absence of rigid status differentials prevail (e.g. the traditional hospital or college). There is a tendency not to place too much emphasis on bureaucratic practices.

4. *Divisional form.* This structure is appropriate for a large, well-established company with a number of different markets. The company could be organized by, for example, product or service referred to earlier, but there is a tendency to adopt machine bureaucracy.

5. *Adhocracy.* This structure could apply to a total organization or a division within it. The organization which is designed to promote innovation operates in a complex and dynamic environment. Employees with expertise, who tend to be attached to project groups with a market orientation, exercise a lot of power and influence. The attachment to the project group conjures up images of the matrix organization examined earlier.

6. *Missionary.* This could be considered to be lacking in features of formal organization. For example, division of labour and specialization is not very pronounced. People are bound together by their shared values.

Formal and informal organizations

A distinction can be made between the formal and the informal organization. Many of the features of organization discussed earlier (e.g. span of control and hierarchy), coupled with the stated objectives of the organization and the roles assigned to individuals, reflect the formal organization. By contrast, the informal organization is flexible with a fluid structure. In the informal organization the degree of informality stems from the interaction of role occupants or employees and it can be harnessed to complement the aims of the formal organization. For example, it could promote a sense of identification with the organization, a sense of belonging and motivation. However, the informal organization has the potential to undermine the effectiveness of the formal organization.

Contingency perspectives

Over the years researchers have studied the form organizations take, and a general conclusion is that structure is determined by circumstances.

Technology and structure

Burns and Stalker (1961) found that mechanistic (bureaucratic) structures had greater relevance when stability prevailed in markets and in the application of technology to operations within organizations. As you would expect, mechanistic structures are characterized by a pronounced vertical and horizontal differentiation, high formalization, centralization and limited upward communication.

Where conditions were unstable, that is markets were unpredictable and there was uncertainty with regard to the application of technology, organic structures were considered more appropriate. In the organic structure, conditions opposite to those applicable to the mechanistic structure applied, as follows:

☐ There was a lesser degree of horizontal differentiation, with greater collaboration between staff at different hierarchical levels and across functions.

☐ There was a lesser degree of formalization, and a greater degree of decentralization.

☐ Responsibilities were less clear-cut, with people interpreting and responding to events in the light of circumstances.

☐ Communication was more likely to take the form of communication networks in which the giving of information and the exercise of control originated not from the apex of the organization but from cells of the organization where the greatest knowledge and expertise resided. Also, lateral communication between employees of different rank, resembling consultation more than command, was considered more important than communication that flowed through formal channels organized on a hierarchical basis.

☐ Community of interest – in current parlance 'shared vision and values' – was a more important influence on behaviour than contractual obligations.

☐ Teams consisting of different specialists (e.g. design, engineering and production) operate better if they are located near each other, and the best way of managing innovative projects is through multi-functional teams led by the same manager from the idea-generation stage through to completion.

The book containing the research evidence of Burns and Stalker has been re-issued by the publisher thirty-three years after it was first released, and was praised recently by a respected journalist in the management field for the quality of its ideas, which he says had a profound impact on contemporary theory and practice (Lorenz, 1994b).

Another researcher interested in factors that determine organization structures was Woodward (1965). She studied the influence exerted by technology. The term 'technology' can be broadly defined to embrace the activities associated with the transformation of various inputs into the output of the organization. In a factory the production system is a technology. In Woodward's research companies were categorized by the types of production systems used; for example, unit or small batch production, large batch or mass production, and process production.

Certain features of organization – e.g. hierarchical level or vertical differentiation, span of control, formalization and standardization – moved in sympathy with the technology adopted. Successful companies in a particular category of production system tended to have similar organization characteristics, and generally speaking organic structures were better suited to unit, small batch and process production companies, while mechanistic structures were most effective when aligned with mass production companies.

In later research Woodward and her colleagues studied the ways in which companies used control systems and how these influenced the design of organizations. Control was viewed from the standpoint of personal control (supervision) or impersonal control (administrative monitoring and control systems), and where it was located (i.e. localized or centrally focused).

Another way of looking at the influence of technology was proposed by Thompson (1967). The categories he used to classify all types of organization are long-linked, mediating and intensive technologies:

1. *Long-linked technology.* Tasks or operations which flow in a particular sequence and are interdependent are referred to as long-linked. This type of production system is found on the assembly line in, for example, a car manufacturing plant whereby one operation has to be completed before another starts.

2. *Mediating technology.* This type of technology includes the tasks and operations involved in linking clients using the services of two different functions of the organization. For example, clients of a bank are treated as depositors in one function and as borrowers in another. The depositors are on the input side of the organization and the borrowers are on the output side. In this example the success of the bank depends on satisfying the needs of disparate groups, and it performs a mediating function in linking units or groups which are otherwise independent.

3. *Intensive technology.* When tasks or operations are geared to tackling problems in conditions where the exact response or solution is unpredictable, we enter the domain of intensive technologies. For example, a firm of management consultants has a number of specialists on its payroll. The firm is invited by a client to conduct an investigation into problems or difficulties experienced by the client. These could be messy problems requiring in the first instance a judgement on their nature and subsequently a decision on which consultant(s), e.g. from marketing, HRM or finance, to allocate to the assignment.

There is no direct link between the system of technology used and structural characteristics of organization in Thompson's research. What he maintains is that the organization arranges its structural characteristics in such a way as to protect the technology from the uncertainty surrounding it. To confront uncertainty, either in the sources of supply of raw materials or in the distribution network, a manufacturing company may adjust structure in a particular way. In these circumstances the technology used could be instrumental in shaping the structure of the organization.

There is also recognition of a connection between technology and structure when it is stated that mechanistic structures are more likely to be associated with companies using long-linked and mediating technologies, whilst the intensive technology could fit the organic structure.

A different interpretation of technology was advanced by Perrow (1970). He emphasized technology based on knowledge rather than production technology. The emphasis is on task variability and problem analysis. The interactions of these variables are shown in Figure 2.1. Where there are a multitude of ways of performing tasks, i.e. there are many exceptions to the general rule, and the approach to the analysis of problems is ill defined because of the complexity of the situation, the job is likely to be

Task variability

		Few exceptions		Many exceptions
Well defined		Routine		Engineering
			1	2
			3	4
Ill defined		Craft		Non-routine

Problem analysis

Figure 2.1 Dimensions of knowledge based on technology.

of a non-routine nature as shown in Figure 2.1 (Cell 4). By contrast, where there are few exceptions to the general rule on job performance, and the approach to problem analysis is well defined, the job is likely to be basic and clear-cut, i.e. routine as shown in Figure 2.1 (Cell 1). An example of a routine job is that of a car park attendant who issues tickets in return for a stated sum of money. The job of a management consultant of some stature or a senior social worker who enjoys autonomy and a lot of scope to interpret situations in conducting assignments could be described as non-routine – Figure 2.1 (Cell 4). The construction of a unique building uses engineering technology, and although it can be undertaken in a ratio-nal and systematic way, there could be a large number of exceptions (Cell 2). Craft technology could be used by an electrical technician who could face a relatively difficult problem governed by few exceptions (Cell 3).

Activities falling into the upper part of the figure lend themselves to systematic analysis, whilst those in the lower part of the figure call for more discretion and intuition. The former are likely to be more compatible with mechanistic structures, and the latter with organic structures.

New techology: In recent years the impact of new technology on organizations has been analysed. Employees at the lower levels of the organization have access to a greater quantity of information owing to the availability of information technology (IT) systems, and the justification for highly centralized structures is difficult to defend. As a result, the cause of decentralization is advanced. However, one has to acknowledge that the growth of IT systems could lead to the pendulum swinging in the direction of centralization. This could arise because senior managers have access to information previously non-existent or difficult to obtain. Because senior managers are better informed about events throughout the or-ganization, there is not the same need as in the past for a number of layers in the hierarchy. As a result, the organization ends up with a simplified and compressed structure having removed layers of middle management which are no longer required (Huber, 1990; Reed, 1989).

In the IT age it is becoming a live issue to support production technology by production systems based on 'just in time' (JIT). Japanese car firms were the first to develop JIT and a number of UK companies followed in their footsteps. JIT is a manufacturing and stock system whereby component parts arrive just in time to be used in the manufacturing process, thereby obviating the necessity to hold stock at the levels required under the old system. There are cost advantages arising from reducing buffer stocks in the warehouse, but because of the reduced stock levels, employees are expected to be flexible and to solve problems as they arise, otherwise the next stage in the process will be adversely affected (Tailby and Turnbull, 1987). In effect JIT can promote employee flexibility and multi-skilling.

Size and structure

The outcome of the Aston Studies (Pugh *et al.*, 1968) indicated that it was size rather than technology that bore the strongest relationship to dimensions of organization structure, such as specialization, formalization and centralization, though technology had an impact closest to its area of influence (e.g. shopfloor). It is easy to appreciate the significance of size. Increasing the number of employees can lead to greater horizontal differentiation (i.e. more specialized activities) and greater vertical differentiation to facilitate the coordination of specialized functions. This sets the scene for greater reliance on rules and regulations (formalization). With growing complexity owing to the above factors, the exercise of personal control by management could become difficult, hence the need to resort to decentralization.

Strategy and structure

The main emphasis in this relationship is that changes in corporate strategy can lead to changes in the structure of organization. It has been suggested that decision makers at top management level make choices about the strategic direction of the organization and that this results in a reshaping of structure (Child, 1972). A major proposition put forward by Chandler (1962) is that as corporate strategy shifts from a position where it is concerned with a single product to being preoccupied with product diversification, the management of the company will tend to develop more elaborate structures in order to achieve an optimum result. Effectively this means starting with an organic structure and eventually adopting a mechanistic structure.

In the light of recent evidence, the strategy/structure proposition is taken a stage further. There is a view that organizations who have embraced an 'innovation' strategy need flexible systems normally associated with organic structures where prominence is given to a loose structure, a low level of division of labour and specialization and formalization, and a pronounced emphasis on decentralization. In different conditions an alternative arrangement could apply. For example, a mechanistic structure might be considered functional when a company goes through a period of rationalization and cost reduction. In this case the suggestion is that there is a significant division of labour, with high levels of formalization and centralization. Finally, where a strategy of what is called 'imitation strategy' applies (where organizations try to capitalize on the best aspects of both an 'innovation' and 'cost minimization' strategy), the result is a combination of both mechanistic and organic structures where tight controls apply to current activities and looser controls to new ventures or developments. Organizations adopting an imitation strategy move into new products or new markets after innovative competitors have proved that a market exists. In essence, they copy the successful ideas of innovators (Robbins, 1992).

Power/control and structure

Very briefly, the power/control explanation states that an organization structure could be determined by the outcome of power struggles among influential competing factions within the organization who are intent on advancing their personal interests. Power may also be derived from sources external to the organization. For example, the funding levels of local government can be influenced by their readiness to adopt flexible structures (including a significant amount of contracting out of work) approved by central government in the UK.

Organizations as open systems

Organizations are not closed systems since they relate to an external environment, such as the financial and legal systems, customers or clients, suppliers, the labour market or regulatory bodies. Therefore, they are open systems. As open systems, organizations can face stable or dynamic environments; the latter are more common nowadays and can create environmental uncertainty. In order to reduce or minimize uncertainty emanating from events such as changing customer tastes, serious challenges from new competitors, threats to sources of supply of raw materials and so on, the organization could modify the way it is structured.

Emery and Trist (1965) examined four types of environment which they referred to as follows:

1. Placid randomized (relatively unchanging).
2. Placid clustered (relatively unchanging, but there are clusters of threats of which the organization ought to be aware).
3. Disturbed reactive (more complex environment, with many competitors).
4. Turbulent field (a rather dynamic environment with a high degree of uncertainty).

The disturbed reactive and turbulent field environments – a common sight at the present time – are more likely to be compatible with an organic structure, while the placid randomized and the placid clustered environments which are becoming increasingly rare nowadays could match a mechanistic structure.

Lawrence and Lorsch (1967) were also interested in the relationship between the environment and organization structure. They studied companies facing different degrees of environmental uncertainty with reference to two dimensions of structure, namely differentiation (horizontal) and integration.

Differentiation exists when those who control different functional units or departments vary in their outlook and objectives. For example, the head of the manufacturing unit has objectives and an orientation at variance with those of the head of the finance unit and this is understandable because they relate to different external sub-environments. A particular sub-environment for the finance unit or function could be the regulatory agency controlling the disclosure of financial information, while for the manufacturing unit or function it could be externally prescribed technical specifications with regard to product quality or safety.

Integration refers to the process of bringing activities together and achieving unity of effort within the organization, and this function is even more important if there is pronounced differentiation.

Successful companies had structures more suited to the demands of their particular environments. Since an organization could be relating to a number of sub-environments, the key to success was to match particular sub-environments with organizational functions. For example, a certain type of functional activity within the organization (e.g. product advertising) faces a dynamic sub-environment, and as a consequence adopts an organic structure, whereas a particular accounting activity interfacing with a relatively stable sub-environment operates within the confines of a mechanistic structure. Another finding from the Lawrence and Lorsch study was that the more diverse the environments faced by the company, the greater the amount of horizontal differentiation within the organization; and that successful companies were those that had established a high degree of integration for coordinating the various functions in the achievement of organizational goals.

When focusing on functions or sub-systems within organizations, we could quite easily turn our attention to the socio-technical systems approach to studying organizations. This approach looks at the organization as an open system structured in such a way as to integrate two major sub-systems, namely the technical (i.e. task) and the social sub-systems. The technical sub-system is concerned with transforming inputs into outputs and the social sub-system relates to the interpersonal aspects of life in organizations. The socio-technical systems approach developed from the research of Trist and Bamforth (1951) when they examined the effects of the introduction of new techniques in British coal-mining many years ago. The expected productivity gains failed to materialize because of problems with the social sub-system due to the splitting up of well-established work groups. Here we see that improvements to the technical sub-system did not produce the desired result because of the adverse effect this development had on the social sub-system.

Box 2.3

AUTONOMOUS WORK GROUPS AT SCOTTISH AND NEWCASTLE BREWERIES

Fork lift truck crews, responsible for loading and unloading delivery lorries and conveying kegs to and from the production line, were closely supervised and had no discretion on how to perform their work. An experiment in job re-design took place in which each crew was formed into a team and allowed to organize how their work should be carried out. A crew would decide how work should be allocated among team members, and were briefed on such matters as the stock position and deliveries. The role of the foreman changed to that of a 'consultant' to the teams when they encountered problems they could not solve for themselves. Features of the new situation were improved communication, regular consultative meetings, better training, a more pleasant physical working environment, and the introduction of a revised payment system. The experiment was considered to be very successful.

(Department of Employment, 1975).

The researchers suggested that the technical and social sub-systems could be integrated through the medium of autonomous work groups. These groups aim to facilitate cooperation between the two sub-systems so that they function for the good of the overall system. Autonomous work groups are related to task redesign, particularly job enrichment referred to in chapter 7, and wider issues connected with group interaction, remote supervision and other aspects of organization design (see Box 2.3). An important feature of the socio-technical systems approach to organization design is the belief in the importance of harmony between the social and technical sub-systems.

Organizational trends

In recent years much has been said about the changes to traditional organization structures that are considered necessary for companies to meet future challenges more effectively. Kanter (1989) maintains that future successful organizations will be post-entrepreneurial. By this is meant that organizations need to take entrepreneurship beyond its present position by combining the creative elements of the role of the entrepreneur and the more disciplined corporate approach which in an HRM sense would entail taking on board a commitment to cooperation and teamwork. There is a need for faster and more creative action within the organization, and for closer partnerships with stakeholders, e.g. employees, suppliers and customers. Organizations need to be flexible and free from cumbersome bureaucratic structure if they are to cope well with changing markets and technology, and the external environment at large. In Kanter's terminology, 'corporate giants . . . must learn how to dance'.

Acceptance of the model of the post-entrepreneurial organization would necessitate the adoption of three main strategies, with a consequent change in values, as follows:

1. *Restructuring to find synergies.* This means that there is an effective rearrangement of the constituent parts of the organization so that the value added by the cooperative effort of the whole is greater than the sum of the individual parts. Such an eventuality could arise when a company goes through a process of downsizing (cutting numbers) of central corporate staff and the removal of layers at middle management level. In the Ford Motor Company's organizational transformation (Ford 2000), referred to earlier in the chapter, there is expected to be a reduction in the average number of layers in several parts of the organization from fourteen to seven (Lorenz, 1994a).

   The manifestation of the restructuring could be seen in changes to the tasks previously carried out by the layer of management which has been removed. Authority could be delegated to lower levels of the organization. This process could be facilitated by giving work groups more autonomy and by enhancing information technology systems to cope with the collection and exchange of information as well as the monitoring of operations.

   In order to react more quickly, large corporations have set up small 'business units' within the organization, and others have contracted out non-core activities (e.g. catering and security) which were previously carried out in-house. The results of these changes can be smaller organizations with flatter and more focused structures concentrating on 'core' business activity. The challenge facing HRM is to ensure that the changes described are introduced without demotivating the employees affected.

2. *Opening boundaries to form external strategic alliances.* As organizations concentrate on their core activities they can benefit from forming short-term strategic alliances with other organizations. These alliances assume various forms and, for example, may involve two organizations in a particular market collaborating on some aspects of research and development of mutual benefit to both of them, but too costly or difficult to undertake alone. In another situation a management consultancy firm and a hospital form an alliance to market consultancy services to other hospitals. The hospital, as part of the health sector, can establish contact with other health sector organizations more quickly and easily than the consultancy firm which supplies the services.

3. *Create new ventures from within the organization* (i.e. ventures based on innovative practices). One way to promote innovation is to commission the formal research and development department, where one exists, to generate new ideas and projects. However, Kanter acknowledges another source from which fertile ideas can spring: essentially the flexibility built into the structure of the organization and the work-force.

   For example, to encourage innovation the organization could establish short-term interdisciplinary teams to undertake particular projects. In this arrangement team leaders would put a lot of emphasis on their advisory role, where they offer support to well-qualified team members, and would prefer empowering people rather than monitoring or controlling their activities in a traditional sense (see Box 2.4). These teams would then disperse on the completion of the projects and subsequently undertake a new set of tasks under a different arrangement.

Another observer of the organizational scene recognizes that companies now operate in a tougher, more competitive and changing environment (Handy, 1989). He sees UK organizations as becoming less labour-intensive and moving towards structures where a central core of knowledge-based workers control the technology and operations of slimmed-down companies. Value is added not through the use of muscle power but through an input of knowledge and creativity. According to Handy, the future organization will have a core of well-informed employees with ready access to relevant ideas and information (i.e. knowledge workers). This is similar to what Drucker (1988) called the information-based organization. The core workers are referred to by Pollert (1988) as a group with permanent employment contracts and job security who are multi-skilled and able to

Box 2.4

EMPOWERMENT

Empowerment is a recent management practice concerned with giving frontline employees more responsibility, resources and authority. It is something that is far more than delegation: in effect it means harnessing the creativity and brainpower of all employees, not just the chosen few such as managers. Properly empowered employees are well placed to maximize their potential, and in the process enhance the competitive advantage of their organization. Empowerment is seen as supportive of a no-blame culture, where mistakes are seen as learning opportunities.

In an Industrial Society (1995) UK survey it was found that the managerial group most enthusiastic about the idea of empowering employees were senior managers. In some cases empowerment was introduced following the appointment of a new chief executive and had the effect of reducing the number of layers of management, normally at middle management level. In certain situations respondents noted other changes such as wider spans of control, managers exercising lesser control coupled with the use of supportive management, and a greater readiness to embrace HRM practices. Finally, the main motive for increasing empowerment at work was to make better use of people's skills, though customer service was also emphasized.

---

perform a variety of functions (i.e. functional flexibility) which may cut across traditional occupational boundaries.

Surrounding the core of knowledge workers would be outside workers – a contractual fringe – operating on a sub-contracting basis and paid a fee rather than a wage. The management of this group (periphery workers) is removed from the organization that is receiving its services. A further consideration is the use of a part-time and flexible labour force. This group of temporary or casual workers are less costly for the organization because their services will only be used to meet particular demands, and released when they are no longer required. In essence the organization is using what Atkinson called 'numerical flexibility' (Pollert, 1988).

Another form of flexibility is called 'financial flexibility' where the organization adapts its labour costs to its financial position (Pollert, 1988). Examples of this would be that the size of the pay packet would be determined by the profits made by the company (e.g. profit-related pay), and relating payment to the performance of specific tasks (e.g. the fees paid to a sub-contractor for doing a particular job).

The changes outlined above will have an impact on the management of human resources. The trend towards information-based organizations and the use of computer-aided production reduces the need for unskilled and semi-skilled production workers. There will be a changing pattern of employment, and an increase in the proportion of the labour force devoted to short-term contract and part-time employees. (Recently, a House of

Lords ruling in the UK parliament supported an EU prescription on rights to certain employment conditions for part-time workers previously the preserve of full-time workers.)

The appearance of flatter organization structures will reduce the opportunities to improve pay through progression within the hierarchy, but such a development offers greater possibilities for the introduction of performance-related pay discussed in chapter 7. The position of the 'core' workers warrants careful attention because their hours of work and the demands on them (e.g. greater flexibility with regard to working practices) are likely to be on the high side. However, we must not lose sight of the likely disadvantages of being a peripheral worker – lack of job security and perhaps very limited training opportunities.

Finally, the 'network organization' is likely to pose a different challenge to the management of the traditional organization. For example, organizations could concentrate on things they do particularly well, outsourcing functions that can be done quicker and more effectively, or at lower cost, by other companies. One company in the network may research and design a product, another may engineer or manufacture it, and a third may handle distribution. This could allow for greater specialization and encourage innovation; it could require less time and effort to be put into planning and coordination now that a number of functions have been hived off (Snow *et al.*, 1992).

Conclusions

Strategy and structure are interrelated and together are crucial for the success of the organization. Determining the nature of the structure of the organization can be an important strategic decision where top managerial influence plays a key role. However, the various environments (e.g. technological, market, economic, political) to which the organization is exposed also play a crucial role in the determination of strategy and structure.

Organizational environments are turbulent and change is always present. This places a great responsibility on the shoulders of strategic HRM to be proactive in developing the organization's flexibility and creativity to capitalize on opportunities and to sustain competitive advantage. Interfacing corporate strategy with strategic HRM has significance in highlighting the importance of the human resource in contributing to organizational success. Therefore, having in place sound structures and processes which allow people to pull together with commitment in a climate of mutual benefit is a laudable aim.

References

Bowman, C. (1990) *The Essence of Strategic Management*. Hemel Hempstead: Prentice Hall International (UK).

Boxall, P. F. (1992) 'Strategic HRM: beginnings of a new theoretical sophistication', *Human Resource Management Journal*, **2**, 60–79.

Burns, T. and Stalker, G. M. (1961) *The Management of Innovation*. London: Tavistock Publications.

Chandler, A. (1962) *Strategy and Structure, in History of the Industrial Enterprise*. Cambridge, MA: MIT Press.

Chee, L. S. (1993) 'Singapore Airlines: strategic human resource initiatives', in Torrington, D., *International Human Resource Management*. Hemel Hempstead: Prentice Hall.

Child, J. (1972) 'Organisation structure, environment, and performance: the role of strategic choice', *Sociology*, **6**, 1–22.

Department of Employment (1975) *Making Work More Satisfying*. London: HMSO.

Drucker, P. F. (1988) 'The coming of the new organisation', *Harvard Business Review*, **January/February**, 45–53.

Emery, F. E. and Trist, E. L. (1965) 'The causal textures of organisational environments', *Human Relations*, **February**, 21–32.

Fombrun, C., Tichy, N. M. and Devanna, M.A. (1984) *Strategic Human Resource Management*. New York: John Wiley.

Hall, D. T. and Goodale, J. G. (1986) *Human Resource Management: Strategy, design, and implementation*. Glenview, IL: Scott, Foresman.

Handy, C. (1989) *The Age of Unreason*. London: Business Books.

Hendry, C. and Pettigrew, A. (1986) 'The practice of strategic human resource management', *Personnel Review*, **15**, 3–8.

Huber, G. P. (1990) 'A theory of the effects of advanced information technologies on organisation design, intelligence, and decision making', *Academy of Management Review*, **15**, 47–71.

Industrial Society (1995) Report: 'Managing best practice', Issue No. 8 (London).

Kamoche, K. (1994) 'A critique and proposed reformation of strategic human resource management', *Human Resource Management Journal*, **4**, 29–43.

Kanter, R. M. (1989) *When Giants Learn to Dance: Mastering the challenges of strategy, management and careers in the 1990s*. London: Unwin.

Larson, E. W. and Gobeli, D. H. (1987) 'Matrix management: contradictions and insights', *California Management Review*, **Summer**, 126–138.

Lawrence, P. R. and Lorsch, J. W. (1967) *Organisations and Environment: Managing differentiation and integration*. Homewood, IL: Irwin.

Legge, K. (1989) 'HRM: a critical analysis', in Storey, J. (ed.), *New Perspectives on Human Resource Management*. London: Routledge.

Lindblom, C. (1969) 'The science of muddling through', in Etzioni, A. (ed.), *Readings in Modern Organisations*. Englewood Cliffs, NJ: Prentice Hall.

Lorenz, C. (1994a) 'Ford's global matrix gamble', *Financial Times*, 16 December, p. 13.

Lorenz, C. (1994b) 'Pioneers and prophets: Tom Burns', *Financial Times*, 5 December.

Mintzberg, H. (1983) *Structure in Fives: Designing effective organisations*. Englewood Cliffs, NJ: Prentice Hall.

Monks, K. (1992) 'Models of personnel management', *Human Resource Management Journal*, **3**, 29–41.

Pemberton, C. and Herriot, P. (1994)' Inhuman resources', *The Sunday Observer* (Business Section), 4 December, p. 8.

Perrow, C. B. (1970) *Organisational Analysis: A sociological view*. London: Tavistock Publications.

Pollert, A (1988) 'The flexible firm: fixation or fact?', *Work, Employment and Society*, **2**, 281–316.

Porter, M. E. (1985) *Competitive Advantage*. New York: Free Press.

Pugh, D. S., Hickson, D. T., Hinings, C. R. and Turner, C. (1968) 'Dimensions of organisation structure', *Administrative Science Quarterly*, **13**, 65–105.

Purcell, J. (1992) 'The impact of corporate strategy on human resource management', in Salaman, G. (ed.), *Human Resource Strategies*. London: Sage Publications.

Quinn, J. B. (1989) 'Managing strategic change', in Asch, D. and Bowman, C. (eds.), *Readings in Strategic Management*. Basingstoke, Hants: Macmillan.

Reed, M. (1989) *The Sociology of Management*. Hemel Hempstead: Harvester Wheatsheaf.

Robins, S. P. (1992) *Essentials of Organizational Behaviour*. Englewood Cliffs, NJ: Prentice Hall.

Snow, C. C., Miles, R. E. and Coleman, H. J. (1992) 'Managing 21st century network organisations', *Organisational Dynamics*, **Winter**, 5–20.

Storey, J. and Sisson, K. (1993) *Managing Human Resources and Industrial Relations*. Buckingham: Open University Press.

Tailby, S. and Turnbull, P. (1987) 'Learning to manage just-in-time', *Personnel Management*, **January**, 16–19.

Thompson, J. D. (1967) *Organisations in Action*. New York: McGraw-Hill.

Trist, E. L. and Bamforth, K. W. (1951) 'Some social and psychological consequences of the Longwall method of coal getting', *Human Relations*, **4**, 3–38.

Tyson, S. and Witcher, M. (1994) 'Getting into gear: post-recession HR management', *Personnel Management*, **August**, 20–24.

Walker, J. W. (1980) *Human Resource Planning*. New York: McGraw-Hill.

Weber, M. (1947) *The Theory of Social and Economic Organisation* (translated by A. Henderson and T. Parsons). New York: Oxford University Press.

Woodward, J. (1965) *Industrial Organisations: Theory and practice*. London: Oxford University Press.

3

Culture and change

There is a relationship between strategy and structure examined in the previous chapter and culture and change which will now be addressed. The structure of an organization is subjected to some form of change periodically and it would be barren without a culture. Likewise strategy and culture can be interactive. Before we discuss organizational culture, the concept of culture at the societal level is briefly acknowledged.

Societal culture

Culture has been a subject of investigation in social anthropology where researchers have sought to understand the shared meanings and values held by groups in society which give significance to their actions. So to understand actions and behaviour at a religious ceremony in a particular country, it would be most helpful to have an insight into the underlying system of beliefs. Nationality is an important factor to consider in the context of values and behaviour. For example, there is some evidence to indicate that the Americans adhere to values associated with individuality, the Japanese are partial to conformity and cooperation in groups, whilst Arabs tend to steer clear of conflict and place loyalty ahead of efficiency. In looking at differences between countries, considerations other than national culture should be given due weight. For example, the legal system and political institutions can shape the national character.

Cultural differences between nationalities were found when the views of a large number of employees spread over many countries but employed by the same organization were solicited (Hofestede, 1980). Hofestede concluded that national cultures could be explained with reference to the following factors:

1. *Power distance.* This factor measures the extent to which culture prompts a person in a position of authority to exercise power. Managers operating in cultures ranked high in power distance (e.g. Argentina) behaved rather autocratically in conditions of low trust, and there was an expectation on the part of subordinates that superiors would act in a directive way. By contrast, in cultures ranked low in power distance (e.g. Canada) a closer and warmer relationship existed between superiors and subordinates, where the latter would be expected to be involved in decision making.

2. *Uncertainty avoidance.* This factor measured the extent to which culture encouraged risk taking and tolerated ambiguity. People in cultures that encouraged risk taking were inclined to take risks and were ranked low in uncertainty avoidance. Such people (e.g. in Hong Kong) encountered less stress from situations clouded with ambiguity and placed less importance on following the rules. By contrast, people in cultures ranked high in uncertainty avoidance (e.g. Iran) tended to be risk-aversive. Features of the behavioural pattern of people displaying risk-aversiveness when confronted by situations high in uncertainty avoidance are working hard, displaying intolerance towards those who do not abide by the rules and staying in the same job for a long time, in order to reduce the high levels of anxiety and stress stemming from conditions of uncertainty.

3. *Individualism–collectivism.* This factor gauged the extent to which culture measured an individual as opposed to a group perspective. In a culture with an individualistic bias (e.g. the United States) there would be a pronounced emphasis on the exercise of individual initiative and performance with a tendency to be preoccupied with the self and the immediate family. By contrast, in collectivist cultures (e.g. Singapore) there exists a broader set of loyalties to the extended family and, where appropriate, to the tribe. In return for loyalty the individual gets protection and support.

4. *Masculinity–femininity.* This factor measured the extent to which culture measured what were called 'masculine' as opposed to 'feminine' characteristics and would be reflected in the type of achievements that are valued. Masculine cultures (e.g. Italy) place much emphasis on the acquisition of material possessions and an ambitious disposition, and there is a clear differentiation between male and female roles. By contrast, the emphasis appears to be on concern for the environment, the quality of life, and caring in feminine cultures (e.g. the Netherlands).

Organizational culture

It is apparent from Hofestede's work, which has been the subject of some criticism, that national cultures impinge on practices within the organization. That provides a cue to direct our attention to a study of organizational or corporate cultures. Shein (1990) defined organizational culture as a pattern of basic assumptions that a given group has invented, discovered or developed in learning to cope with its problems of external adaptation and internal integration. This pattern has worked well enough for the group to be considered valid and therefore is to be taught to new members as the correct way to perceive, think and feel in relation to those problems. An alternative definition provided by Moorhead and Griffin (1992) states that organizational culture is a set of values, often taken for granted, that help people in an organization understand which actions are considered acceptable and which unacceptable. Often these values are communicated through stories and other symbolic means.

Culture became an issue in the 1980s with attempts to unravel the secrets of Japanese business. Certain fundamental values in Japanese society, such as social solidarity, respect for elders and a strong work ethic, influenced behaviour in organizations. Generally the Japanese corporate culture is supportive of seniority-based pay, job security, uniformity in dress and facilities (e.g. canteen), importance of duty, careful attention to employee selection and training, and a quality-driven system of organization and management. However, a direct threat to certain values, e.g. seniority-based pay and job security, has come about as a result of the economic recession in Japan in the early 1990s.

In the early 1980s the economic success of Japan was attributed to a mixture of US and Japanese practices by Ouchi (1981) in his Theory Z, as follows: a predominant concern for people; a guarantee of long-term employment; decision making based on shared values and collective responsibility; a 'clan' approach to participation, with strong social pressures to encourage performance; high trust and faith in the managers' ultimate judgement; and non-specialized career pathways. The end result was mutual commitment, that is employees responded to the commitment made by the employer by a pledge of commitment to the organization.

The corporate welfare and paternalistic aspects of Japanese organizational cultures can be found in a particular ideology. This is the ideology of loyalty to one lord as derived from the Japanese appropriation of Chinese 'Confucian' principles and the feudal legacy (Wilkinson and Oliver, 1992). As stated earlier, in effect societal values in Japan have permeated the fabric of the organization. It would appear that the best course of action by management in the West, who would like to import and use Japanese management practices, is to adapt them to their particular circumstances, rather than transplant them in their entirety.

The relationship between organizational culture and performance in the United States was emphasized by Peters and Waterman (1982) when they associated certain management practices with success. In essence these were: adopt an action-oriented and decisive management; identify and serve the customer's needs; encourage independence and entrepreneurial flair with assistance provided by small cohesive groups; involve people at all times in the management of the enterprise in conditions where top management are seen to be in touch with employees; confine the organization's activities to what it knows best and avoid diversification into unknown territory; avoid complex hierarchical arrangements; and combine central direction with autonomy for the work group.

This research captured the spirit of the times (early 1980s) and offered an American solution to the challenge of Japanese competition. Peters and Waterman felt that the curriculum in business schools with the predominant emphasis on strategy, structure and quantitatively driven systems was ill-conceived. To them success rested on a number of factors, such as those mentioned above, which gave more weight to the 'soft' characteristics of HRM – namely staff, style, systems, skills and shared values. Acceptance of the 'excellence theories' propounded by Peters and Waterman would entail paying more attention to leadership, corporate culture, quality, management of change and, of course, HRM in general. It is easy to find fault with the research of Peters and Waterman, in particular the methodology, but it should be borne in mind that this work attracted the attention of top management and succeeded in shifting the focus of management thinking so that much more weight was given to policy issues in HRM (Guest, 1994).

There have been attempts to relate culture to the design of the organization. In this context four types of organizational culture have been proposed (Harrison, 1972):

1. *Power culture.* A small number of senior executives exert much power in a directive way. There is a belief in a strong and decisive stance to advance the interests of the organization.
2. *Role culture.* There is a concern with bureaucratic procedures, such as rules, regulations and clearly specified roles, because it is believed these will stabilize the system.
3. *Support culture.* There is group or community support for people which cultivates integration and sharing of values.
4. *Achievement culture.* There is an atmosphere which encourages self-expression and a striving for independence, and the accent is on success and achievement.

A modified version of this typology is proposed by Handy (1985) who acknowledges types 1 and 2 above and adds task culture (e.g. utilization of knowledge and technical competency in project teams) and person culture (e.g. personal needs and preferences are seriously considered in the assignment of tasks). The typologies examined here can be described as ideal types within which organizations can be placed. Individuals may fit better into one type of culture than another, as would management functions and organizational features. A criticism levelled at this work is the lack of empirical evidence to support it (Williams *et al.*, 1989).

A typology devised by Miles and Snow (1978) recognizes the potency of managerial ideology and leadership in influencing and shaping the culture of the organization. The three-part typology consists of the following:

1. *Defender organizations.* The major objective is to secure and maintain a stable position in the market for the product or service. There is an emphasis on formal systems where planning and control are centralized and there is a commitment to efficiency and cost reduction.

2. *Prospector organizations.* The major objective is to develop new products and exploit market opportunities. To this end there is an emphasis on flexibility, *ad hoc* systems and creativity.

3. *Analyser organizations.* Careful attention is given to research and development and to steady rather than dramatic growth. There is a tendency to follow rather than lead in the product market.

It is more than likely that different attitudes and beliefs are compatible with the different types of organizational cultures. Also, it is important that structure, strategy and culture blend and harmonize to secure a successful outcome. With regard to strategy, it is known that culture can bolster the strategy of the company and provide the impetus for the development of new products, as has been the case with the US corporation Motorola. Currently, there is an interest in 'reinventing strategy' as a reaction to downsizing, rightsizing and delayering associated with massive cost-cutting (Hamel and Prahalad, 1994). The view is that we should avoid the danger of corporate anorexia, and that companies should be energized and stimulated to create new markets.

There are occasions when organizations feel it necessary to reinforce their existing culture and set in motion a series of events or activities to accomplish this objective. Alternatively, there could be a determination to change corporate culture, and this could have significant implications in terms of modification or revision to strategy, structure and processes within the organization. Before examining ways in which changing culture is prosecuted, it is necessary to develop an understanding of change in organizations.

Change

Change is a phenomenon we encounter in life both inside and outside organizations and it is fair to say that the pace of change has accelerated in recent years. We have witnessed changes in the political landscape of the world with the disintegration of the communist system and the collapse of the Eastern Bloc. This has generated further changes, such as the creation of independent states within the old Soviet Union and of course the unification of Germany. Change is visible in South Africa where power sharing between blacks and whites has replaced the previous system of rule by the white population, and recent international peace initiatives are likely to bring about desired changes in Northern Ireland and in the Israeli-occupied territories.

At the economic level there will be greater competition as barriers to trade between EU countries are removed with the creation of the Single Market. This will be accentuated by the rapid development of global markets. The pace of technological developments is reflected in changes across a broad spectrum. For example, there have been impressive advances in the application of new technology to the office and the factory. Technological innovation also finds expression in the development of new products. Change will also impact on how people perceive careers. Already employee expectations are changing, because now there is recognition of the growing need to have a number of jobs throughout a working life, with much less attachment to the notion of a continuous association with one organization.

It is commonplace in today's world for organizations to bring about a variety of changes to their goals, structures and processes in response to both internal and external happenings or in anticipation of these events. At the strategic level corporate goals could be set or adapted so that the organization is well placed to derive competitive advantage in its market. At the operational level responses or precipitative action to improve efficiency and effectiveness could be reflected in changes to working practices, contracts of employment, systems and structures.

Reactions to change

Change is not a painless process and it is often resisted by employees when they do not share the employer's view. The following are some of the reasons why change is resisted; these could be based on historical justifications:

☐ People perceive that the proposed changes are likely to threaten their expertise, undermine their influence, dilute their power base and reduce the resources currently allocated to their department. If this negative view prevails, efforts to introduce the change could be hindered.

☐ There is a lack of trust between management and employees. This could have arisen because those likely to be affected by the proposed changes did not receive adequate explanations about what is due to take place, or they recall that past changes did not produce the promised benefits.

☐ There are diverse views about the need for change and the anticipated benefits, and this creates some confusion.

☐ People have a low tolerance for change, though it is recognized that there are certain people who thrive on confronting change. Individuals with a low tolerance for change may feel anxious and apprehensive about the uncertainty that accompanies change, and as a result oppose it even though they recognize it is for the benefit of the organization.

☐ As creatures of habit people construe change as uncomfortable because it poses a challenge to established routines to which they have grown accustomed. Also, there could be a sadness at the prospect of severing contact with people who were well liked or discarding established ways of doing things.

☐ People harbour doubts about their ability to cope with the demands of the new situation.

☐ People feel that their future job security and income could be adversely affected by the proposed changes, and this is compounded by fear of a future clouded with ambiguity and uncertainty (fear of the unknown).

Apart from the factors listed above, the organization as a system should be considered. Because of its inbuilt mechanisms, e.g. bureaucratic structures and personnel practices, to maintain stability there is a certain inertia which acts as a counterbalance to change.

A number of measures to overcome resistance to change have been proposed (Kotter and Schlesinger, 1979). Some of the measures which can be viewed as negative, are unlikely to appeal to the HRM specialist; these are 'coercion' in the form of direct threats or force to elicit compliance; or 'manipulation' which amounts to distorting facts and figures so that they look more attractive, or withholding negative data, so that the change scenario is more acceptable to the resisters. The following are the positive measures to overcome resistance to change:

☐ If the source of resistance is poor communication, then action should be taken to communicate with employees specifying clearly the rationale for the change.

☐ A wise course of action is the involvement of those likely to oppose the change in the decision-making process related to it, in particular those who can make a valid contribution to this form of participation.

☐ If people have strong fears and anxieties about the proposed changes, some form of counselling and skills development could be beneficial.

☐ A bargaining process could be mounted where some position is conceded in return for more compliant behaviour on the part of the resisters.

It is understandable that news of profound changes affecting the individual's job or place of work can arouse deep psychological feelings related to self-esteem and achievement, which in turn affect the level of motivation and performance. A 'cycle of coping', which covers five stages and traces the individual's reaction to change, has been proposed (Carnall, 1990). The pronouncements in the cycle of coping which now follow might be viewed as generalizations; however, reflecting on them when considering the management of change could be useful.

Stage 1 is 'denial' as the individual is confronted with the proposal for change. A typical reaction is that change is unnecessary, and there could be an enhancement of the person's self-esteem because of an attachment to the present way of doing things. Where a group is involved, the threat posed by the proposal for change could lead to a reinforcement of the ties between members, and performance remains stable.

Stage 2 is 'defence' and at this stage the realities of the decision to institute change become apparent as early deliberations lead to the formulation of concrete plans and programmes. Faced with this outcome people become defensive in order to defend both their jobs and the way they have executed their duties and responsibilities. This stage produces an adverse effect which manifests itself as a lowering of self-esteem, motivation and performance.

Stage 3 is 'discarding' and, unlike the previous stages which emphasized the past, this stage puts the spotlight on the future. There is a change in perceptions as people realize that change is necessary and inevitable. Although performance is still on the decline, there are signs that self-esteem is improving as people get to grips with the new situation.

Stage 4 is 'adaptation' where people are beginning to come to terms with the new techniques and processes. Naturally it will be necessary to modify and refine the new system and if people are involved in this exercise they are likely to experience an increase in their self-esteem. However, performance still lags behind the growing level of motivation, particularly in situations where it was necessary to have an understanding of new methods and techniques.

Stage 5 is 'internalization' where people finally make sense of what has happened, and the newly adopted behaviour is now becoming part of people's repertoire of behaviour. One could now expect an improvement in self-esteem and motivation and this coupled with the better use of people's abilities could give rise to raised levels of performance.

Managing change

Before setting out to plan change it is well to recognize the existence of a state of equilibrium between the forces for change and the forces against change. In accordance with Lewin's (1951) force field model this equilibrium must be disturbed in a planned way in order to bring about change. This is done by strengthening the forces for change or weakening the forces against change, or taking both courses of action. However, at the beginning it is likely to be a difficult task to identify the forces for and against change. Lewin postulates a model which could be useful as a means of understanding the process of change from the old to the new situation. It consists of:

   Unfreezing → Changing → Refreezing

People are not normally receptive to change when they are locked into a state where they are attached to traditional values supportive of the *status quo* (i.e. they are frozen). It is necessary to unfreeze this state before progress can be made in getting people to adopt new ideas and work methods. The unfreezing stage consists of a number of courses of action, such as highlighting the benefits of moving to the new situation, challenging the *status quo* and the attitudes that underpin it, using appropriate information and discussion in a supportive atmosphere to remove the psychological defences, and facilitating the movement from the *status quo* to the new situation by measures such as advice and skills training.

   After the unfreezing has taken place we move to the changing stage where the planned changes in the work situation are implemented. It is hoped that the anticipated benefits have materialized. If so, the final stage – refreezing – has arrived. At this stage the changes to structure (e.g. the development of a more focused and flexible organization) or processes together with the underlying attitudes and behaviour need to be refrozen so that they can be sustained over time. If this stage is not successfully negotiated, there is the danger of reverting to the previous equilibrium state. On the other hand, if the refreezing has gone ahead without a hitch, then the new situation is stabilized as the driving and restraining forces for change are balanced.

   After examining the way change was managed in fifteen core organizations (though information was also derived from twenty additional organizations), Storey (1992) concluded that there was no single best way to manage change. In fact the approach to adopt was and should be contingent upon organizational and environmental conditions. But the most common approach was for members of the senior management to conceive the change necessary to realize their vision, to ensure that all employees were aware of the proposed changes and to share their vision of the proposed organizational reforms, and that all parts of the organization act in unison, supported by HRM strategies.

By way of example, consider the 'Working with Pride' initiative at the Austin Rover company. Following a period of severe and intense cost-cutting in the early 1980s, top management instigated a programme concerned with quality which ran from the mid to the late 1980s. This entailed direct communication with the work-force, rather than through the trade union representatives, and the creation of groups or 'zones' of workers. The workers were trained in quality control processes so that they could take responsibility for their actions in this area. At the same time a more sophisticated system of recruitment and selection (e.g. psychometric testing) was introduced as a means of assessing the suitability of new employees for working in the changed situation.

A trigger of change which is worthy of note in the case of Austin Rover was the relationship with Honda, which on reflection was beneficial. A trigger for other organizations in the research study was learning useful things from competitors in their market environment.

When reflecting on various prescriptions for managing change by a number of contributors to the literature, the following guidelines could be noted (Armstrong, 1992):

☐ The provision of solid and comprehensive information on the need for change is an excellent beginning, but it is far easier to collect and analyse this information than it is to conceive and execute a plan of action to satisfy that need.

☐ Change will be initiated in a more effective way if it is clearly seen as a crucial component in realizing the corporate strategy for the organization.

☐ It is necessary to appreciate the corporate culture, and the change strategies chosen (e.g. actions and interventions) should be effective in that culture.

☐ A culture of continuous learning for all employees (a learning organization) is supportive of change. An alleged benefit of a learning organization is that it positively encourages acceptance of and belief in ongoing change and development.

☐ Change is best handled on an incremental basis by creating actionable parts of the overall change strategy for which people would be held accountable. This course of action would not be recommended at a time of crisis.

☐ To bring about change that is likely to last requires strong commitment and leadership from senior managers at the apex of the organization.

☐ The leadership skills and temperament of those charged with managing change at all hierarchical levels should be in harmony with the change strategies used and the prevailing organizational conditions.

☐ The system of rewards should be designed in such a way as to recognize success in bringing about change.

☐ The people most involved in managing change are middle managers who must be convinced that the proposed changes are necessary. Getting them on the side of the instigators of the change is by no means an easy task, so they should get as much help and encouragement as possible, including appropriate training.

☐ The people to choose as 'change agents' are those who are likely to accept the challenges and opportunities that change offers.

☐ Change agents acting within an 'organizational development' (OD) framework have a number of behavioural techniques at their disposal, such as process consultation (i.e. helping people to solve their own problems), team-building, counselling, providing feedback and conflict management (see Box 3.1).

☐ Though it is important to communicate the reasons for change, it is also important to listen and take note of the reactions of those affected by the change. This could prove difficult and there are circumstances when it may be necessary to modify the initial plan for change.

☐ Changes to structure and processes can be used as a means to change individual behaviour, rather than trying to change attitudes first and then expecting behaviour to fall into line. The latter is more difficult to achieve.

☐ If people are likely to be better off as a result of the change, but they perceive the opposite to be the case, resistance to change almost certainly will follow. If this situation should arise, it is an example of ineptitude in the management of change.

☐ Driving along the road leading to the end of the process of change can be a bumpy ride. There will be successes and failures, but organizations can learn a lot from the failures.

☐ In an age of unprecedented instability and uncertainty on many fronts (e.g. technology, markets, society), change is ever-present and necessary. The organization bears a responsibility to employees to offer a rationale for change and to do all it can to protect the interests of those affected by change.

Box 3.1

PEOPLE-CENTRED Organizational Development (OD) INTERVENTIONS

People-centred OD interventions, as opposed to task and structural interventions, put the emphasis on changing attitudes and behaviour. Training and development (discussed in chapter 8) could also play an active part in changing attitudes and behaviour. However, there are certain techniques at the disposal of those interested in organizational change and development which will now be considered: these are sensitivity training, process consultation, survey feedback, team-building and inter-group development.

Sensitivity training: This technique is also referred to as encounter groups, or 'T' (training) groups. Its objectives are to give people the opportunity to develop awareness of their own behaviour, how others see them, greater sensitivity to the behaviour of others, and a better understanding of group processes. The main method used to change behaviour is group interaction in an unstructured setting. For example, group members interact in an environment characterized by openness and frankness, and they discuss information about themselves and the dynamics of the group. A trainer or advisor is in attendance but refrains from taking a directional stand. Instead he or she creates a setting where people feel able to express their thoughts and feelings. An outcome from a successfully run 'T'-group would be that people are better able to empathize with others, are better able to listen to others, are less inhibited, are more tolerant of others' point of view, and better equipped to confront conflict situations. The permanency of the benefits is questionable.

Process consultation: This technique bears some similarity to sensitivity training, but it is more task oriented. The purpose of process consultation is for an outside consultant to help a group (e.g. a management group), who is the client, to solve their own problems. Together they diagnose the problem and explore the most likely solution. The consultant is not charged with solving the organizational problem, and neither is he or she required to be an expert in solving the particular problem which could be technical in nature. The consultant's expertise is essentially in the domain of problem diagnosis and developing the most appropriate group dynamics. He or she can help the group locate a technical expert if it is obvious that this type of help is needed.

Survey feedback: This technique could be used to solicit views on a number of issues (e.g. communication, job satisfaction, supervision) from organizational members attached to particular sections or departments. A questionnaire is used to collect this information. When the data is analysed, the results are fed back to the participants in the survey. Management could receive professional help in the analysis and interpretation of the questionnaire responses, and on how best to handle the discussion of the results. Subsequently, in a discussion forum the results of the survey could be used to identify problems and propose solutions.

Team-building: It is natural to focus on team-building as a technique because there are many situations in organizations where members of a team or group frequently work in an interdependent fashion. Interdependency is crucial in teamwork, and so is coordination of the efforts of the group members if a successful outcome is to materialize. The major objective of team-building is to create a healthy climate of trust between members and to foster high levels of interaction. In team-building it will be necessary to make a serious examination of the group's goals and priorities, clarification of each member's role in the group, evaluation of the group's performance, analysis of the problems encountered by the group, and sensitivity to the overall dynamics of the group. During the team-building process different perceptions will surface, and a critical perspective should apply to an appraisal of both the means and the ends in the context of group functioning. In recent years research has indicated that successful team performance rests on 'role heterogeneity', that is different group members are capable of performing different roles within a team (Belbin, 1981; 1993).

Inter-group development: This technique is used to change attitudes and the perceptions that different organizational groups (e.g. finance, marketing) have of each other. Where negative views prevail, this could undermine the quality of interactions and liaisons between teams, and perhaps adversely affect efforts to coordinate activities at the organizational level. In the event of problems with inter-group relationships, one approach to solving them would be to ask each group to meet and list its perceptions of itself, its perceptions of the other group and how the latter perceives it. After the groups have shared the lists, there would be a discussion of similar and dissimilar perceptions. The object of the exercise is to work on strategies that are likely to improve inter-group relations (Mckenna, 1994).

□ In the final analysis it is crucial to obtain the commitment of those who are expected to put change into practice.

Changing culture

In recent years many organizations have felt it necessary to change coorporateculture to ensure survival or to gain competitive advantage. Often this was prompted by the realization that the existing culture did not fit the desired future state for the organization. Forces in the organization's environment could signal the need for a change in culture. For example, in recent years the UK government took action to unleash market forces within the National Health Service and this had a significant impact, particularly in the case of the culture of Hospital Trusts. Apart from the external environmental stimulants, the force for cultural change could come from within when senior executives apply new approaches to management, such as total quality management and process re-engineering (these approaches will be discussed later in the chapter).

Once it has been established that there is a need for change, a first step would be to analyse the existing organizational culture. Next it would be necessary to envisage the desired end state as far as culture is concerned. Certain commentators see the need for strong leadership to permeate the total organization, where 'heroes' recognize the need for change and put in place change agents and construct symbols of change in order to create the necessary momentum (Deal and Kennedy, 1988). The major emphasis in cultural change and development is on trying to change the values, attitudes and behaviour of the work-force.

How does one go about changing culture? According to Schein (1985) the organization can rely on the following 'primary' and 'secondary' mechanisms to change culture.

Primary mechanisms

(a) Matters to which leaders pay most attention

If senior managers place a lot of emphasis on, for example, the control of expenditure or the importance of service to the customer, and this is visible to employees, then a powerful message is transmitted about the significance of this type of activity. Sometimes it may be necessary to mount workshops or discussion groups to get a key message across to all employees as British Airways did with its 'Putting People First' initiative which is dealt with in Box 3.3.

(b) Leader's way of reacting to crises and critical incidents

This could be reflected in the type of situation that is seen as a crisis situation (e.g. a relatively high materials' wastage rate in the manufacturing plant) and the nature of the leader's response to the crisis (e.g. an urgent determination to tackle and solve the problem).

(c) Role modelling, teaching and coaching by leaders

Role modelling occurs when, for example, junior staff copy the behaviour of their seniors and integrate such behaviour into their own pattern of behaviour. This could apply to mannerisms and behaviour such as ways of interacting with valued clients or customers. With regard to teaching and coaching, working closely with people offering guidance and reassurance in a supportive climate has much to commend itself and has value in promoting commitment. There is reference to coaching in the context of management development in chapter 8.

In (a), (b) and (c) prominence is given to the hierarchical role of the leader exercising the right to lead. Some question this type of cultural leadership and point out that if we want cultural change to be effective then there should be wide agreement and ownership among people about the desired change (Torrington and Hall, 1991).

(d) Criteria used for allocating rewards

Recently the visibility of performance in the job as a criterion in the determination of rewards is apparent. At one time loyalty to the organization received greater emphasis as a criterion than is the case today. If the relationship between performance and rewards is highly visible, there is likely to be an expectation that it is functional to strive for improved performance. There is a discussion of performance-related pay (PRP) in chapter 7, and PRP was used by British Airways to reinforce the training interventions it deployed to bring about cultural change; these are described later in the chapter.

(e) Criteria used for employee selection, promotions and termination of employment

The criteria that would apply under this heading relate to what selectors consider important characteristics in hiring staff, the most appropriate work behaviour to secure career advancement, and what to avoid in order to reduce the likelihood of being made redundant.

Redundancy could be used to terminate the employment of employees on a compulsory basis when, for example, performance is unsatisfactory. An alternative way of shedding labour is to offer voluntary redundancy, or early retirement, particularly to those who might have difficulty in fitting into the new culture. It stands to reason that instituting redundancy measures can have a major impact on the lives of those who leave the organization, but also it can adversely affect those who stay. For example, if there is a lack of fairness or compassion in the implementation of the redundancy scheme, resentment can arise and have a negative effect after the change in culture has taken place. The legacy of this type of managerial behaviour could sour future relations between management and workers.

As regards employee selection, the organization could take a conscious decision to recruit workers with attitudes deemed appropriate in the light of the company's culture. This approach has been adopted particularly by Japanese companies setting up operations on a 'greenfield' site. Nissan UK used a rigorous and lengthy selection process when selecting its new work-force (Wickens, 1987). This practice was at variance with the much less exacting traditional practices for hiring shopfloor workers. Nissan's intention was to select a group of employees with values and attitudes compatible with the company's culture. It would appear that the type of person likely to be suitable would be one who is basically cooperative, flexible and certainly not the stereotyped rabble-rouser!

The point to bear in mind is that the organization endeavours to shape behaviour when implementing HRM techniques that utilize the criteria referred to in (d) and (e). An important consideration is the visibility of these criteria in the various decision-making forums.

Secondary mechanisms

(a) Structures, systems and procedures

There could be a fortification of existing structures, systems and procedures or a significant change in them so that the organization is re-positioned to face the future with greater confidence. For example, the desired change might be to create the post-entrepreneurial organization (e.g. flexible and free from cumbersome bureaucracy) as suggested by Kanter (1989) and discussed in chapter 2. Such a transformation, if successful, could bring about a fundamental shift in people's attitudes and behaviour at work.

With regard to changing people's attitudes and behaviour so that they will fit comfortably with the emerging culture, it is suggested in chapter 8 that training and development have a part to play. For example, in teamwork training people are given the experience of working cooperatively in activities away from the actual work situation. This provides them with an opportunity to encounter the attitudes and processes associated with teamwork, and perceive each other's strengths and weaknesses. There is a view that it would be more productive to concentrate on changing behaviour initially in training sessions in the expectation that attitudes will follow the new or changed behaviour. This approach was adopted in Equal Opportunities training programmes because early attempts to develop awareness and acceptance of the need for equal opportunities were seen as unsuccessful in challenging entrenched biases. Subsequently the emphasis switched to training programmes that highlighted appropriate behaviour (e.g. unbiased interview techniques in selection and promotions). The hope is that the new experience will pose a challenge to the biased attitudes, leading to the development of more appropriate attitudes.

Another example of a behavioural change was the 'smile campaign' mounted by a major supermarket as part of a customer service programme. All front-line employees were expected to put on a smile for customers and could face a reprimand if they did not do so (Ogbonna, 1992). In order to motivate employees to undergo the suggested behavioural change, a competition between stores was introduced. Senior managers visited stores before making a judgement on which store offered the best level of customer service. Apart from being profiled in the company's magazine, the winner received a financial reward. Here is an example of the importance of the provision of feedback on performance and the allocation of extrinsic rewards (referred to in 'Primary mechanisms', (d), above) as part of a strategy to bring about changes in attitudes and behaviour within an organization.

(b) Artefacts, façades and physical spaces

These are aspects of the physical environment that convey images which make an impact. For example, a certain impression is created when a person attending a job interview walks into the reception area of the company and perceives an expensively furnished setting. Another manifestation of the physical environment likely to capture the attention of the person and convey a message is the number of open spaces, the layout of the offices and the nature and distribution of office equipment.

When organizations change situations identified in (a) as part of a cultural facelift, they could also change certain aspects of the physical environment so that they blend with the changes made. They may also change their logo (the symbol of corporate identity) if the old one is out of keeping with the changed circumstances.

(c) Stories and legends about important events and people

There could be stories and legends containing a mixture of fact and fiction about heroic deeds in the past which may have contributed in a significant way to the company's success, or alternatively saved the company from disaster. The message is that present employees must not lose sight of dedication to duty and the need to continue with unselfish commitment to the success of the organization. Where accounts of management incompetence or greed circulate, perhaps the expectation is that these are things we should learn from and avoid now and in the future.

(d) Formal statements of philosophy and policy

These could include mission statements which are explicit articulations of the direction in which the organization is going and the values to which it will adhere. These statements should reflect reality and ideally should be reinforced with reference to their practical significance in a discussion forum.

Significance of sub-culture

When organizations are engaged in changing culture it is well to keep in mind that corporate culture is not a uniform phenomenon; in fact an organization could consist of a number of sub-cultures sometimes in conflict with each other and with the overall corporate culture. For example, the culture in the dealing room of a merchant bank could be different from the culture in the department concerned with the management of clients' investment portfolios (see Box 3.2).

Culture change initiatives

Three initiatives or interventions worthy of note are quality circles (QC), total quality management (TQM) and business process re-engineering (BPR). Before examining these initiatives our attention could profitably be diverted to events at British Airways throughout the 1980s in connection with cultural change. These are described in the case study in Box 3.3.

This case illustrates HRM acting strategically. To start with there was a business problem expressed as poor standards of service resulting in a loss-making situation. The solution to the problem was seen as the need

Box 3.2

THE CULTURE OF THE DEALING ROOM

Many dealing rooms in merchant banks and stock broking firms are dominated by one simple system of values: win or be damned. If dealers make large profits for the organization, the rewards – both in a material and psychological sense – are very significant. Not only is personal remuneration substantial, but also the dealers' status in the firm and the market generally is considerably enhanced. However, if the dealers' performance is poor in terms of profits generated or losses sustained, the reverse situation applies. They could feel humiliated and isolated and risk losing their job with detrimental personal consequences. Always in the background is greed and fear, in particular fear: fear of losing the job, and fear of public humiliation. It is fear that prevents dealers from cutting their losses as well as forcing them to get out of profitable positions early.

Dealers live in a unique corporate 'sub-culture', one that encourages over-confidence and insulates them from the outside world. On the trading floor boldness is looked upon as the most important virtue, and the traders' faith in themselves is boosted by their substantial remuneration package. A moment's hesitation or uncertainty could undermine a transaction. Dealers tend to behave as if they are omnipotent, they brag about the size of their deals, and hero status is bestowed on anyone making large sums of money. Because of the high rewards, they are encouraged to take unwise risks.

There is a loss of perspective on outside events, with a tendency for dealers to shield themselves from too much information that could metaphorically lead to paralysis. There is the illusion that the computer screen gives them a window on the outside world, even though it is no more than a series of rapidly changing numbers. Erratic behaviour is condoned if not encouraged, and shouting matches and foot stomping are part of the scene on the trading floor. The dealers display emotional volatility, and this is accepted as long as they are generating good profits. A dangerous cocktail is the mixture of emotional volatility, over-confidence, and access to large amounts of capital.

In addition to tightening up procedures, Weaving (1995) suggests the following action to counteract the culture of individualism, competition, and insecurity symbolized by Baring Securities, Singapore, in early 1995.

□ Create a culture of teamwork in which dealers help each other and share information. When dealers have bad days, colleagues would help them by alerting them to the risk management procedures, coaching them through a bad position, and encouraging them to be more rational.

□ Take steps to build the dealers' self-confidence which should help them admit when they are wrong. With self-confidence they are less likely to fall into the trap of the 'illusion of invulnerability' which is often associated with arrogance.

□ Help dealers to recognize their own particular response to stress – e.g. feeling of panic and a deterioration in rational thinking which could undermine good decision making – and train them on how to manage stress.

□ Institute good management practice exemplified by a competent approach to offering praise, coaching, and the provision of feedback. In the appraisal of performance a broad range of behaviour would be considered, and rewards would reflect behaviour somewhat more varied than a single money-making criterion.

(Griffith, 1995; Weaving, 1995).

Box 3.3

CULTURAL CHANGE AT BRITISH AIRWAYS

In the early 1980s British Airways faced considerable problems – loss making, poor reputation for service to the customer and poor industrial relations. After the appointment of Lord King as Chairman staff numbers were cut from 60,000 to 38,000 by means of voluntary severance and natural wastage. There was a pruning of the number of routes and the sale of surplus assets (e.g. aircraft). There were, however, limits to cost-cutting because fuel prices and airport charges which formed a considerable proportion of total cost were beyond the control of the organization. Given this constraint, competitive advantage had to be gained from other sources.

During the initial cost-cutting exercise staff training was reduced, but in 1983 the people factor was given prominence as a means to overcome the demoralization following the rationalization programme. At this time it was felt that the organization lacked an appreciation of what the customer wanted. This led to an initiative called 'Putting People First' whereby 12,000 customer-contact employees were put through a two-day course, the aim of which was to increase people's self-esteem. The belief was that if employees felt good about themselves, they were more than likely to feel good about dealing with other people.

In addition to the confidence-building exercises and stress-reduction programmes, employees were encouraged to set personal goals and to take responsibility for seeking what they wanted out of life. The overall programme represented a considerable investment for the company. On an ongoing basis employees were involved in activities concerned with the development of ideas for improving customer service using forums resembling quality circles. Also, as a means to generate a greater feeling of belonging and to promote shared interests, profit sharing was introduced.

Although considerable changes had taken place, it was still felt that the management style was too restrictive. Therefore, in 1985 a new programme called 'Managing People First' was introduced, in which 2,000 managers participated over a week. The key themes were motivation, trust, vision and taking on responsibility. A short time later a third major initiative was introduced and this was called 'A Day in the Life'. This was intended to dismantle some of the barriers between different groups in the organization which could act as impediments to change. In order to increase understanding and to encourage collaboration there were presentations to staff on the nature and function of work activities right across the organization, and the chief executive or one of the directors was present at these sessions to indicate top management support.

Staff surveys and customer feedback conveyed that a considerable change in the culture of the organization had taken place. There was a significant increase in customer satisfaction and profitability. However, there was not a unanimous positive reaction to the changes within the organization. Some staff felt there were conflicts between caring and customer service values and the pursuit of profits. Subsequent programmes, such as 'Fit For Business', focused more on commercial skills and activities.

(Hopfl, 1993).

for a culture change, coupled with the development of appropriate employee attitudes and values. The HRM function was active in facilitating the total process which was perceived as long term. The initial change process concentrated on the reduction of costs, with substantial cuts in staffing costs. However, it was felt necessary to go beyond the pruning of expenditure. In fact it was considered necessary to bring about a profound cultural change in order to improve performance.

The process of defining the current culture at the beginning of the programme appeared to be problem-centred but was intuitive in many ways. An in-depth study of culture at the outset was not undertaken. The process of change revolved around training and development activities, although other HRM activities, such as reward management (i.e. profit-related pay), also played a part. The change was active over a decade and is still continuing in various forms. In effect it represents a long-term investment. It is difficult to quantify in financial terms the outcome of the various training and development interventions, but what is obvious is the belief in the value of the culture change and the commitment of top management. This has had the effect of sustaining the change process.

In between the various stages of cultural change and development there was an opportunity to collect relevant information. This activity influenced matters to be considered at the next stage of the process. Among the aspects of culture subjected to change were the attitudes of employees, including their attitudes to customers, management styles and understanding of the activities of different groups and functions within the organization. The experience has left British Airways with a greater capacity to handle change and development in the future.

Returning to the theme raised in the opening of this section, the three initiatives or interventions – QCs, TQM and BPR – will be discussed shortly. But first something should be said about quality. The control of quality was an original American idea enthusiastically taken on board by Japanese business and subsequently adopted by both US and UK organizations. The central idea is that quality becomes the concern of all employees and should be totally immersed in the management process. The latter is characterized by delegated authority and empowerment in all activities connected with quality. The needs and expectations of customers are an overriding preoccupation for those charged with responsibility for quality. It is suggested that one reason for the greater uptake of the idea of quality in Japan was due to the greater scarcity of resources and the resultant need to eliminate waste and maximize getting things right first time (Oliver and Wilkinson, 1992).

Quality circles (QCs)

The QC is a group joined by shopfloor workers to solve problems related to barriers to quality improvement, cost reduction, working conditions, health and safety, etc. The group, normally led by a team leader, consists of five to ten volunteer employees who meet regularly (weekly or fortnightly) to identify and solve problems of the type described above.

In order to equip the QC members to sharpen and develop their problem-solving skills, they are offered training programmes covering topics such as problem definition, statistical analysis, and teamwork and communication skills. In Japan the QC was viewed favourably as a factor in its industrial success, and was imported to the West in the late 1970s.

It is claimed that QCs have a beneficial effect on a number of fronts, e.g. communication, participation, job satisfaction, and personal growth, which leads to increased quality and efficiency. However, there is evidence to challenge this claim. It is suggested that the significance of the QC in Japan has been overrated because the difficulties addressed were relatively trivial; in fact a rather small percentage of 'quality' problems were confronted (Schonberger, 1982). The alleged benefits of the QCs have also been challenged in the United Kingdom. There were low levels of participation – not more than 25 per cent of eligible employees joined QCs – and widespread indifference and often active opposition on the part of employees (Hill, 1991).

Total quality management (TQM)

TQM is a major management philosophy that embodies the major aim of satisfying customers' requirements as efficiently and profitably as possible, to improve performance continually as situations allow, and to ensure that all work activities achieve the corporate objectives and are completed right first time. Quality is seen as the key to the organization's success, and the success of any policy on quality lays firmly on the shoulders of every employee.

To underpin this approach to management would probably require a mixture of soft (e.g. customer care, participation, training, teamwork and performance) and hard factors (e.g. production standards and techniques, and quantitative analysis in the assessment of quality). The proponents of TQM would see it as a total system that fundamentally affects the culture of the organization, rather than as a 'bolt-on' technique which was often attributable to QCs. In the case of QCs the training and cultural change techniques necessary to embed the circles in the values and attitudes of employees were rarely instituted. But TQM is strategically driven by top management and almost prescribes involvement of all employees in matters connected with quality in their jobs. Since TQM emphasizes commitment, trust and self-control within a unitarist perspective, it is consistent with HRM. Also, the introduction of TQM gives HRM the opportunity to play a more strategic role in the organization, such as the creation and maintenance of a supportive culture. It is interesting to note that generally there is a lack of HRM comment in the TQM literature which tends to be concerned with the technical design of systems and solutions (Wilkinson and Marchington, 1994). Nevertheless, Guest (1992) sees

Box 3.4

TQM AT BOSCH

Bosch, a supplier of car components and electronic products to many of Europe's leading car manufacturers, introduced TQM when it opened its first manufacturing plant in the United Kingdom on a greenfield site in Wales in 1990. Many of the company's customers had specific quality demands so it was necessary to have a corporate culture in which quality was firmly ingrained. The values forming part of the culture included a quality product to secure global competitive advantage, continuous improvement of the employees' skills, improved quality of operations and productivity, and ensuring that the company met its responsibilities to customers, employees, suppliers and the local community.

High in the list of priorities was the continuous improvement of employee skills, production methods and productivity, and relations with customers. There was an emphasis on teamworking and team development. This was understandable because the company believed in synergy as applied to the efforts of people – that is, the effect of the group working in concert is greater than the sum of the individual contributions. Teams would be used to tackle problems, to enhance commitment and to further the cause of quality improvement.

The customer–supplier (employee) relationship was emphasized across the board. The supplier would endeavour to deliver to the external customer the appropriate product or service and then ensure that it was delivered 'right first time, on time, every time'. An internal customer is an employee who is a recipient of the company's internal output or service and is entitled to quality customer care. He or she is not the recipient of the finished product or service of the company, but is, for example, the next person on the production line.

The company considered it important that constant feedback flowed from both customers and management to employees to enable them to maintain and improve their standards of performance. The staff newspaper was also used as a vehicle to provide general feedback and reinforcement.

(Fowler *et al.*, 1992).

---

quality improvement as inextricably linked to HRM in the following ways:

☐ Training and development is the normal technique for communicating the importance of quality.
☐ Because the quality and commitment of the employees is crucial in improving the quality of the product or service, there is a need for systematic recruitment, selection and training.
☐ Top management commitment to TQM is a function of the quality and development of management.
☐ Adherence to quality takes root in a process of employee involvement and a flexible mode of operation, and this is likely to be more compatible with an organic type of organization imbued with high trust.

The experience of an organization which adopted TQM as a key feature of a corporate culture the company wished to establish is reported in the case study in Box 3.4.

Although TQM has its supporters as an effective intervention in changing and developing culture, it has been the subject of criticism. It is argued that it is questionable whether employee empowerment or greater autonomy is a reality. On the basis of a case study of an electronics manufacturing company where TQM was adopted, it was clear that problem-solving teams worked on problems identified by management, and the implementation of the solutions and any deviations from the standard format for the execution of a task led to the exercise of management control (Sewell and Wilkinson, 1992).

Business process re-engineering (BPR)

BPR has been defined as 'a radical scrutiny, questioning, re-definition, and re-design of business processes with the aim of eliminating all activities not central to the process goals' (Thomas, 1994). As a process of change that questions the way activities are carried out in the organization, BPR focuses on core business (i.e. activities that add value), leaving non-core activities to be contracted out.

A special characteristic of BPR from an organizational design perspective is that it advocates a departure from the rigid compartmentalization of processes in hierarchical organization arranged on a functional basis, which can lead to unacceptable delays in processing tasks (e.g. executing orders from customers), to acceptance of the cross-functional project team approach which is similar in some respects to matrix organization and project management. It poses a direct challenge to the division of labour and the need for hierarchical control. The proponents of BPR point to advantages in terms of speed of response, quality, delayering and the scope to apply information technology to handle the complex inter-dependent and cross-functional processes. In the early 1990s IBM intro-duced a new management structure after the arrival of its new chairman and chief executive. Shortly afterwards the focus was on business processes, i.e. the way the company carried out the multitude of tasks related to forming and maintaining customer relationships. The main justification for the company's adoption of BPR was to satisfy the needs of customers more effectively (Kehoe, 1994). An application of BPR to a US insurance company appears in the case study in Box 3.5.

In this case job enlargement (explained in chapter 8) and job enrichment (explained in chapter 7) were experienced by those who participated in the new system. This would suggest that some form of empowerment took place, but this is not always the case. For example, a High Street outlet in the United Kingdom, Argos, instituted change processes which resulted in the simplification and de-skilling of tasks.

Box 3.5

BPR AT MUTUAL BENEFIT LIFE

Before BPR was introduced the company dealt with new applications for insurance by using a complex administrative process in which applications went through thirty steps, five departments, and were handled by twenty people who performed simple repetitive tasks. The total process could take any time from five to ten days to complete.

After the implementation of BPR the situation changed radically. All new applications were dealt with individually by case managers, with the exception of the most complicated cases. The case manager had at his or her disposal an information technology workstation utilizing a database and an expert system which was invaluable as an aid to decision making. The end result was that the time taken to process each application was reduced by three to five days and the administrative capacity to handle applications nearly doubled. A reduction in staff amounting to one hundred posts led to considerable savings.

(Hammer, 1990).

There are some parallels between BPR and TQM, since both interventions include major organizational and cultural changes. Both require vision and commitment from top management as well as gaining the commitment of employees. Some recent applications of BPR have taken root in greenfield sites. This has inbuilt advantages, as we saw in the Bosch case earlier, because the company can select a work-force compatible with the culture it wishes to adopt and avoid the problems connected with changing the outlook of an existing work-force. First Direct, an autonomous offshoot of Midland Bank, set out to establish a new system of banking involving processes different from traditional banking, and considered it more appropriate to recruit a new work-force with terms and conditions of employment and industrial relations practices different from those in the parent company, but more functional from its own point of view.

It would appear that BPR does not draw on a particular mix of HRM practices. The prevailing circumstances within an organization are likely to determine the most appropriate mix. However, the following HRM practices are likely to occupy a prominent position: recruitment and selection; job redesign and rewards; training; team-building; transformational leadership; and counselling.

Opponents of BPR are quick to point out that its claims to success are wildly exaggerated and would no doubt get some satisfaction from the fact that the Mutual Benefit Life Corporation, referred to by Hammer earlier in Box 3.5, collapsed shortly after the appearance of his article in 1990. They would also point out that there is very little in BPR that has not been incorporated in other management and organizational approaches, such as matrix organization and TQM. Some argue that it is a cost-cutting and restructuring technique at a time when the prevailing management emphasis is switching to growth. In other words, its focus is on corporate mechanics, not on vision or strategy, and left to its own devices it will drive out all strategies except cost-minimization (Lloyd, 1994).

Culture and HRM

HRM adopts a unitarist position, which espouses the view that it is in the interests of organizational members to work together towards the achievement of common goals without the intrusive influence of conflict. It takes the view that it is to the benefit of employees, in terms of rewards and job security, for the organization to achieve its goals successfully. In taking this stand HRM is supporting a particular view of organizational culture, which could be seen as management-driven, where conflict does not exist and common interests prevail.

This could pose a dilemma because HRM also espouses a flexible approach to job design. This could mean greater control by employees over their work, including greater responsibility for the outcome of their effort, as well as greater group autonomy through, for example, quality circles and autonomous work groups. Apart from specific initiatives in job design, HRM is partial to the removal of layers within the organization which has the effect of pushing decision making further down the organization. This results in reducing managerial control over employees. In addition, HRM expects effective and dedicated performance from members of the organization when it stresses the need for employees to be creative and innovative in pursuit of higher performance standards, and to commit themselves to hours at work over and above their contractual hours.

The challenge for HRM is to reconcile the unitarist perspective with the pluralist perspective of greater individual and group autonomy. The reconciliation of these two positions is unlikely to be an easy task. Can we create an organizational culture in pluralist conditions where there can be reasonable harmony between the interests of the organization and the interests of employees to pursue objectives based on self-interest which may not be in congruence with company objectives?

Finally, there have been a number of criticisms of the role of culture in HRM. Above, it is acknowledged that in the pluralist perspective, managerial control is removed to a certain extent, and subordinates are empowered, thereby creating conditions for a greater diversity of views. In such a climate is it realistic to assume that a uniform culture with strongly held shared values and beliefs can co-exist with 'deviant' values held by individuals? According to Willmott (1993) the conditions for the expression of heretical views, or the adherence to competing values by individuals or groups, could be severely limited if the uniform culture is strong.

Referring to strong cultures to which organizational members subscribe, it is suggested that a disadvantage could be reduced flexibility and adaptation to changing environmental conditions because people subscribe to cultural norms more suited to the previous conditions than to the changed conditions (Legge, 1989). However, one should not be left with the impression that, generally speaking, weak culture is synonymous with flexibility. It may be that the metaphor of relative strength is not the best way to conceive cultures.

Conclusions

It should now be clear that the organizational culture and attempts to change and manage it are legitimate concerns of HRM. Culture is closely linked to strategy and structure and influences activities such as recruitment, selection, appraisal, training and rewards, which are covered in subsequent chapters. Changing culture is a prolonged and costly process. For example, the Rover Motor Car Company spent fifteen years trying to gain acceptance for its changed philosophy of management. In HRM terms the latter is based on mutual commitment which has the potential to increase cooperation and performance and lead to competitive advantage.

HRM is closely associated with the management of organizational change and development. It plays an important role as a facilitator of change, but it must be continually aware that people in the organization can be either a positive force or a barrier to change. Organizations introduce change in order to increase competitive advantage or effectiveness. Setting up the right strategies and systems is part of this process, but it is equally important to energize and enthuse the employees to implement the strategies.

References

Armstrong, M. (1992) *Human Resource Management: Strategy and action*. London: Kogan Page.
Belbin, R. M. (1981) *Management Teams: Why they succeed or fail*. London: Heinemann.
Belbin, R. M. (1993) *Team Roles at Work*. Oxford: Butterworth-Heinemann.

Carnall, C. (1990) *Managing Change in Organizations*. Hemel Hempstead: Prentice Hall.

Deal, T. and Kennedy, A. (1988) *Corporate Cultures*. London: Penguin.

Fowler, A., Sheard, M. and Wibberley, M. (1992) 'Two routes to quality', *Personnel Management*, **November**, 30–34.

Griffith, V. (1995) 'Hero one day, villain the next', *Financial Times*, 3 March, p. 13.

Guest, D. (1992) 'Human resource management in the UK', in Towers, B. (ed.), *The Handbook of Human Resource Management*. Oxford: Blackwell.

Guest, D. (1994) 'Human resource management: opportunity or threat?', in *Survival and Quality, Annual Course Proceedings 1994*, Indoe, D. and Spencer, C. (eds.). Educational and Child Psychology, **11**, 5–10.

Hamel, G. and Prahalad, C. K. (1994) *Competing for the Future*, Boston: Harvard Business School Press.

Hammer, M. (1990) 'Re-engineering work: don't automate, obliterate', *Harvard Business Review*, **July–August**, 104–112.

Handy, C. (1985) *Understanding Organisations* (3rd edn). London: Penguin.

Harrison, R. (1972) 'Understanding your organization's character', *Harvard Business Review*, **May–June**, 119–128.

Hill, S. (1991) 'Why quality circles failed but total quality management might succeed', *British Journal of Industrial Relations*, **29**, 541–568.

Hofestede, G. (1980) *Cultures Consequences*. Beverly Hills, CA: Sage Publications.

Hofl, H. (1993) 'Culture and commitment: British Airways', in Gowler, D., Legge, K. and Clegg, C. (eds.), *Case Studies in Organizational Behaviour and HRM*, 2nd edn. London: Paul Chapman.

Kanter, R. (1989) *When Giants Learn to Dance: Mastering the challenge of strategy, management, and careers in the 1990s*. London: Unwin.

Kehoe, L. (1994) 'Down in the dirt to clean up IBM', *Financial Times*, 5 December, p. 8.

Kotter, J. P. and Schlesinger, L. A. (1979) 'Choosing strategies for change', *Harvard Business Review*, **March–April**, 106–114.

Legge, K. (1989) 'Human resource management: a critical analysis', in Storey, J. (ed.), *New Perspectives in Human Resource Management*. London: Routledge.

Lewin, K. (1951) *Field Theory in Social Science*. New York: Harper and Row.

Lloyd, T. (1994) 'Giant with feet of clay', *Financial Times*, 5 December, p. 8.

McKenna, E. F. (1994) *Business Psychology and Organisational Behaviour*. Hove: Lawrence Erlbaum Associates, Publishers.

Miles, R. E. and Snow, C. C. (1978) *Organizational Strategy, Structure, and Process*. New York: McGraw-Hill.

Moorhead, G. and Griffin, R. W. (1992) *Organizational Behaviour*, 3rd edn. Boston, MA: Houghton Mifflin.

Ogbonna, E. (1992) 'Organization culture and human resource management: dilemmas and contradictions', in Blyton, P. and Turnbull, P. (eds.), *Reassessing Human Resource Management*. London: Sage Publications.

Oliver, N. and Wilkinson, B. (1992) *The Japanization of British Industry: New developments in the 1990s*. Oxford: Blackwell.

Ouchi, W. G. (1981) *Theory Z: How American business can meet the Japanese challenge*. Reading, MA: Addison-Wesley.

Peters, T. and Waterman, R. (1982) *In Search of Excellence*. New York: Harper and Row.

Schein, E. H. (1985) *Organizational Culture and Leadership*. San Francisco: Jossey Bass.

Schein, E. H. (1990) 'Organizational culture', *American Psychologist*, **45**, 109–119.

Schonberger, R. (1982) *Japanese Manufacturing Techniques*. New York: Free Press.

Sewell, G. and Wilkinson, B. (1992) 'Empowerment or emasculation? Shopfloor surveillance in a total quality organization', in Blyton, P. and Turnbull, P. (eds.), *Reassessing Human Resource Management*. London: Sage Publications.

Storey, J. (1992) *Developments in the Management of Human Resources*. Oxford: Blackwell.

Thomas, M. (1994) 'What do you need to know about business process re-engineering', *Personnel Management*, **26**, 28–31.

Torrington, D. and Hall, L. (1991) *Personnel Management: A new approach*, 2nd edn. Hemel Hempstead: Prentice Hall.

Weaving, K. (1995) 'Sweeping fear from the floor', *Financial Times*, 3 March, p. 13.

Wickens, P. (1987) *The Road to Nissan*. London: Macmillan.

Wilkinson, A. and Marchington, M. (1994) 'TQM: instant pudding for the personnel function?', *Human Resource Management Journal*, **5**, 33–49.

Wilkinson, B. and Oliver, N. (1992) 'HRM in Japanese manufacturing companies in the UK and USA', in Towers, B. (ed.), *The Handbook of Human Resource Management*. Oxford: Blackwell.

Williams, A., Dobson, P. and Walters, M. (1989) *Changing Culture*. London: Institute of Personnel Management.

Willmott, H. (1993) 'Ignorance is strength, freedom is slavery: managing culture in modern organizations', *Journal of Management Studies*, **30** (4), 515–552.

4

Employee resourcing: human resource planning

Employee resourcing, the process of acquiring and utilizing human resources in the organization, consists of a number of specialist activities which need to act in harmony to ensure that human resources of the right quantity and quality are available to meet the overall objectives of the company. The specialist activities referred to are human resource planning, which is dealt with in this chapter, and recruitment and selection which are examined in chapter 5. These activities are operationalized in the context of strategic human resource management, a topic discussed in chapter 2. As was stated then, strategic human resource planning is an approach which links the management of human resources to the organization's overall strategies for achieving its goals and objectives.

A starting point for human resource planning is to assess the future needs of the organization for employees, noting the blend of skills required. As stated earlier, human resource planning is part of the framework set by the interaction of strategic human resource management and corporate strategy. By contrast, traditional manpower planning was concerned principally with making sure that the organization had the right number of employees in the right place at the right time. Human resource planning has not rejected this perspective; however, it has changed our understanding of it. In traditional manpower planning a strong quantitative bias was evident, with an orientation towards dealing with 'hard' problems and their solution. But in human resource management, with its strong emphasis on people as a key resource, there is the recognition that the 'hard' problem approach has to be supplemented by the 'soft' problem approach. In the latter case qualitative issues connected with employee creativity, innovative practices, flexibility, messy problems and so on are taken very seriously.

The anchor of human resource planning comprises three facets as follows:

1. Demand for human resources, which can be gleaned from the strategic human resource plan.
2. Utilization of human resources in a cost-effective and efficient manner.
3. Supply of human resources manifested in the current number of employees (internal supply) and the potential pool of suitable applicants external to the organization (external supply).

There is a dynamic interplay between the three facets mentioned, and the overall process is mediated by happenings within the organization (internal environment) and forces external to the organization (external environment). Both environments generate turbulence where change is omnipresent and has to be managed.

Demand for human resources

Demand for human resources can be defined as the number of staff required to meet the organization's future needs, as well as the composition of the work-force in terms of the necessary skills. For example, an expansion of the organization's activities could result in recruiting extra staff with the appropriate skills. On the other hand, an organization may be planning to reduce staffing levels because of an anticipated fall in the demand for the company's product(s). Of course rationalization of staffing levels could also be prompted by other considerations such as scope to cut costs, or improve working practices, which offers the opportunity to maintain the existing output, or in some cases to increase output, with fewer employees. As was mentioned earlier, competitive forces emanating from the external environment can have a material bearing on the magnitude of the demand for human resources. This could be reflected in a reduction of staffing levels, as well as changing the character and skills associated with the jobs that remain, and is illustrated in the case presented in Box 4.1.

This illustration shows how organizations need to devise and carry out strategies in order to confront threats from the external environment. The increased competition from building societies, coupled with customer expectations of low charges and quality of services, brought about a need to reduce costs but to maintain levels of service. A method to achieve this was greater use of new technology. As a consequence, there has been a

Box 4.1

DEVELOPMENTS IN THE BANKING SECTOR

Increased competition from building societies, the effects of losses on bad debts, low inflation and a low interest rate environment put considerable pressure on banks to cut their costs. The traditional approach to banking was paper- and labour-intensive. The use of cheques, for example, reached its peak in 1991. In order to be processed, a cheque would be dealt with initially at the bank receiving it and would pass through a number of people before ending up at the home branch of the customer who wrote the cheque. In order to reduce costs, a strategy has been adopted to change the labour-intensive processes of banking through the introduction of new technology.

Since 1991 the use of cheques has been declining and banks commissioned national advertising to encourage customers to use card transactions. By 1993 70 per cent of cash withdrawals were made from automatic teller machines. Much of the need for 'backroom' activity and paperwork was removed by the introduction of new technology, and most of the major banks became involved in rationalization programmes to reduce staff numbers in branches. The industry employed 400,000 people at the beginning of the 1990s and Brian Pitman, Chief Executive of Lloyds Bank, predicted that there would be 100,000 job losses during the 1990s (Hamilton, 1993).

The jobs which remain will be more concerned with sales of financial services rather than carrying out banking processes which are no longer labour-intensive. In some areas, employee reward is being linked to sales targets.

---

reduction in staffing levels in order to avoid over-staffing. This has resulted in a significant reduction in demand for human resources, and led to a preoccupation with the quality of the human resources. For example, it was felt that the staff needed new information technology skills, and to develop their abilities in customer relations, sales and knowledge of the products and services offered by the bank.

The traditional approach to calculating the demand for human resources is to make use of ratios. An example of a simple ratio is as follows. A ratio of 4:1 is used in a research and development department within a company. In this particular situation that means four scientific officers to one technician. The company decided that an extra four scientific officers will be appointed, in which case it must set aside funds for a new technician as well.

A first step when using ratios in the example given is to decide on the number of new scientific officers that the company requires. To assist with this task, data are collected and projected into the future, and this can be presented diagrammatically using trend analysis (see Figure 4.1).

Projection A in Figure 4.1 shows a constant ratio. This means that in every situation the work of four scientific officers will require the work of one technician. Projection B indicates that in certain circumstances the ratio may be variable. In this case there are 'economies of scale', which means that although the first 4 scientific officers need a full-time technician,

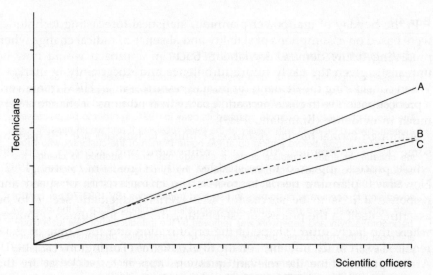

Figure 4.1 Staff ratios: A = constant ratio of 4:1, scientific officers:technicians; B = variable ratio – 'economies of scale'; C = constant ratio of 6:1, e.g. because of the introduction of new technology.

in a larger department of 20 scientific officers, 3 rather than 5 technicians are needed. This could occur because of efficiency gains from the technicians working as a team, or from them specializing, and becoming expert in particular tasks. Projection C indicates achieving a different ratio because of implementing a change, for example, the introduction of new technology, which results in each technician being able to service 6 scientific officers.

This type of analysis, as Torrington *et al.* (1991) point out, can also be used to plot the number of employees needed against projected demand for production. For example, there could be a ratio of 4 scientific officers to 1 million units of production per annum. Therefore, if production was to be raised from 4 million units to 6 million units, the complement of scientific officers would need to rise from 16 to 24 (where a constant ratio was applied).

The use of ratios in calculating the demand for human resources was more prevalent when the influence of trade unions was pronounced. They were used in union–management negotiations on staffing levels. However, in the competitive conditions of the 1990s a more flexible approach is called for. This means assessing particular requests on the basis of merit. A more flexible approach may involve achieving the same level of output with a reduced number of staff through gains in productivity, the introduction of new technology, or it may involve changes to job design such as job enlargement.

In the heyday of manpower planning, statistical forecasting techniques were based on assumptions of stability and absence of radical change when predicting future demand for labour. Such an approach would now be unrealistic given the likely future turbulence and uncertainty in markets. When considering the demand for human resources in an HRM framework a preoccupation with customers and quality in conditions of change is very much in evidence (Bramham, 1989).

Although formal human resource planning techniques are still used by some large companies, they lack refinement and accuracy and the whole process appeared to be studded with pragmatism (Storey, 1992). Nowadays, planning needs to possess the characteristics of speed and response if it is to be successful. Managerial judgement seems to be asserting itself in the process of establishing demand for human resources where the likely future shape of the organization and the range of skills required exert much influence on the final outcome (Torrington et al., 1991). At the present time the relevant questions appear to be 'What are the business needs?' and 'What is the ideal complexion and size of the human resource factor to meet those needs?'

Utilization of human resources

Establishing the demand for human resources cannot be achieved without considering the way employees' skills and talents will be used. Utilization of human resources impacts directly on the demand for staff. For example, a company improves its systems of work as part of a programme to make better use of its employees. As a consequence, there are now more staff than are needed to process the workloads. The end result could be a need for fewer staff, and could lead to voluntary or involuntary redundancies. However, if opportunities exist elsewhere within the company there could be a redeployment of all or some of the staff who are superfluous to requirements.

An increasing trend has been the use of computer-aided design and production in manufacturing. This trend has reduced the number of human resources needed to carry out processes which used to be labour-intensive. It has also had an effect on the quality of employees required, since people with particular skills are needed to create and maintain the systems.

Another trend has been the use of teamworking arrangements. Small groups of employees take responsibility for the total production of goods or services where individuals had previously specialized in small sections of the production process. This has an implication for the skill levels of the employees, as in a team they need to be able to carry out a wider range of tasks to complete the process. This type of utilization of human resources is linked to quality approaches and the devolvement of responsibility from supervisors and middle managers to the teams who actually carry out the work.

There has been a long tradition of trying to foster efficiency and effectiveness of the operations of an organization through work study and related management services techniques. The basic approach is to subject to detailed analysis the way tasks are undertaken and then to make recommendations for the improvement of systems and the better utilization of staff. The forerunner of present-day work study was the research undertaken by Taylor (1947), the father of scientific management. He examined the tasks undertaken by employees in order to establish how wasted time could be eliminated, and how human effort and work techniques could be better used. His approach was to observe employees engaged in the performance of tasks and to document and analyse their movements. On the basis of his analysis he postulated action strategies for improving techniques, making better use of time, and introduced training and incentives, with a view to increasing productivity. Taylor's intentions were felt to be more partial to the interests of management and detrimental to the interests of workers according to commentators such as Braverman (1974).

An example of a present-day work study exercise carried out in a secretarial pool of a Buildings and Estates Department of a Local Authority is shown in Box 4.2. A number of outcomes following the adoption of the recommendations of this work study report can be identified. Work was re-designed and systems were changed. Secretarial pool operators spent less time correcting small mistakes and more time on producing finished reports to the required standard. The changes also had an impact on the way the professional members of staff worked. This resulted in a reduced demand for staff in the secretarial pool.

A close reading of the case will convey certain weaknesses of objective methods in a work study exercise designed to examine the utilization of human resources. If the initial raw data had been used for decision making with respect to staff reductions, there would have been a reduction of operators of 40 per cent. In exercises of this nature it is necessary to go behind the raw data, and try to detect the reasons for what is happening. In such circumstances the factors at play can be deep-rooted at both psychological and social levels. These can relate to factors of motivation and performance (which are addressed in chapter 7) and factors relating to the individual's resistance to change (which were addressed in chapter 3).

Prominence was given earlier to the role of work study as a technique to quantify the utilization of human resources. But a question to ask is: does this technique live up to the expectations of its adherents? Some

Box 4.2

WORK STUDY IN A SECRETARIAL POOL

The department produced a large amount of documentation. This included plans, reports on the state of buildings, repairs and maintenance needed, tender documents for contracting outside building work, orders and invoices. Most of the work was carried out by professional and officer-level employees, but the word processing was largely carried out by the secretarial pool which was staffed by twenty people. Their work was checked by the professional staff and was edited before being sent out.

A management services analysis was undertaken of the output produced. A sample of the work was taken and the number of key strokes (letters, punctuation marks, use of the space bar, etc.) needed were counted for the sample. The results from the sample were extrapolated to give an estimate of the number of key strokes needed for the total output. This was compared with the typing/word processing speeds required of staff recruited to the secretarial pool. The result was that 60 per cent of those currently employed should have been able to produce the total output if they were to work constantly at the rate of which they were capable.

However, at times of high pressure the pool could not deal with the workload and temporary staff were needed to supplement them. It was important to discover the reason for the disparity between the actual and the potential outputs. Staff were interviewed and it was found that a considerable amount of time was spent editing reports and documents. This required going through the document in great detail and picking out specific changes. The result was that it could take two hours or more to make a relatively small number of key strokes while editing. Some documents were edited several times.

This raised the question of why there was so much editing. Editing followed changes made by professional staff once they had seen a typed copy of their document. The changes were mainly related to the originator of the document wanting to see a material change rather than errors made by the secretarial pool being corrected.

A 'right first time' approach was introduced to the department and the result was that the need for editing was substantially reduced. Professional staff were also given greater access to word processors so that they could edit their own work. As a result the secretarial pool received less work, and what they received could be quickly put into the official format and produced to the required standard.

The initial analysis showed an overstaffing rate of 40 per cent, but further investigation had been required to understand the reasons behind the problems. Over a period of time, reductions of 30 per cent were made in the secretarial pool through natural wastage and relocation of staff within the authority, and the need for use of temporary staff was removed.

---

people would harbour certain reservations. Workers can disguise their capacity to produce when they are being observed and assessed. Naturally they are very conversant with the various facets of the job, and when they are assessed by the work study practitioners in order to set standards of work and output, it could be in their interest to under-perform. By so doing they create a situation whereby softer targets or standards are allocated to them.

In contemporary reflections on the scientific management approach, of which work study is a part, there has been a challenge to the 'carrot and stick' approach where control by management features strongly. An approach more acceptable to a human resource management perspective would be to concentrate on worker motivation where the emphasis would be on creating enriched jobs and greater self-control so as to provide employees with more scope for self-fulfilment. It is in this climate that appraisal systems which focus on personal/self-assessment have emerged which seek to encourage people to realize their potential. Performance management is discussed in chapter 6.

Finally, making a judgement about human resource utilization currently involves a greater recognition of the importance of the qualitative approach (i.e. obtaining soft data from managers and workers about the reasons behind what is done and future intentions), though the quantitative approach highlighted in the case in Box 4.2 is still relevant.

Human resource supply

The next stage of human resource planning is to evaluate the supply of labour. This is done by reference to the amount of labour needed as a result of having calculated the demand for labour (examined earlier in this chapter). The approach to human resource supply has two parts to it: internal and external supply.

Internal supply

When reference is made to the number of employees already employed by the organization we speak of the internal supply. The first step is to report on key characteristics of the internal supply as follows:

☐ Age.
☐ Grade.
☐ Qualifications.
☐ Experience.
☐ Skills.

Before conducting exercises, such as the above method of profiling, policy decisions taken by the organization with respect to expansion or contraction should be kept firmly in focus. For example, if contraction is contemplated (e.g. downsizing referred to in chapters 2 and 3) it may be decided that employees aged 50 and over could be considered for early retirement. Therefore, it is felt necessary to profile staff by age and grade. However, when this exercise is completed and the analysis shows that a substantial number of senior and middle managers are over the age of 50, it would appear necessary to reconsider the policy on early retirement, because releasing a large number of managerial staff over the age of 50 could strip the organization of most of its experienced managers.

If conditions suggest that an increase in the supply of managers from within the organization is needed, then the organization has to pay attention to 'succession planning'. This calls for an assessment of the actual performance of the person in his or her position, with that person's potential for promotion firmly in mind. It normally entails a formal plan to broaden the person's knowledge and experience of many aspects of work in a particular area, or/and training in skills at the technical and human relations levels. One has to guard against the misuse of succession planning where it is seen to disadvantage certain groups.

Where the decision about which individuals gain access to this form of development is a matter of managerial judgement, it is important to ensure that there is parity between the judgements of different managers. Conscious or unconscious bias on the part of the manager could result in criteria being used which unfairly discriminate against particular groups. For example, if a manager regards an aggressive or 'macho' style of management as preferable, this may give unwarranted advantage to men over women in terms of who is seen as having the potential to make a good manager.

Traditionally, upward movement was a feature of career progression (the linear approach). As organizations move to flatter structures (see chapter 2) with fewer layers of management, the potential for gradual movement upwards is reduced, and lateral moves (e.g. moves to different positions in a work group at the same level) are entertained. Obviously this can create greater employee versatility as new skills are learnt and familiarity with new roles within the group or team grows. Metaphorically, career ladders give way to career climbing frames, where sideways and sometimes downward moves become increasingly a feature of employee development within organizations.

An organization could be contemplating a reduction in the internal supply of labour because of a reduced demand for the services of all those currently employed. It is felt that labour is superfluous to requirements in one or more sections. A variety of conditions could have contributed to this state of affairs, including the advent of new technology which has reduced the labour-intensiveness of operations. A programme of redundancy is mounted because reliance on natural wastage would not be good enough to get rid of the surplus. It is also important for management to control the outward flow of skills, experience and knowledge from the organization rather than leaving this solely to the choice of individual employees, as the outcome may be the loss of important skills and the retention of employees who are not as valuable to the organization.

The law on redundancy must be considered by the organization, because there are legal provisions which state that the company must make every reasonable attempt to find a comparable position for an employee whose job ceases to exist. Therefore, if a situation arose where the organization is reducing staffing levels in one section, and expanding numbers in another, those whose positions are redundant should receive first consideration for the newly created vacancies over those external to the organization.

Inevitably during the process of collecting and analysing data on the internal supply of labour we encounter the staff turnover rate, which could indicate that the organization has problems. The formula used to compile this rate was given in chapter 1. The rate in itself is relatively uninformative, but what is useful is the comparison of rates across sections or departments. For example, if in a department of fifty staff, ten left in the previous year, that is a rate of 20 per cent. This may signal grounds for concern if most other departments in the organization have a rate of 5 per cent or less. In certain industries a high staff turnover is normal. For example, catering staff and kitchen workers have a tradition of staying in a job for a relatively short period of time.

It is always a good idea to establish the reasons why the turnover rate is on the high side (or exceptionally low). Reasons for high turnover can include a local competitor offering better conditions and benefits, or general dissatisfaction in a department, due to, for example, job insecurity or very poor management. Similarly, it is a good idea to learn more about a group of employees who entered the organization together. An example of such a group is a cohort of graduates recruited as trainee managers. The progress of the group could be analysed at regular intervals to see how many completed the training, how many achieve certain levels of performance and grades, and how many leave the company. Cohort analysis using statistical techniques can be used to explore the extent of wastage or loss due to turnover. One such technique is Bowey's (1974) stability index, which takes account of the length of service:

$$\frac{\text{Sum of months served (over 'N' period) by staff currently employed}}{\text{Sum of possible months service (over 'N' period) by a full complement of staff}}$$

$\times 100 = \%$ stability

This formula measures the experience of current staff as a proportion of the maximum experience that could have been gained over the period ('N') being examined if all the staff had been in constant employment for the whole period.

The following example may serve to clarify the use of this index. A group of 20 management trainees is recruited by an organization, and after 2 years Bowey's stability index is to be calculated. The sum of the possible service/experience in months is:

20 (people) × 24 (months) = 480 person months

This supplies the figure for the bottom of the equation (the denominator).

The current management trainees have the following profile: 5 have served 24 months; 5 have served 12 months; and 10 have served 6 months. This indicates that some members of the cohort have left and been replaced during the 2 years. The 15 members of staff who have less than 24 months' experience are replacements. The total number of months served by the current employees is 240. If these figures are inserted into the equation (240/480 × 100) the stability is 50 per cent. This would indicate that the group is not very experienced, it has amassed only half the possible experience it could have gained in the time period. This level of staff stability would be likely to be seen as relatively low.

Further analysis may be undertaken to establish the pattern of leaving. A wastage or stability rate may be distorted by a disproportionately high (or low) number of people passing through one particular position or a specific job type. If this were found to be the case, it would indicate that there may be a problem with the particular job or position which is not general to the whole department. It would be important to discover the reasons behind this phenomenon.

Quantitative techniques, such as Bowey's stability index, are a vital part of the planning of the internal supply of labour. However, they should not be viewed as the ultimate explanation, but as a starting point for further explanation. As mentioned earlier when focusing on the application of quantitative techniques, we need to go behind the statistics and try to establish the reasons for a particular result or trend. With regard to cohort analysis, what contributed to a high rate of turnover in a particular situation? It could be that employees are leaving to take up better posts elsewhere, or to broaden their experience, or to escape from an unpleasant atmosphere within the organization.

This type of qualitative information can be obtained from 'exit interviews' with those leaving the organization. Exit interviews are probably best conducted by a personnel or human resource specialist who is likely to be seen as less threatening and as someone to whom one can divulge frank views. A departing employee is often able to voice criticisms about many facets of the organization and its management, views one would not expect to hear from a person who plans to remain in the organization. The latter may be reticent about voicing criticism because of a belief that such action would be damaging for one's career and future remuneration. Of course, a departing colleague could also express complimentary views. Therefore, the exit interview provides useful information not readily available from other sources.

External supply

If the organization cannot draw on an internal supply of labour when extra staff are needed it will need to recruit from the external labour market. The external supply of labour will be discussed with reference to the following:

1. Tightness of supply.
2. Demographic factors.
3. Social/geographic aspects.
4. The type of employee required.

Tightness of supply

A tight supply of labour arises where there are relatively few external candidates with the requisite abilities to do the job. By contrast, a loose supply indicates a large number of able candidates are available. Given the current relatively high level of unemployment in the United Kingdom, one might conclude that the external supply of labour is high (loose). While this may be the case in a quantitative sense, the picture is more complex when viewed qualitatively. For example, the particular skills and abilities required by the organization are not necessarily found among the unemployed.

Guest (1994) reports that expertise in some areas of information technology is in very tight supply. According to the Federation of Recruitment and Employment Services, demand exceeds supply by 3:1 for IT staff. This has resulted in companies engaging in gazumping, i.e. offering higher salaries to potential recruits than the recruits had already agreed with competitor organizations, in order to attract the supply of labour they need. Where the organization experiences difficulty in attracting people with the necessary skills, it may resort to the use of sub-contractors or consultants to overcome the shortage. This could be a one-off arrangement or alternatively a continuing relationship.

An alternative to recruiting people with the necessary skills is to recruit people with potential and train them to the required standard. This does involve the cost of training and carries the risk that their potential will not be realized. It can be time-consuming to train people and, particularly for small organizations who do not have training systems already established, this course of action could be prohibitively expensive and difficult. However, there are advantages to training people internally. It can lead to an increased sense of commitment on the part of the employees, the training could be directly related to the organization's needs, and it is a form of investing in people and treating them as assets. There is more detailed discussion of training in chapter 8.

Demographic factors

Demographic changes (e.g. the number of young people entering the labour force) affect the external supply of labour. In 1982 there were 3.7 million young people in the age group 16–19; in 1994 the figure was 2.6 million (Skills and Enterprise Network, 1994). This change (approximately one-third) will affect the supply of labour to organizations who have traditionally recruited young people and trained and developed them by the use of the training process and exposure to the organization's ethos or culture. The stated demographic change will alter the age composition of the work-force, and will force employers to review their recruitment policies. The outcome of such a review could be to give more consideration to employing older workers who will constitute a higher proportion of the work-force than hitherto.

The composition of the work-force is also likely to experience a change in its gender composition. The *Labour Force Survey* (Department of Employment, 1994) showed that women are now making up 45 per cent of the total UK employed population. A comparison between 1984 and 1994 indicates a rise of 3.3 per cent (0.7 million) in the total number of employees. This is composed of a fall of 0.5 million men, and a rise of 1.2 million women in employment. This trend of an increasing proportion of women in employment will put pressure on organizations to become more 'family friendly'. In the future, progressive organizations are likely to employ more women and older workers. This will entail the application of appropriate strategies of recruitment, retention and training.

Another factor to note is the change in EU legislation which has increased the potential mobility of labour within the EU. Under this legislation workers are free to undertake employment in other member states. On the demographic front it should be noted that the proportion of young people in the population will decline even more sharply in Germany and Italy. It could be that this will result in a net movement of skilled workers out of the United Kingdom to take up positions in Europe (Hendry, 1994). However, this predicted outcome is subject to varying influences, e.g. linguistic skills, culture and economic growth.

During the economic recession of the early 1990s the predicted effect of demographic changes was not too evident, particularly when the unemployment level among school-leavers and graduates is noted. (In 1992/93 the 16–19 age group had an unemployment figure of 18.8 per cent,

Box 4.3

B&Q AND THE 'GREY REVOLUTION'

The DIY store, B&Q, had traditionally recruited school-leavers to serve in its shops. Demographic changes prompted the personnel department to initiate a policy of employing older workers. This 'grey revolution' (Jetter, 1993) started with a new store in Macclesfield where all the recruits were over 50.

Recruitment took place through advertisements in the national press and two open days held locally. It was felt that older people would have more experience of DIY and would be able to encourage customers who were unsure of their abilities. The initial training was lengthened from four to eight weeks to allow for slower learning. However, this was found to be unnecessary, and it was reduced to the normal period.

The selection policy was thought to contribute to above average profits, a massive reduction in 'unattributable stock loss' and a very low absentee rate. Staff turnover was 50 per cent below average and customer satisfaction was significantly higher. The manager felt that there was a collective determination to prove that older people can perform.

---

and the 20–24 age group a figure of 15.6 per cent. These compare with an overall rate of 9.9 per cent; Skills and Enterprise Network, 1994.) However, when the recovery in the economy is well established the effects of the demographic changes could be felt. Recognizing the implications of the demographic changes for the organization, B&Q, a UK do-it-yourself store, created a personnel policy to employ older people (see the case in Box 4.3).

Reflecting on the B&Q case, one feels that certain prejudices about older workers are unfounded. In particular, older workers are able to learn as effectively as younger workers given the right conditions. Sickness absence is not higher than that for younger workers, and the profitability of the organization is not adversely affected.

Social/geographic aspects

The external supply of labour is influenced by socio-geographic factors. In certain parts of the United Kingdom (e.g. North of England, Scotland, Wales), where rapid decline of the older industries has taken place, there are large pools of labour with skills. This has prompted industrialists to consider moving their operations to these areas. Among the other factors influencing a company's decision to move to an area where an adequate supply of suitable labour exists are the quality of the transport system and access to the market for its output.

Many Japanese companies which have invested in the United Kingdom have done so in greenfield sites where there is high unemployment (Wilkinson and Oliver, 1992). For example, Komatsu, who manufacture earth-moving vehicles, set up their operation in the North-East of England. In the case of many of the Japanese consumer electronics companies, the company was not attracted by skills which already existed in an area, but was more concerned to recruit inexperienced labour. The selection process has been principally concerned with testing candidates' teamwork ability and their attitude to cooperative modes of working, as well as numeracy and dexterity skills.

Type of worker
The category of worker is another variable to consider when discussing the external supply of labour. Graduates and professional staff are more prepared to move location for a job than blue-collared skilled and semi-skilled workers. As was stated earlier, freedom of movement of labour within the EU is now enshrined in legislation, but in practice it is management and professional workers for whom mobility is a greater reality because of the attractive remuneration packages on offer. Initiatives have been taken by the EU to increase mobility in the labour market (Hendry, 1994). These initiatives include promoting common vocational standards, transferability of qualifications, and student exchanges.

Internal v. external supply

Using the internal supply of resources as a source of labour has certain advantages over the external supply. Those already employed in an organization are well placed to understand the way things are done and how the different parts of the organization fit together, and to appreciate the nature of the culture. The people responsible for selecting internal candidates for vacant positions have access to more comprehensive information relating to their abilities, track record and potential achievement than they would have if they were selecting people originating from the external labour market. Drawing on an internal supply of labour to fill vacancies, whereby the internal candidate receives a promotion, sends a powerful signal to employees that the organization is committed to their advancement and development.

However, one must be aware of certain disadvantages associated with drawing on an internal supply of resources. Although there may be more information about internal candidates at the disposal of selectors, it is not always free of bias. Also, there is greater likelihood of more negative information about internal candidates being available, whilst external candidates are better placed to conceal information about their past failures and difficulties. Finally, internal candidates could be steeped in the culture of the organization: if this culture is risk-aversive and conservative, it could act as a constraint when innovative practices and initiatives are required of the successful candidate. An external candidate could feel less inhibited where the introduction of fresh ideas to work practices and job performance is highly desirable. But for this to happen it may be necessary to change the corporate culture.

One way in which companies bring about a change in culture is by tapping the external supply of labour (Williams *et al.*, 1989). This could be reflected in an attempt to create a work-force with values and attitudes compatible with the desired corporate culture. For example, Toshiba aimed to increase cooperation and flexibility on their shop floor. This was done by carefully wording their recruitment literature, which referred to 'assembly operators' rather than to specific jobs, and through the use of a video shown to candidates offering themselves for employment so that they could engage in self-selection if they felt comfortable with the projected organizational environment on screen. Therefore, candidates with a flexible attitude, who were prepared to take on a variety of tasks, were selected rather than people who wanted to assume only one specific and fixed role.

Conclusions

Human resource or manpower planning has always been an area of interest in personnel and human resource management. Emphasis has been placed on different parts (hard and soft) of the planning process at different times in its history. The approach taken has largely reflected the business environment and the state of development of the subject. It is important to strike a balance so that no area of the planning process is neglected.

HRP is concerned with proactively analysing the external environment and making the best possible use of employees. In these ways HRP can provide an input to the organizational strategy by outlining the possibilities and costs of current and potential work-force configurations. It maps out the implications of strategic decisions for subsequent HRM activities such as recruitment and development. Therefore, HRP can be seen as an important linking factor between strategy and operation.

References

Bowey, A. (1974) *A Guide to Manpower Planning*. London: Macmillan.
Bramham, J. (1989) *Human Resource Planning*. London: IPM.
Braverman, H. (1974) *Labour and Monopoly Capitalism*. New York: Monthly Review Press.

Department of Employment (1994) *Labour Force Survey, No. 8*. London: Department of Employment.

Guest, D. (1994) 'Gazumping comes to the jobs market', *The Times* (Business Section), 22 July, p. 32.

Hamilton, K. (1993) 'Axing the bank clerks', *Sunday Times* (Business Section), 10 October, p. 4.

Hendry, C. (1994) 'The Single European Market and the HRM response', in Kirkbride, P. S. (ed.), *Human Resource Management in Europe*. London: Routledge.

Jetter, M. (1993) 'The wisdom factor: B&Q's employment of older people', in McIntosh, M. (ed.), *Good Business*. Bristol: SAUS.

Skills and Enterprise Network (1994) *A Summary of 'Labour Market and Skill Trends 1993/94'*. London: Department of Employment.

Storey, J. (1992) *Developments in the Management of Human Resources*. Oxford: Blackwell.

Taylor, F. W. (1947) *Scientific Management*. New York: Harper and Row.

Torrington, D., Hall, L., Haylor, I. and Myers, J. (1991) *Employee Resourcing*. London: IPM.

Wilkinson, B. and Oliver, N. (1992) 'Human resource management in Japanese manufacturing companies in the UK and USA', in Towers, B. (ed.), *The Handbook of Human Resource Management*. Oxford: Blackwell.

Williams, A., Dobson, P. and Walters, M. (1989) *Changing Culture*. London: IPM.

5

Employee resourcing: recruitment and selection

Recruitment and selection is the planned way in which the organization interfaces with the external supply of labour. Recruitment is the process of attracting a pool of candidates for a vacant position, and selection is the technique of choosing a new member of the organization from the available candidates. The processes of recruitment and selection incur significant costs, so it is natural for organizations to pay attention to these activities from a cost-effective viewpoint. For example, placing advertisements and using the services of managers in selection interviewing can be costly. It is also costly if the person selected to fill a particular vacancy does not perform satisfactorily in the job. Sub-standard performance on a production line can lead to having to correct a mistake, and a lack of skill in interacting with a customer could lead to a loss of business. Within a workgroup a poor performer can affect the rhythm and output of the team.

Certain advantages are said to accrue from external recruitment. It offers the organization the opportunity to inject new ideas into its operations by utilizing the skills of external candidates. When internal promotions have taken place, external recruitment could be used to attract candidates to fill positions which have been vacated by insiders. Also, external recruitment is a form of communication, whereby the organization projects its image to potential employees, customers and others outside the organization.

Prerequisites to recruitment

Recruitment and selection needs to be underpinned by solid preparatory work in the form of engaging in job analysis and preparing a job description and job specification.

95

Job analysis

This is done by a process of analysis to find out what is involved in the job that is now vacant. To start off this process one could interview the previous job-holder as well as his or her supervisor and other staff connected with him or her in the natural course of events. This approach has value in describing the tasks which constitute the vacant post, and highlights the reporting relationship (to the job-holder's superior) and other forms of liaison (e.g. with colleagues). There is also a tradition in job analysis whereby the job-holder may be asked to keep a work diary so that a record of how time is actually spent is available. When conducting a job analysis exercise one should keep firmly in mind the justification for the job in the light of current and future organizational needs. Therefore, corporate strategic considerations are a guiding force.

Job analysis will normally take place when a position becomes vacant, but as organizations become more flexible it can be an ongoing process of updating so as to enhance the adaptability of the organization. Job analysis provides the fundamental information which will subsequently be used in formulating the job description and job specification, i.e. information about the tasks that are carried out and the skills and attributes needed to achieve successful performance.

Job description

Having defined the job after analysing it, the next step is the preparation of a job description. This should contain an outline of the job, the tasks involved, the responsibilities and the conditions. A job description is a foundation stone for a number of human resource practices, ranging from selection to pay determination and training. But the traditional job description is now being challenged with the advent of the 'flexible' job description. This has become popular for some organizations, particularly those influenced by Japanese management practices in the early 1990s. The flexible job description will normally outline the nature of the tasks, and mention 'competences' and skills required for the job-holders; but it will not specify which team or group they belong to, nor will it state the precise nature of their responsibilities. The reason for the open-ended nature of the job responsibilities is to provide flexibility in the event of changes in the emphasis or direction taken by the organization.

Note the reference to competences above. The comparatively recent move towards underlining the importance of competences shifts the emphasis away from closely specifying tasks to be carried out towards stating the abilities and skills required of the job occupants. By taking this line of approach it is hoped that the individual and the organization will utilize the flexibility to adapt to new job requirements and situations. Also, the rigidity imposed by specifying a closed set of duties and responsibilities is removed.

Job specification

Job specification is used to describe a process whereby the information contained in the job description is used to assist in profiling the type of person capable of successfully executing the tasks associated with the job. A traditional approach to help with this exercise of matching job applicants and jobs is Rodger's (1952) seven-point plan:

1. Physique (health, appearance).
2. Attainments (education, qualifications, experience).
3. General intelligence (intellectual capability).
4. Special aptitudes (facility with hands, numbers or communication skills).
5. Interests (cultural, sport, etc.).
6. Disposition (likeable, reliable, persuasive).
7. Special circumstances (prepared to work shifts, excessive travel, etc.).

To make the seven-point plan operational would mean specifying essential and desirable characteristics under each of the above headings. More modern interpretations are likely to place emphasis on skills, work attitudes and interests apart from the above factors. In particular, restrictive personality requirements and criteria such as having a 'likeable' disposition could introduce an element of bias into the process, and so tend to be treated very carefully.

An alternative person specification is the five-fold grading system proposed by Munro Fraser (1958):

1. Impact on others (through physique, appearance, mode of expression).
2. Acquired qualifications (education, training, experience).
3. Innate attitudes (quick to grasp things, appetite for learning).
4. Motivation (sets goals and is determined to achieve them).
5. Adjustment (stable with high threshold for stress, relates well to others).

The central fact to note is that the preparation of a job specification is critical as a step in the process prior to recruitment because it tells us about the type of person needed to fill the vacant post. It provides a benchmark on the desirable qualities and important qualifications below which the organization must not go. In many cases current practices are modifications of one or more of the above systems.

Key result areas

It is now customary to pay attention to making explicit 'key result areas' for the job around the time the job specification is prepared. In this approach, getting results is heavily underlined, and so the emphasis is on outputs, and not on inputs. Outputs could be expressed in the form of quality, quantity, time and cost. A feature of 'key result areas' is that objectives are set for the new recruit, in accordance with stated criteria (e.g. quality/quantity of output), and this can provide the basis for subsequent performance appraisal.

Increasingly the language used in job specifications tends to reflect recent cultural shifts in human resource management (e.g. creative management of change, performance-oriented), so words such as initiate, achieve, stimulate, etc., seem to have wide currency.

Another recent development with respect to the format and content of the job specification is to highlight critical competences likely to be associated with successful job performance. A competency would refer to an underlying individual characteristic such as ability to communicate, to solve problems, to delegate effectively and to act as a good teamplayer. An elaboration of what we mean by competences appears in Box 5.1. There is further discussion of competences in a training and development context in chapter 8.

Before leaving the discussion of job specification it should be mentioned that the process so far should be considered within a framework of equal opportunity. This means keeping in mind that all job applicants should be given the chance to demonstrate their abilities irrespective of their sex, ethnic origin, disability or age where these factors are considered irrelevant to job performance.

Recruitment

In this section the spotlight will be on how to attract applicants, the sources of recruitment, and the shortlisting of candidates.

Box 5.1

COMPETENCES

Increasingly organizations are considering competences as an important feature of recruitment and selection, because of their association with good performance in an organizational role. The Training Agency (1989) defined competence as the ability to perform the activities within an occupation or function to the standards expected in employment.

The emphasis is on performing with the necessary level of skill to a desired standard, and national qualifications (e.g. Certificate in Management) can act as a means of verification and endorsement to ensure that the standard is achieved. This can be of assistance to selectors. For example, a person with a Certificate in Management is deemed to possess a range of specified competences in a number of areas (e.g. human resource management, financial decision making and information technology).

Of course there will be certain elements of competence not assessed by national awards, and organizations are expected to compensate for this omission when they analyse jobs. For example, London Transport carried out a competency-based analysis of the position of supervisor, and now bases recruitment and selection around such criteria as written and oral communication, planning and organizing, customer awareness, quality consciousness and attention to detail. Within these general headings, more specific criteria are identified. For instance, a person competent in oral communication is able to convey information and instructions that can be easily understood, and a person competent in planning and organizing has the ability to prioritize work and plan or schedule it. The above competences must be kept firmly in mind when assessment of skills is made during the formal selection process.

Attracting applicants

Now that the organization has a good idea of the profile of the candidate suited to the vacant position, the next step is to attract the attention of suitable applicants. The job specification will be used as a basis to create a shortened profile of the ideal candidate and likewise the job description will be used to extract information on the duties and responsibilities of the job-holder. This information is then used to advertise the position and to send an 'information pack' to applicants. This is an important stage in the process because the primary aim of the organization is to attract a sufficient number of good candidates. It should be noted that it is disadvantageous to attract too many candidates, because sorting out large numbers of applications is time-consuming and costly. Also, it is disadvantageous to attract too few applicants because the organization is faced with insufficient numbers, which limits choice.

Sources of recruitment

How does the organization go about finding suitable applicants? A number of options are open to it. Before exercising its options, a decision will be made on whether to handle the process internally or externally. In certain situations the personnel department or human resources function has the resources and competency to mount a recruitment campaign. One might expect this to happen where the job is fairly routine and applicants are in plentiful supply, but it could apply to other situations as well. External recruitment could run concurrently with activity to advertise vacancies internally, thereby encouraging internal candidates to apply. The following are examples of situations where the organization uses external agencies.

Job centres

A job centre is a free external service which the organization could find to be of great assistance. It will advertise the job and help with shortlisting suitable candidates. This can be most helpful where there is a large pool of available candidates.

Recruitment agencies

These agencies are likely to have a list of suitable applicants in their files, and charge a certain percentage of the salary attached to the job for rendering the service. They will be responsible for advertising the vacant position and shortlisting candidates. The obvious advantage to the organization using the services of recruitment agencies is the saving of time; and the small organization without an adequate personnel or human resource function has the advantage of having specialist advice and assistance available. The disadvantages are the cost involved, and the fact that control of such an important process is outside the organization. Another drawback might be that some agencies do not adhere to the organization's equal opportunities policy and its implementation in a way the organization would do when dealing internally with job applicants.

Executive search agencies

When the organization wishes to fill a very senior position, or a highly specialist position where applicants are in short supply, it may resort to the use of search agencies. These agencies charge very high fees, but organizations using them believe that the benefits will outweigh the cost. To derive benefits will certainly necessitate providing the search consultant or headhunter with a thorough job specification related to the vacancy.

Casual callers

These are respondents who read vacancy notices at, say, a factory gate, and could be attracted by the image of the company as an employer. They may show a reluctance to register with a job centre or agency, or to respond to a newspaper advertisement.

Friends or relatives of existing employees

The advantage of introductions through friends or relatives already employed in the organization is that the prospective employee gets an insight into the nature of the job and conditions within the company. However, it is important to bear equality of opportunity in mind because if certain groups (such as ethnic minorities or women) are under-represented in the current work-force, they may also be underrepresented in the friends and relations of the current work-force.

Schools, colleges, universities

Organizations which have traditionally taken on young people directly from the education system have operated a number of processes to recruit from this source. These processes include the 'milk round' where employers would visit universities publicizing their vacancies and interviewing final year students. Some employers have built up links with schools, encouraging visits and supporting education. Other employers, such as the Royal Navy and some large electronics companies, have funded the education of students on the understanding that the graduates or diplomates will work for the organization following completion of their courses.

Advertisements

A popular source of recruitment is an advertisement in national, provincial or local newspapers, or specialist magazines or journals. The organization could liaise directly with the media, or use the services of advertising agencies. The latter, who receive their commission from the media, can offer advice on advertising copy and choice of media, and may be better placed than the typical organization to book advertising space at short notice.

It is important to give serious consideration to the contents of the advertisement. For example, there would be an emphasis on the necessary qualifications and experience; duties and responsibilities; the organization where the job is located; salary (unless negotiable); method of application; and closing date for applications. Any special requirements such as non-standard hours or travel arrangements might be included to facilitate a decision to act one way or the other.

The advertisement is effectively projecting the image of the company, and as such it is a selling document; it is selling the company and the job in order to elicit a good response. The language used in the advertisement and the style of presentation should have intrinsic appeal. In the final analysis it should be uppermost in the recruiter's mind that the potential applicant has the choice to apply or not to apply. Therefore, what appears in the advertisement should assist rather than hinder the applicant in deciding whether or not he or she is interested in joining the organization.

Telephone 'hotlines'
In most cases the first major contact between a candidate and the organization after receiving the appropriate information will be a written submission in the form of either a completed application form or a curriculum vitae (CV). An alternative first contact is a telephone 'hotline'. This may be publicized through an advertisement, and candidates will be encouraged to contact the organization to discuss the vacancies, conditions of work and so on. This has the advantage of facilitating a speedy response and can encourage a larger pool of recruits, which may be important if there is a tight external supply of labour.

Open days
Some organizations use open days to encourage recruitment. Potential candidates are invited to come into the organization to meet managers or team leaders, and to see what working for the organization involves. This allows people to decide whether or not they are attracted to the vacant positions and to the organization, and it can encourage them to enter the next phase of recruitment.

As with telephone hotlines, open days can be useful where there are a number of similar vacancies and a relatively tight supply of labour.

Shortlisting

The outcome of the recruitment process is to produce a shortlist of candidates whose background and potential are in accordance with the profile contained in the job specification. If there are large numbers of applicants, this can be a time-consuming process. Those engaged in the shortlisting exercise will hopefully be making good use of the information provided by candidates on a well-designed application form, although in some situations candidates are asked to submit a CV instead of completing a pre-printed form.

An advantage of the CV is that it allows candidates to state their qualifications, experience, etc., in a way which could reflect their written communication skills. However, one should be aware of the fact that some candidates may receive professional help with the preparation of a CV. A problem with a CV as opposed to a standard application form is that the candidate specifies the information to include or exclude, whereas with the application form it is the organization that controls events and requires information relevant to organizational needs. The application form could be considered more reliable, because all applicants are forced to divulge information under set headings.

Whatever approach is adopted, the organization will be looking for information on the person's age, marital status, nationality (which can reflect the need for a work permit), education, qualifications, training, experience, present salary, special qualities, state of health, leisure interests and reasons for leaving; and the candidate is normally given the opportunity to provide any additional relevant information. Some employers provide less elaborate application forms for applicants seeking manual work. Although the application form is designed with selection firmly in mind, the completed form also serves another purpose. It can be used as an input to the personnel records of the successful candidates who join the organization. At this stage additional information, such as the national insurance number, may be required.

Selection

Selection is referred to as the final stage of the recruitment process when a decision is going to be made on who the successful candidate will be. As you can imagine, this is an important decision and should be made in an impartial and objective way, drawing on some or all of a number of selection techniques. These can be listed as follows:

1. Interviews.
2. Psychological tests.
3. Work-based tests.
4. Assessment centres.
5. Biodata.
6. References.
7. Graphology.

Interviews

Interviewing, either on a one-to-one basis or by interview panel, could be considered the most popular selection technique. Interviews offer the opportunity for a genuine two-way exchange of information which can be useful in judging whether or not the interviewee will relate well to colleagues and fit into the culture of the organization. According to Shackleton and Newell (1991), 90 per cent of their sample of organizations always use at least one interview in their selection process.

Interviews are said to have low validity but they continue to remain popular (Lewis, 1985). (The issue of validity will be examined later.) The crux of the matter with conducting interviews is not the irrelevance of interviewing as a selection device; it is the widely held view that the process itself is carried out in a flawed way. So what are the dysfunctional aspects of selection interviews?

☐ Subjective unsound judgements are made by untrained interviewers.

☐ There is a tendency for interviewers to arrive at a judgement early on in the interview, and this could be perceived as unjust by the interviewee who picks up this impression from the nature of the questioning and body language.

☐ Where interviewers have prior unfavourable biases about interviewees, there is the danger of highlighting negative data about the candidates so that it fits the biases. The 'halo' effect is where the interviewers are positively disposed towards interviewees because they like or are attracted to them. The result is that the interviewers look more benignly on the answers of the candidates instead of judging the raw content of what they say. The 'horn' effect is the reverse of this, where interviewers are predisposed to 'hear the worst' in what the candidates are saying. If a number of interviewers are involved (e.g. a panel interview), it is hoped that such individual biases will be reduced.

☐ There are many times when a consensus view does not emerge from a panel of interviewers, simply because interviewers see different things in the same interviewee.

What can be done to mitigate the worst effects of the selection interview, and improve its overall standing?

1. Set in motion a training programme for those who conduct interviews, be they managers, supervisors or 'personnel' specialists, using closed-circuit television. In such a setting the trainees would receive coaching in good practice.

2. Ensure that the appropriate documentation (i.e. job specification, job description, completed application form or CV) is circulated to the interviewer or interview panel members well in advance, and carefully studied before the start of the interview.

3. The venue should be suitable for conducting interviews, and the furniture in the interview room should be appropriately arranged.

4. A reasonable amount of time should be allocated for the interviews, and generally each interviewee should receive the same time allocation.

5. Where appropriate, open-ended, job-related questions, which require more than a yes/no response, should be asked of interviewees. The information received can be summarized and relayed to the interviewee to check that a correct understanding has been gained.

6. Normally towards the end of the formal questioning, the interviewee should be given the opportunity to ask his or her own questions, and be free to make observations.

7. Complement the information gleaned from the interviewee with the outcome of psychological tests where used, and references (preferably written). (There is a discussion of tests and references later in the chapter.)

8. Using panel rather than one-to-one interviews can reduce the amount of individual interviewer bias (such as the halo and horn effects), and can yield more information than where one interviewer is trying to take in all the information being disseminated. However, interview panels should not be so large that they become intimidating for the interviewees. Between three and five interviewers would be seen as normal.

The selection interview is a process which is evolving on a continuous basis. The discussion above concentrated on the structured interview, with some manifestations of an unstructured orientation when the interviewee has been given a modicum of control to ask questions and raise issues. This can be a useful approach to encourage a genuinely two-way exchange of information.

One particular approach to interviewing is called the situational interview (Latham et al., 1980). Here critical on-the-job incidents are identified and recorded following a job analysis exercise. Questions are then prepared to elicit the views of the interviewees on these events. For example, an interviewee is asked 'what would you do in a particular situation?' The answers are entered on a form and rated on a five-point scale. Studies by Latham et al. (1980) and Latham and Saari (1984) have shown the situational interview to be more valid and reliable than unstructured interviews.

Another development in the selection interview, which is worthy of note, is the patterned behaviour description interview (PBDI) (Anderson and Shackleton, 1989). The interviewer probes major life change events in order to ascertain the interviewee's reasons for taking the reported career direction. The aim is to create a 'picture over time' to help with predicting the candidate's likely reactions to future career challenges and changes. Patterns of behaviour could relate to educational choices, ways of approaching particular problems and opportunities at work, and decisions about career development. A pattern may emerge in which candidates are either more proactive or reactive to situations, or information may be gained on whether they deal with problems aggressively, assertively or passively. The emerging pattern is compared with the pre-established desirable pattern of behaviour.

A recent development is 'competency-based interviewing' (Johnstone, 1995). Instead of looking at what the candidates have achieved, the focus is on how they achieved the results they claim. With competency-based interviewing, the interviewer is looking for specific traits reflected in past achievements. To identify those traits, interviewers are instructed to look for STARs – an acronym that stands for Situations, Tasks, Actions and Results. This is likely to unfold as follows: first, examine the job specification to establish what the job requires. For example, a managerial job could require the exercise of leadership skills, or the ability to make a presentation at a senior level, or skills in promoting interaction in teams. Having identified the relevant roles, the candidates are asked whether they played such roles or found themselves in such 'situations' in the past or previous job. Once interviewers have found an appropriate situation in the candidates' past, the next step is to identify the 'tasks' they were responsible for, followed by identifying the 'actions' they took if a problem arose, and finally what effect or 'result' the action(s) had.

Psychological tests

Two of the more important psychological tests (often referred to as psychometric tests) used for selection purposes are intelligence tests and personality tests. The justification for considering both intelligence and personality tests in the field of selection is the belief that scores on those tests have some validity in predicting future job performance.

Intelligence testing

If an organization gave intelligence tests to recruits, which took the form of tests of numerical and verbal ability, and found from experience that good test scores were associated with good subsequent performance in the job, then we could conclude that there is a high correlation between a particular test of intelligence and job performance. Tests of verbal and numerical ability, with questions on vocabulary, similarities, opposites, arithmetical calculations, etc., are often referred to as general intelligence tests. When people score highly on these tests they are said to have a good capacity to absorb new information, pass examinations and pick up things quickly and perform well at work. But it should be noted that a particular test may only be valid for a particular type of job or activity.

Apart from general intelligence tests, there are aptitude tests and attainment tests. Aptitude tests can measure specific abilities or aptitudes (e.g. spatial ability, manual dexterity, numerical ability, verbal ability) and are used to gauge the person's potential. It should be noted that individuals differ markedly in their ability to do certain things – for example, the ability to learn to do tasks requiring eye–muscle coordination.

Attainment tests, which are sometimes called achievement tests, measure abilities or skills already developed by the person. For example, a word processor operator could be tested for speed and accuracy on a typing test prior to the interview for a secretarial post.

Personality tests

There is a recognition that personality has a bearing on the competence of the individual to perform effectively at work, and that personality defects can nullify the beneficial aspects stemming from having the appropriate aptitude or ability. It goes without saying that a highly motivated, psychologically well-adjusted employee is of greater value to a company than an employee who is emotionally unstable and demotivated.

As a broad statement we could refer to personality as that part of us that is distinctive and concerned more with our emotional side and how it is reflected in our behaviour. By contrast, intelligence is concerned with the cognitive or thinking side of us, though, of course, there are some areas of overlap. For example, in Cattell's (1963) sixteen personality factors (16PF) inventory or test, *one* factor refers to intelligence. Other factors deal with mainstream personality, such as emotional stability, submissiveness, controlling, timidity, risk taking, roughness, confidence and so on.

After the administration of a test, such as Cattell's 16PF, a profile of the job applicant is produced. There are a number of personality inventories on the market with the same basic aim as Cattell's 16PF, such as Saville and Holdsworth's occupational personality questionnaire (OPQ). When personality is assessed, using one of the published tests, the next step would be to compare the resulting profile with some standard profile believed to be appropriate or relevant to the job for which the candidate is being considered. Obviously a good fit would be advantageous, but one must be aware of the extreme difficulty of creating the standard or ideal profile of a job occupant.

When a person is completing a standard personality questionnaire the organization would like to think that honest responses are given, and that the respondent avoids giving socially acceptable answers. In practice there could be problems meeting these conditions, as there could be difficulties in establishing clear links between certain personality traits and job outcomes (good performance).

The characteristics of a good psychological test should be noted:

☐ The measuring device is able to discriminate between individuals.

☐ The test is reliable and valid (this will be explained later).

☐ The test is properly standardized, whereby it has been used on a significant sample of the population to which it is related. Individual scores are then compared with norms derived from that population when interpreting the results.

Overview

Certain assumptions underlie the administration of psychological tests:

1. There is the belief that there are significant differences in the extent to which individuals possess certain characteristics, e.g. emotional stability, intelligence, motivation and finger dexterity.
2. There is a direct and important relationship between the possession of one or more of these characteristics and the ability of the person to do certain jobs.
3. Selected characteristics can be measured in a practical sense and an evaluation can be made of the relationship between test results and job performance.

The value of selection test scores to predict future job performance has been the subject of much debate in recent times, with challenges to the validity of such exercises (Blinkhorn and Johnson, 1990). Some might object to the narrow focus, when personality test scores only are used, because of the failure to consider other relevant factors that influence behaviour, e.g. demands of the immediate environment. Others point out, again in the context of personality, that there can be a danger of recruiting the same or similar personality types and producing a situation where there is a lack of variety in the personality composition of work teams.

Whatever the shortcomings of psychological testing, there has been a growth in their use in the field of selection over the last decade. In the mid-1980s 65 per cent of organizations in one survey never used personality tests (Robertson and Makin, 1986); in another survey that figure fell to 36 per cent in the early 1990s, with 27 per cent of organizations using them for more than half their vacancies (Shackleton and Newell, 1991). The size of organization seems to be an important variable in mediating the use of tests. In a further study 59 per cent of large organizations (employing more than 2,000 people) used personality tests and 74 per cent used aptitude tests; the figures for smaller companies were 41 and 62 per cent respectively.

Work-based tests

When an organization needs to assess the level of candidates' competence in particular areas, behavioural tests can be used. These are sometimes referred to as 'in-tray' tests because the candidates are presented with a representative sample of the work they would be doing if appointed, i.e.

a sample of what they might find in their 'in-tray', and are required to undertake the typical tasks associated with the job. The quality of their work is then assessed. Normally the test will have a time limit. Candidates will have to prioritize the work they are presented with and carry out as many tasks as they can. For a secretarial position, this may include typing sample correspondence, dealing with enquiries (presented verbally or in writing) and so on. This approach has also been used in the selection of social workers, where candidates joined in the examination of hypothetical cases to decide on the appropriate programme of action or care.

Work-based tests are valuable in that they provide evidence of the candidate's competence in actually carrying out specific tasks. However, as the situation of the test is simulated, rather than real, certain factors may affect the performance of candidates. Candidates may perform poorly if they are nervous or lack the background information and experience they would have if they were actually in the job.

There is a further question to raise and that is, what is being assessed? Work-based tests concentrate on the current competences of candidates. However, where the organization is concerned with flexibility and the future potential of candidates – a stand which would be compatible with an HRM perspective – it would be necessary to use other selection techniques as well.

Assessment centres

Assessment centres, which are events rather than places, use a variety of selection methods in order to increase the likelihood of making a good decision. The methods used include the interview, psychometric tests, and individual and group exercises such as role playing and task simulations, including in-tray exercises referred to earlier.

Before assessment commences the organization should ensure that the relevant job specification and competences are spelled out and are available. The assessment assumes an individual form when psychometric tests are administered and the candidates are interviewed individually. But an important part of the assessment centre is the evaluation of the candidates' interactive and interpersonal skills in a group exercise. This is done by a number of trained assessors, many of whom are line managers within the organization. One reason for having a number of assessors is to minimize bias in the assessment process. Also, a number of assessors are needed to observe closely the behaviour and interactions of the various candidates. Because a number of methods are used, and it is an intensive process, it stands to reason that the overall exercise is time-consuming (say two or three days) and costly.

Normally one finds that assessment centres (or development centres when applied to management development) are used by large organizations to select key staff, and this could include graduate entrants. The cost of mounting an assessment centre for selection purposes is justified if it is effective in channelling a flow of able employees into the organization. A spin-off of the assessment centre could be the provision of feedback to candidates who have gone through the process which helps them to build on their strengths and tackle their weaknesses. Finally, assessment centres have high validity as a selection device.

Biodata

When candidates apply for a job in an organization they normally complete a standard application form or submit a CV. In these documents one would expect to find certain 'biographical' information related to age, education, personal history, and current and past employment. When one uses biographical information or biodata in a systematic way as a selection tool, a questionnaire is used to collect information on a large number of successful performers in the job, and the data are then correlated with the data from candidates. From this exercise could materialize an awareness of biodata (e.g. a certain type of qualification) that is associated with career success. Particular features of a person's biographical profile could receive a higher score than others because of such features' prime importance in influencing good performance. The basic assumption of this approach is that if we know enough about people's life histories we can improve selection by being better able to predict the likely future performance of candidates.

To operationalize the biodata approach the specially designed questionnaire, with weighted items, is used for each candidate. A score is given for responses under each item, and individual item scores are then summed. This technique can be used at the shortlisting phase or later at the time of a structured interview. The discriminating factor in either case is the score given.

There are certain advantages stemming from the use of the biodata approach. It is a useful technique when it is necessary to screen a very large number of applications in response to an advertisement. It is relatively objective and underlines the importance of using a systematic approach to compiling biographical information as a means to improving selection decisions. An obvious disadvantage is the large amount of time needed to ascertain the key biographical items in the first instance, as well as the cost of such an exercise.

There are certain potential dangers in the use of biodata. The features of personal background which are accorded the status of highly rated desirable features might be biased against certain minority groups. For example, bias could occur where the sample of employees from whom the biodata profile is drawn (by which the candidates will be judged) is an unrepresentative group, or has distinctive features which could unfairly exclude others. For instance, if all the successful performers coincidentally had a particular type of family background, to use this as a discriminating factor would introduce bias.

Finally, a study found that 20 per cent of organizations used biodata as a selection device for some vacancies, but only 4 per cent used it for all their vacancies (Shackleton and Newell, 1991).

References

A candidate for a job is normally asked to nominate more than one referee. One function of a reference is to provide confirmation that the information provided by the candidate is true, another is to provide a character reference. Normally, a reference is taken up when the applicant appears on a shortlist and is seriously considered for the particular job, though there are times when a 'long' shortlist is prepared, and a reference has a part to play in the production of the final shortlist.

Some candidates are not too keen for a potential employer to approach their current employer with a request for a reference unless a job offer is on the table. They may not want their present employer to know that they wish to move on. Others might positively welcome their current employer being approached, even though they have not received a job offer, because they feel that being considered seriously for another job of some significance is something they would like their current employers to hear about.

References are considered to be an important input to the selection process where honesty and moral rectitude are crucial considerations. But there are cases where the information contained in references is of doubtful value, particularly when referees provide little beyond confirmation of the dates of employment. Obviously references have greater value when informative data on the candidate's track record are provided and the contents of the application form are verified. A reliable form of reference is one that has been prepared specifically in response to a list of relevant questions posed by the potential employers.

A drawback of references as a selection device is that the applicant nominates the referee(s), and he or she is unlikely to choose a person who will provide a negative assessment. In practice referees are often hesitant to express negative views about a person in writing; although some would feel less inhibited in this sense if asked to provide a reference over the telephone. Generally, the validity and reliability of references are rather

Box 5.2

GRAPHOLOGY IN SELECTION

Exponents of handwriting analysis believe that graphology can show the potential and ability of a person not apparent from the normal scrutiny of a CV or completed application form. The British Institute of Graphologists claims that analyses from trained graphologists are generally described by clients as extremely accurate and compare favourably with other methods of personality assessment, such as psychometric testing.

A graphologist will require a candidate to submit at least a page of spontaneous writing in fountain or ball-point pen, preferably on unlined paper. The content of the submission is unimportant, but the writer is told not to copy a piece of text as this impedes the flow of writing. Precise rules are followed to measure the writing size, slant, page layout and width of letters and pressure on the paper. These measurements are interpreted to reveal the emotions and talents of the writer. Apparently the degree of pressure on the page conveys the writer's level of energy.

Nowadays, more than 75 per cent of French companies use graphology as a standard selection procedure, and its use by Swiss companies is even higher. Graphology is also used regularly by companies in countries such as Germany, Austria, Belgium, Holland and Italy. Job advertisements in continental European newspapers frequently ask for handwritten letters, and applicants expect their handwriting to be analysed. Therefore, it is not surprising to find many continental European companies having in-house graphologists on their staff.

(Altman, 1995).

---

poor (Reilly and Chao, 1982; Hunter and Hunter, 1984), but they are still popular in the United Kingdom. Shackleton and Newell (1991) found that 74 per cent of the UK organizations surveyed always used references as opposed to 11 per cent of organizations in France.

Graphology

Graphology is a technique which makes predictions about future performance on the basis of handwriting analysis. Although not very popular in the United Kingdom, it has greater acceptance in France (Shackleton and Newell, 1991) (see Box 5.2). A recent report by the British Psychological Society expressed serious reservations about its effectiveness as a selection device (McLeod, 1994).

Validity and reliability

Validity measures how successful a selection technique is in predicting the future performance of the job occupant. Before we can measure validity, criteria have to be established as to what constitutes successful performance in the job, and also what constitutes successful performance during, for example, the interview process or test. Measuring performance on a psychometric test, for example, is not too difficult, but measuring performance when another selection device is used (e.g. the interview) is much harder. Statistical methods are used to relate measures of performance during the selection process to measures of subsequent job performance.

A valid selection process could be expressed as follows: those who score highly on a selection test perform better on the job than those registering lower test scores. A statistical relationship showing the correlation between test scores and indicators of performance could amount to +1 (a perfect positive correlation) or the opposite −1 (a perfect negative correlation), and 0, where there is no evidence of correlation and no predictive value (i.e. the selection method is no better at predicting performance than reliance on pure chance). In practice, a very good figure for correlation would be 0.5–0.6, and a range between 0.3 and 0.4 would be acceptable. Finally, one should realize that ascertaining the validity of a selection method is by no means an easy task, and psychologists use different types of validity.

The reliability of a test is the extent to which it measures consistently whatever it does measure. For example, all candidates for a job are subjected to the same tests and are questioned by the same interview panel, and if the procedures remain the same, the selection methods are said to be reliable. If a test is highly reliable it is possible to put greater reliance on the scores individuals receive than if the test is not very reliable.

An example of an unreliable test is as follows: a person is examined on two separate occasions, using a finger dexterity test. He or she scored highly on the test on the first occasion, and was placed near the top of the group. However, without any material change in factors affecting the individual that person scores badly on the test on the second occasion and is placed near the bottom of his or her group.

Reliability of tests is something one might consider in the context of the implementation of an equal opportunities policy. It is important that all candidates have an equal chance to express themselves and show their competences.

Cost effectiveness

It is important that the selection techniques used are cost-effective. As was mentioned earlier, the cost of a selection decision mistake can be very high and this has to be balanced against the cost of extensive procedures to minimize mistakes. Consequently, many organizations will use assessment centres (which are costly) for managerial jobs and other positions considered important, but would not incur the same cost for lower level positions in the organization. Similarly, biodata and psychological tests can be expensive to set up and use because the services of specialist professionals will generally be required. As a result, they tend to be used for the more senior positions.

Conclusions

The processes of recruitment and selection interact with other HRM systems. In particular they are part of the way human resource plans are implemented and they provide input to the training and development functions of the organization. As recruitment involves advertising, publicity and corresponding with members of the public it needs to be implemented in a way which supports the image of the organization.

Employee selection has attracted considerable research and scholarly attention. As a result there has been extensive critical debate about the effectiveness of selection methods. There is now a wide range of techniques available, and the human resource manager should be aware of each technique's strengths and weaknesses so that the best method for the job and the organization can be chosen.

Traditionally, human resource managers have felt that their expertise in this area is an important part of their professionalism. Increasingly, however, organizations are devolving aspects of recruitment and selection work to line and functional managers. This means that there is a change in focus from providing a high quality inclusive service, to providing support so that other managers can carry out the process legally, effectively and efficiently.

As increases in the flexible use of the work-force occur, recruitment and selection need to adapt to changing circumstances. This can entail speedier approaches to attracting temporary workers and the use of specialist agencies. It is important that these changes do not reduce the quality and fairness of the procedures.

References

Altman, W. (1995) 'The write way to a job', (Business Recruitment Feature), *London Evening Standard*, 24 January, p. 34.
Anderson, N. and Shackleton, V. (1989) 'Staff selection decision making into the 1990s', *Management Decision*, **28**, 5–9.

Blinkhorn, S. and Johnson, C. (1990) 'The insignificance of personality testing', *Nature*, **348**, 671–672.

Cattell, R. B. (1963) *The 16 PF Questionnaire*. Champagne, IL: Institute for Personality and Ability Training.

Hunter, J. E. and Hunter, R. F. (1984) 'Validity and utility of alternative predictors of performance', *Psychological Bulletin*, **96**, 72–98.

Johnstone, H. (1995) 'Beat the interview blues', (Business Recruitment Feature), *London Evening Standard*, 8 March, p. 46.

Latham, G. P. and Saari, L. M. (1984) 'Do people do what they say? Further studies of the situational interview', *Journal of Applied Psychology*, **65**, 422–427.

Latham, G. P., Saari, L. M., Pursell, E. D. and Campion, M. A. (1980) 'The situational interview', *Journal of Applied Psychology*, **65**, 659–673.

Lewis, C. (1985) *Employee Selection*. London: Hutchinson.

McLeod, D. (1994) *Graphology and Personnel Assessment*. Leicester: The British Psychological Society.

Munro Fraser, J. (1958) *A Handbook of Employment Interviewing*. London: Macdonald & Evans.

Reilly, R. and Chao, G. (1982) 'Validity and fairness of some employment selection procedures', *Personnel Psychology*, **35**, 1–62.

Robertson, I. and Makin, P. (1986) 'Management selection in Britain: a survey and critique', *Journal of Occupational Psychology*, **59**, 45–57.

Rodger, A. (1952) *The Seven-point Plan*. London: National Institute of Industrial Psychology.

Shackleton, V. and Newell, S. (1991) 'Managerial selection: a comparative study of methods used in top British and French companies', *Journal of Occupational Psychology*, **64**, 23–36.

Training Agency (1989) *Training in Britain: A study of funding, activity, and attitudes*. London: HMSO.

6

Employee development: performance management

Frequently judgements are made, both formally and informally, about the performance of employees at work. In an informal system we are aware that superiors are continually making judgements about their subordinates' performance on a subjective basis. By contrast, superiors could resort to using formalized appraisal techniques when assessing the performance of subordinates, and these judgements are considered to be more objective. In formalized systems the terms 'performance appraisal' and 'performance management' are used. Both refer to a process whereby managers and their subordinates share understanding about what has to be accomplished, and the manager will naturally be concerned about how best to bring about those accomplishments by adept management and development of people in the short and long terms. Also, performance would be measured using the techniques discussed in this chapter and it would be subsequently related to targets or plans. In this way the subordinate receives feedback on his or her progress.

However, a distinguishing feature of performance management is its integrating strength in aligning various processes with corporate objectives: for example, the introduction of performance-related payment systems and the mobilization of training and development resources to achieve corporate objectives (Bevan and Thompson, 1991).

Aims of appraisal

The following aims might be considered when examining a performance appraisal system:

- Set targets which are acceptable to those whose performance is going to be appraised and do so in a climate characterized by open communication between superior and subordinate and strive for partnership in action.
- Use reliable, fair and objective measures of performance, compare actual with planned performance, and provide feedback to the appraisee.
- Where performance is sub-optimal, after going through the previous step, signal the need to specify and agree with the appraisee a personal improvement plan which could be based on an assessment of the person's training and development needs.
- Make provision for the allocation of both extrinsic rewards (e.g. performance-related pay) and intrinsic rewards (e.g. opportunity to enhance one's skills) following the assessment process.
- Subscribe to desirable outcomes in the form of employee fulfilment, full utilization of the individual's capacity, change of corporate culture (where appropriate), and the achievement of organizational objectives in conditions where there is harmonization of individual and organizational objectives.
- Recognize that performance management is at the heart of the general management process.

Appraisal techniques

Certain techniques are available to evaluate the performance of the employee. This section briefly reviews the major techniques in use.

Written report

The appraiser writes a narrative about the strengths, weaknesses, previous performance and potential of the appraisee, with suggestions for improvement. It is important that the appraiser is perceptive with reasonable writing skill.

Critical incidents

The appraiser highlights incidents or key events that show the appraisee's behaviour as exceptionally good or bad in relation to particular outcomes at work. This exercise would depict desirable behaviours as well as behaviour that signals a need for improvement.

Graphic rating scales

This is a popular appraisal technique and, unlike the written report and critical incidents techniques, it lends itself to quantitative analysis and comparison of data. A set of performance factors is identified, including such characteristics as quality of work, technical knowledge, cooperative spirit, integrity, punctuality and initiative. The appraiser would go through the set of factors rating them, for example, on a scale 1 to 5 where the highest number would denote the best rating. This technique is economical in the time devoted to its development and use, but it does not provide the depth of information provided by the other techniques described above.

A variation of the graphic rating scales is the 'behaviourally anchored rating scales', where descriptions of the type of behaviour associated with each point on the rating scale is clearly stated. Behaviourally anchored rating scales specify job-related behaviour associated with each performance factor along a continuum. The appraiser then selects the appropriate point on the continuum for each performance factor. For example, an appraisee, who is a middle manager, is rated as 4 under the performance factor referred to as 'leadership'. The statement of behaviour associated with this point on the continuum or scale is 'exceptional skill in directing others to great effort'. By contrast, a rating of 1 on the same continuum could be described as 'often weak in command situations; at times unable to exert control'.

Multi-person comparison

This technique, which is a relative rather than an absolute measure, is used to assess one person's performance against one or more other individuals. It comprises three well-established approaches, namely individual ranking, group ranking and paired comparison.

☐ *Individual ranking*. This approach orders appraisees from the best to the worst performer with no provision for ties.

☐ *Group ranking*. This approach requires the appraiser to place appraisees in particular categories which reflect their performance. For example, a person who performed exceptionally well would be placed in the top 10 per cent, while a person who performed very poorly would be placed in the bottom 10 per cent.

☐ *Paired comparison*. This approach allows for the comparison of each appraisee with every other appraisee. Appraisees are paired and each person is rated as either the stronger or the weaker individual. When the exercise of paired comparisons is completed, after all appraisees have been paired with each other, each appraisee is given an overall ranking score which reflects the stronger points. Although this approach permits everybody to be compared with everybody else in a particular organizational setting, it can be difficult to handle when large numbers are involved.

Multi-person comparisons can be used in conjunction with one of the other techniques in order to mix the best features of the relative and absolute measures. For example, a graphic rating scale could be used alongside an individual ranking approach.

Multi-rater comparative evaluation

One example of this technique is an assessment centre which was examined in chapter 5 in connection with selection. It can adopt a comparative evaluation approach, using multiple raters. When used in the context of management development, it is often referred to as a 'development centre' where the appraisal of managerial abilities and skills with a view to establishing the suitability of subjects for promotion can take place over a few days. The total appraisal process consists of interviews, psychometric testing, simulations of relevant work activities, peer appraisals and appraisals by trained assessors.

Management by objectives

Objectives are agreed and formulated at the beginning of the period under review, and the appraisee is given the necessary assistance and training to facilitate the achievement of those objectives. At the end of the period there will be an appraisal of performance and new objectives are set.

Self-appraisal

As a rider to the discussion of the major appraisal techniques which are frequently used by superiors in evaluating the performance of subordinates, consider for a moment the practice of self-appraisal in the context of employee development. Michelin, the tyre manufacturer, introduced on a pilot basis a self-appraisal scheme as a means of empowering workers, enhancing teamwork and raising awareness of quality. The pilot scheme covered thirty workers who were asked to complete appraisal forms on which they evaluated themselves against criteria such as attendance, productivity, quality, safety, teamwork and commitment.

The completed appraisal forms were then used as a basis for a discussion with the managers of the participating workers. Freeing the managers from form-filling meant they had more time for communication with their subordinates. It was concluded that the workers who participated in the self-appraisal scheme were not backward in coming forward with criticisms of themselves, more so than if the managers conducted the appraisals. It is the company's intention to expand the scheme (Huddart, 1994).

Different perspectives

There are two main perspectives on the performance appraisal process; one is evaluative and the other is developmental (Anderson, 1992). An evaluative appraisal amounts to making a judgement about the appraisee and this follows a historical analysis of the latter's performance over the period under review. The judgement is made after comparing the appraisee's performance against previously established objectives or targets, or against all operational items on the job description. This type of appraisal could be linked to the allocation of extrinsic rewards, such as pay.

A development appraisal sets out to identify and develop the potential of the appraisee with the spotlight on future performance, and could be linked to career planning and management succession. A major aim is to establish what type of knowledge and skill the individual should develop. After identifying the appraisee's development needs, appropriate development objectives can be established. Because it is necessary for the appraisee to be open and frank about his or her perceived personal limitations and difficulties encountered in performance, it is necessary for this type of appraisal to be imbued with a high level of openness and mutual respect between the appraiser and the appraisee; also, there ought to be an avoidance of restrictive bureaucratic control.

The two performance appraisal perspectives stress the need for feedback on both good and bad performances and they underline the importance of indicating future personal development. By doing so they acknowledge the part played by motivation in feedback sessions; for example, being recognized for good performance or being told where there is scope for improvement has real motivational significance. Further discussion of the evaluative and developmental perspectives follows.

Evaluative appraisal

Performance factors were briefly referred to earlier when examining appraisal techniques. Here we will have something more to say about them. When engaged in performance-related behaviour the employee is concerned with the behavioural, social and technical aspects of the job. The appraiser, normally the immediate supervisor or manager, with perhaps assistance from a human resource specialist, has to establish what aspects of employee performance should be examined, and what combination of objective and subjective appraisal techniques should be used. In research undertaken by Income Data Services, London (IDS, 1989) it was concluded that the performance factors most usually appraised were as follows:

☐ Knowledge, ability and skill on the job.

☐ Attitude to work, expressed as enthusiasm, commitment and motivation.

☐ Quality of work on a consistent basis with attention to detail.

☐ Volume of productive output.

☐ Interaction, as exemplified in communication skills and ability to relate to others in teams.

Other performance factors which were less commonly used consisted of the following items: flexible mode of operation; ingenuity in tackling problems; capability to act with little supervision; skill at managing others; conversant with job requirements; track record at meeting performance targets; attendance record and punctuality; ability to plan and set priorities; and awareness of health and safety regulations. Obviously there is an overlap between some of these factors and key factors listed above (e.g. job knowledge, ability and skill).

Those involved in the appraisal of performance will pay a lot of attention to the choice of both performance factors and techniques. They will be interested in the outcome of the appraisee's performance. This could be something tangible like a quantitative record of the employee's output, or more qualitative like the display of appropriate behaviour. What should be avoided is the recording of personality traits which are not connected to actual behaviour on the job.

A feature of the evaluative appraisal is the link between the outcome of the appraisal process and pay or financial benefits. Proponents of this association are likely to point out that it is equitable and has real motivational effect. Employees are likely to consider the appraisal process as being significant because good performance is recognized and rewarded, but poor performance is not rewarded. Also, a performance-oriented culture is fostered (Anderson, 1992). By contrast, opponents of the process of linking pay to appraisal feel that the purpose of the performance review is blurred, that it is almost tantamount to a pay review, and that performance appraisal should be separated from a review of pay.

According to Anderson (1992), pay assumes a position of overriding importance when it is linked to performance: appraisees try to extract from their boss performance targets that are easily attainable; the appraisee's behaviour is too narrowly focused on those targets to the detriment of a broader view of performance in order to receive good ratings; appraisees show an inclination to conceal negative information about their perform-ance; and those charged with performance appraisal give appraisees a higher ranking when they know a lower ranking would disadvantage them in financial terms.

When looking at the relationship between pay and performance appraisal it is wise to consider the influence of culture. In an organizational culture supportive of individualism and achievement there could be firm expectations on the part of employees that the appraisal process should coincide with the review of pay. An example of such a culture would be the dealing arm of a stockbroking firm (see Box 3.2, p. 67). The dealers are likely to welcome a situation of loose organizational control with a minimum amount of guidance from above. The outcome of the appraisal process would form an input to the activity connected with the determina-tion of rewards. It is unlikely that the organizational culture would be supportive of conditions where performance appraisal and the review of pay take place at different times.

There are circumstances where, at the target-setting stage, the perform-ance appraisal process is used to transmit organizational values or culture. The latter could then be reinforced at the evaluation of performance stage when acceptable behaviour in which the organizational values are enshrined is recognized and rewarded. A company subscribing to this viewpoint could be concerned with encouraging appropriate behaviour (e.g. reliability, cooperativeness, able team-player, good attendance record, enthusiastic, efficiency-conscious and being a good example to others in improving methods and practice) with less emphasis on actual output. This was the approach adopted by Polaroid in its appraisal process when determining who should be promoted (Townley, 1989).

It appears that compliance is exacted from the subordinate in return for some advantage or reward when the evaluative appraisal is used, and the process has ingrained in it images of a power relationship between the superior and subordinate. Such an arrangement could run counter to a system of industrial relations where collective bargaining has taken root. In such circumstances there could be trade union resistance. Now we seem to have moved into territory where the performance appraisal system is seen as a medium of management control and manipulation. However, not everybody would take that view because there is a body of opinion that considers that the appraisal process can create a performance culture that gives due recognition to the individual's actual and potential performance and development needs.

Development appraisal

In this type of appraisal the interview features prominently, with the emphasis on the future development of the appraisee. The provision of open and constructive feedback is used to create the right motivational disposition. In practice the appraisee could gain sight of the appraisal forms and say what he or she thinks of the performance of the person carrying out the appraisal (the appraiser). We now appear to be moving towards emphasizing a partnership between the manager and the subordinate in the appraisal process. The importance of personal objectives, which flow from corporate objectives, being agreed by both the appraiser and appraisee as realistic and challenging is strongly advocated, with the rider that appraisal techniques should be appropriate measuring devices of actual performance and kept under review (Williams, 1991).

One should also note the reinforcing qualities of solid feedback in an appraisal session when good behaviour is praised and deficiencies identified, though this is something that should happen on a periodic basis and not just once a year. Where deficiencies have been found, steps should be taken to prepare a performance improvement plan to help the appraisee rectify the deficiencies and build on his or her strengths; self-development should be encouraged in these circumstances.

There is no doubt about the status of development appraisal: it is an integral part of the management process. It is suggested that counselling should be coupled with the normal deliberations associated with running the appraisal process. This occurred at IBM in a climate supportive of employee development, with the added dimension of determining merit pay (Sapsed, 1991). Introducing pay determination into the development appraisal is unlikely to be the normal practice in organizations that subscribe to the basic tenets of assessment aimed at development. Apart from counselling and developing a relationship of mutual trust and respect, the manager might give serious consideration to empowering his or her subordinates so that they have the opportunity to stretch their capabilities in a problem-solving context.

Given the recent developments in HRM whereby ownership of the appraisal process has moved from the personnel function to the appropriate manager, it is imperative that the latter is trained in operating the techniques of appraisal. When using the appraisal data to diagnose development needs the manager will be expected to use counselling and communication skills, including effective listening, and perhaps, in appropriate circumstances, inviting the appraisee to practise upward appraisal (see Box 6.1). If the manager is found wanting in the utilization of these skills, this could signal the need for a skill-based management development experience for the manager. Where a number of different but

Box 6.1

UPWARD APPRAISAL

This is a bottom-up approach to appraisal whereby subordinates rate superiors and has been used by organizations such as British Petroleum (BP), British Airways, and Cathay Pacific Airlines. It is felt that subordinates are well placed to gain a solid view of the strengths and weaknesses of their boss. A representative view could materialize from the combined ratings of a number of subordinates. For this system of performance management to work well requires it to be efficient and equitable in an appropriate cultural setting. For example, a prerequisite is that the organization feels it can trust employees to be honest, fair and constructive. Also, there should be a firm belief in the value of two-way communication within the organization.

Upward appraisal is not without its problems. One has to recognize that some subordinates could feel somewhat inhibited when asked to offer a frank and fair view of their superior for fear of reprisal. Others might show an aversion to rating at either the upper or lower ends of the rating scale, instead they settle for the unadventurous middle point of the range. Sometimes the suggestion is made that subordinates should come forward with anonymous ratings, and therefore might feel less inhibited. However, there could be a downside to such an approach when subordinates avail themselves of the opportunity to be vindictive towards a superior who has been putting pressure on them to reach exacting performance standards.

Finally, subordinates would need training on how to conduct appraisals, and from the organization's point of view it is desirable that subordinates' ratings are acted upon. The latter could necessitate a significant change of corporate culture.

(Furnham, 1993).

complementary appraisal techniques are used, as found in a development centre (discussed earlier), the manager could find him- or herself rubbing shoulders with a number of other suitable assessors.

Before looking at the problems associated with appraisal, we shall turn our attention to a case dealing with the introduction of performance appraisal in British universities, which appears in Box 6.2.

In this case the introduction of a performance appraisal system took place against a backcloth of greater organizational change aimed at increasing efficiency and managerial control within British universities. This is an example of the use of an HRM process as part of a wider strategy for change within an organization.

Problems with appraisal

Appraisal has many strong points when it is well conceived and executed as a process for providing systematic judgements to support pay reviews, promotions, transfers and the provision of feedback on actual

Box 6.2

PERFORMANCE APPRAISAL IN BRITISH UNIVERSITIES

In 1985 the Committee of Vice-Chancellors and Principals (CVCP) circulated the Jarratt Report. This report examined the structures and systems operating in British universities in the earlier part of the 1980s. Given the labour-intensive nature of these institutions, the report paid particular attention to the way employees were managed, and identified the lack of appraisal systems and succession planning. It concluded that a formal performance review procedure would be to the benefit of both the staff and the universities, and that an appraisal system should have the following objectives:

☐ To recognize the contribution of individuals.

☐ To help the development of individuals.

☐ To make the most effective use of staff.

There was a recognition that, given the nature of the work of academic staff, there were potential problems with the measurement of academic work. Also, there was the expectation that the trade union, the Association of University Teachers (AUT), would oppose changes which attempted to quantify academic work and intrude into academic freedom by solidifying hierarchical control. In negotiations with the universities the AUT adopted the position that an appraisal system geared to the development of staff and non-judgemental in nature would be acceptable.

A set of guidelines governing appraisal systems was produced with scope for local adjustments in its implementation. The guidelines incorporated the following:

☐ The scheme is applicable to all staff and is viewed as a joint exercise involving the appraisee and the appraiser.

☐ The heads of department would be closely involved in the evaluation of the performance of their staff.

☐ The scheme should serve a developmental purpose, and critical to this orientation would be the improvement of performance by the provision of feedback to appraisers.

☐ The appraisal reports would be filed and could be released to 'promotion' committees.

The guidelines did not make specific statements about the arrangements for monitoring and evaluation, or how training and development would be carried out. These were matters to be determined locally. Most of the implemented appraisal systems involved staff completing self-reporting forms on their progress over a twelve-month period in the light of their stated goals. The outcome of this exercise would be jointly reviewed with the manager, when new goals would be set and documented.

(Townley, 1993).

performance, with pointers to performance improvement through changes in attitudes, behaviour and skills. Also, as mentioned earlier, it provides an opportunity for counselling and can sow the seeds for personal development. However, one has to acknowledge a number of potential problems associated with performance appraisal as follows:

☐ Poorly designed appraisal forms compounded by some irrelevant items.

☐ Insufficient time is devoted to preparing for the event, completing the appraisal forms and ensuring the necessary training is undertaken.

☐ Feedback given to subordinates is deficient in a number of respects.

☐ Action strategies (e.g. training) that stem from the appraisal are not seriously entertained.

☐ Unreliable judgement because of subjectivity on the part of the appraiser, despite efforts to minimize it. One way to minimize subjectivity and promote objectivity is to make sure that there are explicit previously agreed performance criteria against which judgements are made. Also, a senior manager could take responsibility for overseeing a number of appraisals to check that differences between the ratings that individuals receive are not due to appraiser bias.

☐ Target setting and use of techniques leave much to be desired.

☐ Where the appraiser acts as both judge and counsellor, this could give rise to confusion as well as leading to certain difficulties for the appraisee. For example, the appraisee is subjected to an evaluative appraisal at which past performance is assessed and rewards determined, and then there is a switch to a development appraisal; in such circumstances there could well be a reluctance on the part of the appraisee to be open and frank about past mistakes and problems. Randell *et al*. (1984) argue that the solution to this problem would be to arrange different meetings for the different types of appraisal, with a different appraiser for each meeting. The development appraisal might be conducted by a manager from another department or by a human resource specialist in training and development.

Conclusions

Performance management has an evaluative and developmental dimension to its make-up, and is crucial in both linking rewards to performance and providing a platform for the development of employees. Over-concentration on the assessment of performance can work to the detriment of effort aimed at establishing the development needs of the individual in an open and honest way. The manager, as an appraiser, may encounter difficulties in reconciling the roles of 'judge' and 'mentor'. Managers need to develop the skills of coping with such tensions in their roles. In some organizations this problem is solved by having different managers carry out performance and development appraisals.

Appraisal provides the context in which managers can seek to ensure that there is acceptable congruency between the objectives of the individual and those of the organization. Although one recognizes the part played by performance management in the determination of rewards, we believe that if treated as a way of providing feedback on progress and of jointly agreeing the next set of aims, the appraisal can have a positive effect on individual motivation.

References

Anderson, G. (1992) 'Performance appraisal', in Towers, B. (ed.), *The Handbook of Human Resource Management*. Oxford: Blackwell.

Bevan, S. and Thompson, M. (1991) 'Performance management at the crossroads', *Personnel Management*, **November**, 36–39.

Furnham, A. (1993) 'When employees rate their supervisors', *Financial Times*, 1 March.

Huddart, G. (1994) 'Firm runs self-appraisal', *Personnel Today*, **17 May**, 1.

IDS (1989) *Common to All*. IDS Study no. 442, December.

Randell, G., Packard, P. and Slater, J. (1984) *Staff Appraisal: A first step to effective leadership*, 3rd edn. London: Institute of Personnel Management.

Sapsed, G. (1991) 'Appraisal the IBM way', *Involvement and Participation*, **February**, 8–14.

Townley, B. (1989) 'Selection and appraisal: reconstituting social relations', in Storey, J. (ed.), *New Developments in Human Resource Management*. London: Routledge.

Townley, B. (1993) 'The introduction of a performance appraisal system', in Gowler, D., Legge, K. and Clegg, C. (eds.), *Cases in Organizational Behaviour and Human Resource Management*, 2nd edn. London: Paul Chapman.

Williams, S. (1991) 'Strategy and objectives', in Neale, F. (ed.), *The Handbook of Performance Management*. London: Institute of Personnel Management.

7

Employee development: reward management

The purpose of managing the system of rewards within the organization is to attract and retain the human resources the organization needs to achieve its objectives. To retain the services of employees and maintain a high level of performance, it is necessary to increase their motivation and commitment. In effect the organization is aiming to bring about an alignment of organizational and individual objectives when the spotlight is on reward management.

In an HRM context reward management is not restricted to rewards and incentives, such as wages or salaries, bonuses, commission and profit sharing, which relate to extrinsic motivation. It is also concerned with non-financial rewards which satisfy the employee's psychological needs for job variety and challenge, achievement, recognition, responsibility, opportunities to acquire skills and career development, and the exercise of more influence in the decision-making process. The non-financial rewards can be equated with intrinsic motivation. Later in the chapter there will be a brief examination of motivation theories. A valid question to ask at this stage is how does the organization determine the level or magnitude of reward?

Determination of rewards

Traditionally, many reward systems have been determined by collective bargaining whereby management and employee representatives (usually trade union officials) negotiate wage rates for large groups of employees. In certain UK organizations, such as hospitals in the National Health Service and local authorities, pay grades were established for groups of employees on a national basis. For example, a nurse assuming a particular set of responsibilities in the South of England would be on the same grade as a nurse shouldering identical responsibilities in the North of the country despite differences in the cost of living between the two regions. However, it should be noted that there is a special cost-of-living allowance for those working in London.

Underlining this approach to wage determination is the use of a technique called job evaluation. Job evaluation could be described as a process used at the level of a company or industry to determine the relationship between jobs and to establish a systematic structure of wage rates for those jobs. It is concerned with 'internal relativities'; that is, that individuals doing the same type of work would receive equal rewards. Job evaluation is only concerned with the assessment of the job, not the performance of the job occupant, and it goes without saying that the preparation of reliable job descriptions is a prelude to embarking on administering job evaluation schemes. Job evaluation measures differences between jobs, and places them in appropriate groups and in rank order. Schemes of job evaluation can be classified as either the quantitative or the non-quantitative approach:

1. Quantitative – factor comparison;
            – points rating.
2. Non-quantitative – ranking;
                    – job classification.

Factor comparison

Different jobs are ranked against agreed factors such as minimum level of education, level of skill, task difficulty, supervisory responsibility, level of training and decision-making responsibility. These are referred to as criteria, each with a scale 1 to 5, against which jobs are placed in rank order. A factor comparison system is more applicable to the evaluation of clerical and administrative positions than to more senior positions with more pronounced problem-solving characteristics.

Points rating

Job evaluation systems based on points rating require an analysis of factors common to all jobs and at one time were widely used. The factors commonly used include skill, responsibility, complexity and decision making. Each factor is given a range of points to allow the award of a

Table 7.1 The Hay–MSL system

Level	Factor
1	Purpose
2	Accountability
3	Activities
4	Decision making
	Context
	Relationships
5	Knowledge
	Skills
	Experience

maximum number of points. The relative importance of a factor is the weighting it receives which is determined by the number of points allocated to it, and is related to the level at which the factor is present in the job. For example, the well-known Hay–MSL system identified 9 factors common to all jobs at different levels as shown in Table 7.1.

Levels 1, 2 and 5 are key indicators for senior jobs, and 3, 4 and 5 are key indicators for all other jobs. In the evaluation of jobs, using the Hay–MSL system, three characteristics are considered, namely 'know-how', 'problem solving' and 'accountability'. When jobs are matched against these criteria a numerical exercise is undertaken and points are awarded. Generally, the more important the job, the greater the number of points.

To make schemes, such as the above, operational requires a lot of preparation and effort. Although these schemes help in the design of graded salary structures, whereby the scores obtained by a particular job under each factor are aggregated, and have the appearance of objectivity, they can be highly subjective. Among the disadvantages of the points rating system are the following:

☐ That the evaluation of all jobs, or even just 'benchmark' jobs, can be a complex, time-consuming and costly exercise. Benchmark jobs are a small number of jobs covering the range of jobs subjected to evaluation and considered by the evaluators to represent a good example of the right relationship between pay and job content.

☐ That the assessment is static and not dynamic because the analysis refers to a moment in time.

Ranking

This procedure involves comparing jobs on the basis of, for example, knowledge/skill, discretionary features of decision making and task complexity, and then arranging the jobs in order of importance, or difficulty, or value to the organization with the appropriate levels of pay. To begin with the most and least important jobs are identified, followed by ranking all jobs within this framework. In this hierarchical arrangement 'benchmark' jobs are established at key points and the remaining jobs are put in position around them. Establishing the position of the most and least important jobs is relatively easy but deciding on the position of the middle range jobs can be difficult. In a ranking exercise it is important to be aware of the potential for the introduction of bias or prejudice on the part of evaluators, and to avoid the pitfall of assessing the performance of the job occupant rather than evaluating the job itself.

Job classification

Jobs are placed into a number of grades in which differences in skill and responsibility are accommodated. The differences in skill and responsibility embrace areas within a job such as required knowledge, training and type of decision making. A definition of a job grade should be sufficiently comprehensive so as to permit a comparison of a real job description with the corresponding grade definition. The job classification approach with a predetermined number of grades and a pay structure to match is relatively straightforward and inexpensive. However, using the job classification approach with a large number of grades can consume a lot of time and it cannot cope with complex jobs, often found at the more senior levels, which do not fit comfortably in one grade.

Other systems

A more recent system is the single factor approach called 'competence and skill analysis'. The competence or skill requirements of a job are analysed using an appropriate technique. The relevance of the individual's competence to the needs of the organization is emphasized simply because there is no point in rewarding employees for knowledge and skills which have no operational significance for the organization. This approach has particular value in situations where the deployment of skills has a material bearing on outcomes, as in the case of the jobs of scientific and professional staff, and could be suited to modern conditions of flatter organizational structures where there is an emphasis on flexibility, multi-skilling and teamwork. This system, as a non-analytical approach to job evaluation, would be difficult to use in equal value claims and is likely to be unsuitable when used in organizations with firm bureaucratic structures. (An equal value claim arises when an employee asserts that his or her job, though different, is equal in nature to a job that has been given a higher rating. The first legal case in the UK governed by the Equal Pay Act 1970 (ammended 1984) was Haywood *v* Cammell Laird Shipbuilders, where a cook's work was found to be equal to that of a printer, carpenter and thermal insulation engineer).

Advantages and disadvantages of job evaluation

The advantages and disadvantages of job evaluation should be acknowledged. As to the advantages, it is said to be an objective, fair (free from managerial influence) and logical approach in the determination of a pay structure. With regard to objectivity, the point should be made that this could be undermined if job descriptions were prepared subjectively. It is worth noting that job evaluation is often viewed favourably by industrial tribunals as a foundation for a reward system that is visible and amenable to adjustment when correction is necessary.

As to the disadvantages, there could be a problem where the objectivity of the evaluators is questioned; it could also be costly to install and maintain. In connection with maintenance, it should be noted that upgradings following the evaluation could mean extra expenditure but savings on downgradings may not follow where protected grade status exists for current employees. The validity and reliability of job evaluation is called into question. One particular bone of contention is that the initial choice and weighting of 'benchmark' jobs is arbitrary (Armstrong, 1991).

Wickens (1987) is critical of the rigidity of job evaluation systems and of the attitudes that underpin them. He feels they result in a level of bureaucracy which runs counter to the notion of flexibility and adaptability ingrained in HRM thinking. Job evaluation operates on the assumption that there is a collection of tasks performed by a job occupant working in a stable reporting relationship in a traditional bureaucratic organization. But as new organizational forms emerge, epitomized by delayering and flattening of structures, employees will be required to be more flexible and versatile in the work domain. This rules out a demarcation of jobs mentality and introduces a recognition of the need for flexible job descriptions and acceptance of frequent changes to job boundaries. In such circumstances the level of stability required by job evaluation no longer prevails. This could herald the advent of simplified job evaluation systems, for example, Nissan's fifteen job titles.

Another matter to consider in connection with traditional job evaluation systems is that while it may seem equitable to offer the same reward to different individuals doing the same job on a particular grade, one has to recognize the possibility of variations in their performance. Therefore, one can challenge the fairness of a system that dispenses a uniform rate to workers irrespective of their level of performance. Apparently, a criticism more valid in the past than at the present time is that job evaluation reinforced discrimination, particularly sexual discrimination, among employees (Cowling and James, 1994). This arose when greater weightings were given to factors supportive of men, e.g. physical strength or having completed an apprenticeship, while aspects of women's work, such as dexterity or caring, received a lower weighting.

External influences

The 'internal relativities' emphasis outlined in the previous section when examining job evaluation is no longer the overriding consideration when it comes to the determination of rewards. It appears that external market and environmental conditions are now of greater importance. Over the past decade the political environment has had an impact on the determination of rewards. Since 1979 employment legislation in the United Kingdom has weakened the power of the trade unions. The system of the 'closed shop', where everyone doing a particular job governed by a trade union agreement is required to join the same union, is illegal. A large number of employers have taken steps to move away from collective bargaining systems to more individualized reward systems. Performance-related pay, which will be discussed later in this chapter, is a good example of this trend. It is a payment system which takes into account the quality of performance on the job instead of being specifically related to a wage or salary grade.

External competitiveness, rather than internal equity which is associated with job evaluation schemes, is now a live issue in the determination of rewards. This is evident when organizations set out to adopt market-driven reward systems where the rate for the job reflects the rate required to attract recruits rather than being based on a payment system which is underpinned by an internal grading structure.

There are a number of 'sources of information' on the levels of pay and employment conditions which prevail in competing organizations in the labour market. These would include official national statistics on incomes and economic data; incomes data services from private agencies; company surveys whereby HRM specialists solicit relevant information on remuneration from their counterparts in other organizations; groups of organizations which are committed to the exchange of information on remuneration on a frequent basis; and data collected from external job advertisements and from external job applicants.

It is important to compare like with like, and to do so necessitates the preparation of a job description, and not reliance on a job title alone. Of the sources of information listed above, it would appear that well-conceived exchanges of information on pay between companies are highly effective if they are based on reliable job descriptions. Apart from the competitiveness of the remuneration package on offer, one should endeavour to ensure that it is fair. Finally, the role of performance appraisal, which has been discussed in chapter 6, should be considered in the context of the determination of rewards.

Types of reward system

There is a variety of schemes on offer, such as the following:

1. Time rates.
2. Payment by results.
3. Individual/group performance-related pay (including profit-related pay).
4. Skill/competency-based pay.
5. Cafeteria or flexible benefit system.

Time rates

When a reward system is related to the number of hours worked it is referred to as a payment system based on time rates; this is common in collective bargaining. Time rates can be classified as an hourly rate, a weekly wage, or a monthly salary. Traditionally, factory workers received a weekly wage and it is common for office workers to receive a monthly salary. By contrast, part-time employees receive an hourly rate. As stated earlier, jobs have grades attached to them following job evaluation and each grade has a particular level of pay associated with it. Within a grade it is common to have an incremental scale in which employees move along on the basis of one point each year until the maximum of the scale is reached. This system rewards experience rather than performance; in effect the employee receives an incremental award normally on an annual basis for serving time in the job. Time rates place the main emphasis on the value of the task (the work system process) as influenced by job evaluation, and not explicitly on the value of the skills and abilities the employee brings to the job, or on the quality or quantity of performance.

A stated advantage of the time rates system is that it is open to inspection and equitable in the sense that employees doing the same job will be on the same grade, though there could be differences in income owing to staff being on different positions on the incremental scale. Other advantages are the following:

☐ The system encourages the retention of human resources by creating stability, knowing that there are gradual increases in rewards within given grades. The rationale is that employee retention and the stability of the labour force offer staff the chance to enhance their skill and efficiency over time with obvious cost advantages.

☐ The system is relatively easy to administer and allows labour costs to be predicted.

☐ The system does not emphasize quantity of output to the detriment of quality.

A criticism levelled at the time rates system is that whilst theoretically costs of output decrease as the competence of employees grows, employees have no motivation to become more productive. For example, a worker receiving a wage of £200 a week increases output dramatically from 100 to 200 units per week. This clearly is to the advantage of the organization but not to the employee in monetary terms. The reward received by the employee in the example is the same whether the output figure is 100 or 200. This raises the issue of why an individual should want to be a good performer if good and bad performers on a particular grade receive the same pay. Another matter to consider is that the traditional form of progression up the hierarchy from one grade to the next by way of promotion or career development has to be revised in the light of de-layering and flatter organizational structures.

Payment by results

One way to address the criticisms levelled at the time rates system is to introduce a payment by results (PBR) scheme. PBR links pay to the quantity of the individual's output. A forerunner of PBR is the piecework system where pay is linked to the number of units of work produced. This was common in manufacturing industry; for example, if the piece-rate is £2 per unit and a worker produces 200 units of output, the income received is £400. Any figure above or below 200 units would lead to more or less than £400. Another example is the commission received by sales representatives, and this depends on sales volume. The rationale usually put forward to support the PBR scheme consists of the following:

☐ The employee is motivated to put in extra effort because by doing so he or she will receive additional income.

☐ Although there is an absence of overall equity in the sense that not everybody doing the same job will receive the same level of income, there is fairness in that the level of reward is related to the level of production.

☐ There are likely to be cost advantages since wages are directly linked to production and less supervision is required.

Prior to the introduction of a PBR scheme, method study techniques are used to establish the best procedures to do the job. Then rates of pay are fixed after calculating the time taken to complete the tasks by the employee working at the appropriate or correct speed. As a general principle, in accordance with the British Standards Institution 100 Scale, one could expect that an employee on a PBR scheme working at the correct speed should be able to earn a third more than a colleague on a time rates system (Cowling and James, 1994).

When considering the measurement of output it has to be acknowledged that in certain jobs output cannot be easily measured. Managerial jobs and many jobs in the service sector do not have easily quantifiable output. For example, a swimming pool attendant's pay could not be based on the number of lives saved. In this example the output is not controlled by the worker (the attendant). Obviously the expenditure of effort and the exercise of skill are critical variables when it comes to life saving, but factors such as the number of swimmers in the pool and their levels of expertise are outside the control of the swimming pool attendant.

It is likely that PBR schemes geared to the individual will stimulate the quantity of output, but management must be on its guard in case increased output is at the expense of quality. An example of an adverse impact on quality is a dramatic increase in the scrap rate following an increase in a PBR worker's output in a factory. Therefore, if there is a PBR scheme in operation, there are obvious advantages in having quality control mechanisms firmly in place. Apart from the question of quality, the following reservations should be noted:

☐ As was stated above, it could be difficult to measure output in certain jobs.

☐ In the drive to increase production, safety standards may be compromised.

☐ Passions could be aroused between workers and management if the PBR scheme is viewed by the workers as a device to obtain greater effort from them without commensurate reward, and where they have to haggle over money. If workers feel that they have been short-changed, there is the inclination to withhold critical information about job performance.

☐ In a climate of suspicion and distrust between trade unions and management, the trade union representatives may use the PBR scheme, particularly in relation to pay, as a means to put pressure on management and create conflict.

Taking a positive view, it is suggested that PBR schemes can be effective where they are well conceived, where work measurement and output measurement are possible, where good prior communication and consultation with employees have taken place, and where there is a healthy rapport between management and workers (Cannell and Long, 1991).

Performance-related pay

Unlike payment by results examined in the previous section, performance-related pay (PRP) considers not only results or output but also actual behaviour in the job. The individual's performance is measured against previously set objectives or compared with the various tasks listed in the job description, using performance appraisal techniques discussed in chapter 6. Following this assessment, normally conducted by the manager, with or without professional assistance, there is an allocation of rewards. Rewards linked to performance could consist of a lump sum, or a bonus as a percentage of basic salary, with quality of performance determining the magnitude of the percentage increase; or alternatively accelerated movement up a pay scale. In connection with the last, excellent performance might, for example, justify a movement upwards of two points on the scale, whilst poor performance could result in staying at the current level. Some incremental pay scales have a bar at a particular point, beyond which there is entitlement to discretionary points. To go beyond the bar and benefit from the discretionary points, it would be necessary for the individual to receive a favourable performance evaluation. It should be noted that management reserves the right to award discretionary points.

Certain conditions are said to be necessary for a PRP scheme to be effective (Applebaum and Shappiro, 1991):

☐ In order to make the measurement of performance a meaningful activity, it is essential that there should be sufficient differences between individuals on the basis of performance.

☐ The pay range must be of sufficient width to accommodate significant differences in the basic pay of employees.

☐ The measurement of performance must be a valid and reliable exercise, and it must be possible to relate the outcome of the measurement process to pay.

☐ Appraisers are skilful in setting performance standards and in conducting appraisals.

☐ The culture of the organization is supportive.

☐ The remuneration package offered is competitive and fair, and the organization is adept at relating pay to performance.

☐ Mutual trust exists between managers and their subordinates, and managers are prepared to manage with an eagerness to communicate performance criteria and face making difficult decisions.

Whilst the above conditions are supportive of PRP schemes, it is possible to encounter conditions, such as the following, which produce a negative impact (Applebaum and Shappiro, 1991; Goss, 1994):

1. No attempt is made to relate individual performance to organizational objectives.

2. Appraisals are not conducted fairly, because either output is difficult to measure or the appraiser is incompetent.

3. Openness, trust, joint problem solving and commitment to organizational objectives are adversely affected by the introduction of PRP schemes.

4. The introduction of PRP schemes produces adversarial conditions when it creates supporters and opponents of such schemes.

Having examined the conditions necessary for the introduction of PRP schemes, and being aware of conditions likely to produce a negative impact, it is legitimate to ask what are the advantages and disadvantages of such schemes? First we shall note the following advantages of individually based PRP schemes (Goss, 1994):

☐ Incentives are linked to meeting targets or objectives, as well as to the quality of performance as perceived by superiors. Linking pay to performance that lends itself to measurement is considered fairer than awarding across-the-board cost-of-living increases which do not discriminate between high and low performers.

☐ Where employee performance can be measured and the amount of money available to reward performance is sufficient to motivate effort, it saves money if the organization targets rewards on those who perform.

☐ High performers are attracted to PRP cultures in the knowledge that pay is linked to productive effort, and that poor achievement is discouraged.

☐ Employees receive useful feedback on their performance.

☐ There is an emphasis on a results-oriented culture, with the accent on effort directed at activities that the organization values.

The following could be considered disadvantages of individually based PRP schemes:

1. Behaviour is rewarded, which one would expect to occur anyway in accordance with the employment contract. The argument goes that good performance is expected and provision is made for it, and where there is poor performance it is the job of management to sort it out.
2. Open communication between managers and subordinates could be discouraged, because subordinates are less likely to divulge information on personal shortcomings just in case such disclosures act to their disadvantage.
3. The rewarding of self-centred individualism can undermine the co-operation and teamwork which are necessary for coping with today's climate characterized by complexity and interdependency (Pearce, 1991).
4. The growth of managerial control over subordinates is promoted, with the effect of isolating the individual; this could affect teamwork.
5. Poor performers are punished; this is unfortunate because it is in the organization's interest to motivate this group in order to improve their performance.
6. The existence of trade union opposition could sour relationships between management and the representatives of the workers. Sometimes trade unions object to the individualistic nature of rewards which run counter to the spirit of collective bargaining, and there is currently a view that too great a part is played by subjective managerial judgement in the determination of rewards. With respect to the latter, there is the fear that equitable criteria are not applied objectively to all employees.

Though PRP schemes are heavily endorsed by a number of practitioners, their motivational significance has been challenged (Thompson, 1993; Kohn, 1993). The results of a survey of managers at British Telecom indicated that the PRP scheme was unfairly administered and there was scepticism of its effect on performance; in fact the payments made had an adverse effect on performance (IRS, 1991). Recently, British Telecom suspended its PRP scheme for managers, following a pay comparison study in which it was established that the company was paying its managers between 11 and 14 per cent above remuneration levels for managers in similar jobs in outside organizations (Taylor, 1994). This line of action was driven by the need to keep costs in check and to retain competitiveness. The importance of external comparability in the determination of rewards is evident in this situation.

Group PRP schemes

These schemes, which link rewards to outcomes such as meeting budget targets or organizational profitability, are said to avoid the threat to cooperative modes of working associated with individually based PRP schemes by de-emphasizing the individualistic nature of rewards. According to Murlis (1994), team-based pay seeks to eliminate the divisive nature of individually based PRP schemes. The group PRP schemes include the exercise of share options (see Box 7.1) and profit sharing. A group scheme related to profit is called profit-related pay.

Box 7.1

RISK-FREE OPTION FOR DIRECTORS

The use of share options by directors of large companies, particularly the privatized public utilities in the UK, is a contentious issue. Much criticism has been levelled at share option schemes. In a recent editorial in the *Financial Times* it was stated that even though the cost of such schemes is not a charge to the company's profit and loss account under current accounting conventions, they do have a cost. These rewards are inadequately related to management performance and send a poor signal to employees who are not included in the scheme. A finding from a recent survey by the National Institute of Economic and Social Research in the UK suggests that there is little obvious link between the rewards generated by such schemes and company profitability or total shareholder returns.

Share option schemes are attractive to the recipients. If the company's shares increase in value, the directors stand to gain, but if they decrease they merely lose a potential profit opportunity. By contrast, shareholders incur genuine losses in the latter situation. Share options fail the key test of a good incentive scheme, which is that the interests of shareholders and managers should be as closely aligned as possible. There is a growing feeling that share incentive schemes should be reserved for exceptional performance, and not for meeting the requirements of a normal job.

(*Financial Times*, 1995).

Profit-related pay
The original idea was that by linking pay to profits, companies could make their wage costs variable. Employees would be given an incentive to work harder, and in good times would reap the rewards, while in bad times they would share the pain, though it is possible to design schemes so that

the employees are safeguarded when profits fall. Companies can use profit-related pay as a bonus paid in addition to existing salary, or by getting employees to swap part of their salary for profit-related pay. A major reason why many companies who use profit-related pay, such as Boots, have done so is because it is a more tax-efficient means for paying bonuses.

The tendency now is for schemes to cover all or most employees as opposed to senior grades as in the past. According to the recruitment manager at Boots, 'the scheme gives our workforce a greater stake in the business. It means they switch off the lights at night and don't keep the machinery running, and may have lessened pay claims' (Kellaway, 1993). Profit-related pay may not be suitable for all companies. The companies that have little to gain from such schemes are those with very low-paid workers – who pay little tax – or where profits are so volatile that they are impossible to predict. Some companies steer clear of profit-related pay because they prefer incentive schemes based on individual rather than group performance. But other companies, such as Boots and the Halifax Building Society, view profit-related pay as an addition rather than an alternative to individual incentives (Kellaway, 1993).

Among the alleged benefits of group PRP schemes are the following:

☐ Employees identify more closely with the success of the organization, and this has obvious advantages in terms of commitment and improved organizational performance.

☐ There is a breaking down or removal of the 'them' and 'us' barrier.

☐ Cooperation and working together for mutual benefit is encouraged.

☐ There is an awareness of the link between performance and organizational profitability, leading to a greater awareness of costs and their impact on performance. This realization is beneficial to the organization when wage claims are submitted.

☐ When adverse trading conditions, such as a recession, hit the organization the element of profit devoted to pay can fall. Such an eventuality is a preferable alternative to laying off employees.

☐ Group pressure could raise the performance levels of poor performers.

A disadvantage of group-based schemes, where rewards are linked to company profitability, is that the employee may see the rewards as too distant from individual effort, more so because of having to rely on others as well as the influence of external factors (e.g. competitors and markets).

Cases where management rewarded employees for working as members of teams or groups appear in Box 7.2.

Box 7.2

GROUP-BASED REWARDS AT PEARL ASSURANCE AND THE
AUTOMOBILE ASSOCIATION IN THE UK

Pearl Assurance was unable to pass on the cost of significant salary increases to its customers because of the prevalence of acute market competition and economic conditions of low inflation. Therefore, it had to give serious consideration to the most appropriate remuneration system in these circumstances. Previously, a performance-related pay system was in operation, but when salary settlements were below 3 per cent of payroll cost, managers under this system had little scope to use their discretion and reward staff on the basis of merit.

Team-based pay was introduced and it was the job of the heads of the sections or teams to meet and rank the performance of each section, and to determine the pay increase each section was to receive. Then each head was expected to evaluate the performance of individuals as team-players and exercise discretion in the award of individual salary increases.

(Trevor, 1993).

At the Automobile Association team-based incentives were introduced following the creation of a flatter organization structure. The aims of teams of thirty were to provide high quality service and maintain a quick response rate, but it was proving difficult to create team spirit because teams spent much of their time on the road with a high level of individual autonomy.

Targets were set for teams covering such criteria as the number of jobs completed at the roadside, the average time to complete the job, and the average time to respond to a Relay call when the motorist's car had to be transported to his or her home or to a garage. The performance of teams was measured against the above criteria, and teams competed in leagues. The winners received tangible prizes, such as outings and vouchers to use in stores, coupled with the intrinsic reward of the status stemming from being the winning team. The winners were announced quarterly and annually.

(Pickard, 1993).

Skill-based pay

The schemes examined above have concentrated on the 'outputs' of work activity, such as volume and quality of production or profit. By comparison, skill-based pay places the emphasis on 'inputs' which consist of knowledge, skills and competences injected into the job by employees. In the distant past the craftsman received differentiated rewards at different stages of his career. As he moved from apprentice to master the development of skill was reflected in increased reward. In the not too distant past the growth of mass production systems accompanied by advances in technology gave rise to the simplification of work and to a significant amount of deskilling which had the effect of maintaining a steady demand for unskilled workers.

In the current climate the march of new technology has meant that there is a contraction in the number of unskilled jobs and a growth in the demand for multi-skilled workers. This has been brought about by a team-based approach towards work and the need for flexibility in manning arrangements. To foster a multi-skill capability in the labour force calls for the acquisition and use of more skills than required hitherto. In order to provide an incentive to employees to broaden their skill base, some employers are linking rewards to skills' acquisition and deployment.

According to IDS (1992), before introducing a skill-based system there should be good planning, a fair amount of consultation and employee participation, as well as training directed at the acquisition of new technical skills and teamworking skills. Subsequently, rewards would be linked to both skills' acquisition and use, and perhaps also to the level of performance directly associated with the deployment of those skills if such an exercise is possible. If it is not possible, then an organization can only hope that skills will be utilized in a manner compatible with high levels of performance.

A point to note in connection with skill-based pay is that management is well placed to use rewards to encourage and support changes in behaviour (i.e. acquisition of a broader range of skills) which are necessary to implement contemporary changes in organizational design and functioning. Also, the operation of a skill-based pay system requires attention to skills to be rewarded, setting the right rate of pay, providing the appropriate level of training, putting in place the necessary procedures, and ensuring that sufficient time is invested wisely in the process.

The cases shown in Box 7.3 stress the growing importance of skill-based pay. In the UNISYS case, the main emphasis is on the input of skill, but there is also an aspect of performance assessment. In the IBM case the interaction between organizational design and rewards is highlighted.

Cafeteria or flexible benefit systems

These systems are a way of managing rewards that are gaining in popularity in the United Kingdom, and are established in the United States where they are referred to as 'flexible benefits'. In Australia they are called 'packaged compensation', and in the United Kingdom they are known as the 'cafeteria' system. Since they are substitutes for pay, they must be calculated within an overall remuneration or compensation package.

Their popularity in the United States has no doubt been prompted by tax advantages, unlike the position in the United Kingdom, and mainly comprise life and accident insurance, medical and dental care, and care for children. In addition, the growing costs of healthcare for companies in the United States motivated them to take flexible remuneration

Box 7.3

SKILL-BASED PAY AT UNISYS AND IBM

UNISYS moved away from a performance-related pay scheme to a skill (competence)-based pay scheme. Behaviour was assessed using criteria such as teamwork, customer orientation, innovative practices, accountability and motivation. Employees were assessed using these criteria and were placed in four categories, with different levels of reward associated with each category.

(Huddart, 1994).

IBM introduced changes to its pay structure involving a move towards skill or competency-based rewards and sensitivity to job market pay rates. The rates attached to particular jobs are linked to market pay rates within a system of general job categories. The number of levels of jobs in the management and professional area was reduced from twelve to four. The newly created four levels represent broad bands containing a range of jobs within which individual employees move around from one area to another within the organization. Moving in this way means there is no change to the cost of the remuneration package because the employee remains within his or her broad pay band.

The new approach to pay has been influenced by IBM's changed philosophy linked to work design and career structures. The 'job for life' culture and automatic annual pay rises have been challenged. The intention is to create a 'human growth' culture where individual competence is recognized and rewarded. This will put pressure on employees to be concerned with their development and employability so as to secure their future with the company.

(North, 1993, 1994).

---

seriously. Companies give employees pre-tax 'flex credits' which they could use to meet the cost of health benefits.

In the United Kingdom flexible benefits have captured the imagination of human resource practitioners as a means of providing employees with a degree of choice over the form which their remuneration takes, and as a useful measure in the recruitment and retention of human resources. A cafeteria system in the United Kingdom could be made up of such benefits as the company car, additional holiday entitlement, private health insurance, membership of social clubs, modification to working hours, special pension arrangements, mortgage loan subsidies and other benefits. Scottish and Newcastle Breweries offer a package covering ten separate benefits, including the company product in the form of wines and spirits. The scheme allows an executive earning, say, £50,000 p.a. to increase his or her salary to £60,000 p.a. if no benefits were taken. Alternatively, the salary could be as little as £37,000 p.a. if the optimum benefits cover was utilized.

Employees exercise choice when selecting a range of benefits from a menu which they consider important and to which they are entitled.

Box 7.4

CAFETERIA SYSTEM AT BHS

A first step at BHS was to give top management more say over the composition of their pay and benefits. The scheme started with over 50 managers and by 1993 was extended to 400 managers who were in possession of company cars. An example of how the scheme works is as follows.

A particular male manager earns £35,000 p.a. The cash value of his benefits is £8,115. The latter provides a ceiling for his benefits, from which can be chosen between one and three times his salary level in life insurance cover, from four levels of private medical care, and from four levels of annual holiday entitlement between twenty-two and thirty days. In addition, there is a choice of a free company car, the opportunity to buy long-term disability insurance, an optical cover plan which subsidizes contact lens purchases and eye tests, and a dental care plan. Benefits in excess of his entitlement can be obtained, in which case there is a reduction of the appropriate amount from his salary.

Taking benefits less than his entitlement could mean an increase in salary by an amount equivalent to the reduction in benefits. The only benefit the company insists that managers take is the minimum level of holiday. The human resources manager at BHS is reported as saying that the package on offer has proved popular and that this system of reward 'is a fairly progressive recruitment tool; to be honest people love it'.

(Donkin, 1994).

Although a number of schemes apply to executive and managerial staff, there is evidence to indicate that these schemes are becoming progressively available to other employees (Woodley, 1993). This may not apply universally within an organization, certainly not for two companies – BHS (Retail Stores) and Scottish and Newcastle Breweries – who have avoided introducing flexible benefits throughout their work-force, mainly because those further down the organizational hierarchy have fewer benefits, such as company cars, to choose from. At Scottish and Newcastle Breweries a scheme was introduced around 1992 which initially covered seventy or eighty employees with an intention to extend it through all 2,000 managers who have company cars (Donkin, 1994).

BHS was one of the first companies in the United Kingdom to introduce the cafeteria system when a new chief executive, educated in the United States, joined the company in 1990. Details of the scheme appear in Box 7.4.

The following are issues to consider when adopting cafeteria or flexible benefit systems in the United Kingdom (IDS, 1991):

☐ Flexibility in the way remuneration systems are determined is necessary because of demographic changes (e.g. using the services of more women and older workers). However, it should be noted that the economic recession of the early 1990s and the continuing high levels of unemployment have largely nullified the effects of demographic change.

☐ If flexible benefit systems are too individually based, there is a danger that teamwork will be undermined.

☐ Every effort should be made to communicate the total benefits portfolio.

☐ Those who participate in the scheme have the advantage of choosing benefits considered relevant to their needs from a menu which is publicly available. This could have a beneficial effect on commitment.

☐ The position of spouses/partners with careers should be considered in order to avoid duplication of certain benefits (e.g. health insurance).

☐ When flexible benefits are costed, there is greater awareness of the costs of employing people.

☐ Full advantage should be taken of the potential of information technology in the administration of schemes in order to keep the costs of operation within reasonable levels.

☐ The costs of schemes should be kept under review; in particular, the administration of schemes when employees choose benefits which happen to be in great demand as an alternative to under-utilized benefits.

☐ The tax implications of schemes should be considered.

☐ The schemes may be more appropriate to situations where non-unionized labour exists. There is a belief that trade unions may consider such schemes as a potential threat to standard remuneration packages. In appropriate circumstances it would appear sensible to involve the trade unions in the various deliberations.

☐ A feature of the schemes in the United Kingdom is their flexibility and individual bias, but in the United States the major attraction seems to be the tax implications and medical insurance cover.

Other matters to consider are that flexible remuneration arrangements are useful for multi-national companies looking for ways to manage expatriate costs; that companies get rid of the perks-driven mentality of employees who expect certain entitlements as a right; and that employees who take part of their total income by way of flexible benefits experience a cost advantage (Donkin, 1994). In connection with the latter, it would be more economical to acquire, say, private medical cover through a company's group plan than on an individual basis out of personal disposable income.

Relevance of motivation theories

Those with responsibility for designing reward systems will benefit from an understanding of motivation theories. Work motivation theories delve into psychological explanations about what motivates people in formal organizations. Therefore, motivation and rewards are connected because rewards are given on the understanding that employees are motivated to commit themselves to perform to satisfactory levels at the work-place.

Pay as an important component of a system of rewards has been singled out by Thierry (1992) as having psychological and social significance, because it sends a number of messages to employees, quite apart from its status as a desired material reward. Pay says something about the appropriateness of the employee's work behaviour, it is a symbol of recognition and it conveys what the organization thinks of the person's behaviour. In addition, pay performs the following roles (Thierry, 1992):

1. It satisfies personal needs (e.g. provides an escape from insecurity, creates a feeling of competence, and opens up opportunities for self-fulfilment).
2. It provides feedback on how well a person is doing on a variety of fronts and it acts as an indicator of that person's relative position in the organization.
3. It is a reward for success in controlling others where the individual has a supervisory or managerial position.
4. It conveys a capacity to spend in the sense that pay reflects purchasing power in the consumer market.

In the above situational interpretation of pay it is clear that a reward could mean different things to different people. For example, one person desires a certain level of income to satisfy his or her security needs, to another person money serves as a means to portray his or her relative success at work, and to a third it is a means to provide spending power compatible with expectations of status.

For the greater part of this century researchers in work motivation have stressed the importance of different factors in the motivation of workers, though in some cases there was a convergence of view.

Economic man
Money as a major motivating factor was endorsed by Taylor (1947), the founder of scientific management, in the earlier part of this century. People were seen to be motivated by self-interest and were keen to accept the

challenge to maximize their income. From the organization's point of view, the opportunity to maximize production rested on creating reward systems (e.g. piece rates, payment by results) where financial returns (extrinsic rewards) vary with levels of output. The greater the level of output, the greater the level of individual reward.

Human relations

The 'economic man' school of thought gave way to the human relations perspective expounded by Mayo (1949). Following a series of experiments on the social and environmental conditions at work, the importance of recognition and good social relationships at work as motivational factors contributing to morale and productivity was heavily underlined.

Need theories

Next to appear on the scene were the need theories principally represented by Maslow (1954) and Herzberg (1966). Maslow arranged human needs in the form of a hierarchy with basic needs (e.g. hunger, security and safety) at the lower end, self-actualization needs at the top, and ego and social needs in the middle. The individual moves up the hierarchy as lower needs are satisfied, and it should be noted that a pressing need is a powerful motivator of behaviour until it is satisfied.

Basic pay, sick pay and pension entitlement could satisfy security needs, and a work environment where hazards are well controlled could satisfy safety needs. The provision of sports and social clubs, which facilitate interaction at work, and works outings could satisfy social needs. Position in the organization and symbols of success, such as a valuable company car, have relevance in the context of satisfying status and recognition needs. An experience whereby the individual acquires key knowledge and skills, and successfully completes an exacting and challenging assignment, could contribute to the satisfaction of self-actualization needs. Finally, adequate pay has significance at the lower end of the hierarchy, although one should take note of the broader interpretation of the psychological implications of pay attributed to Thierry (1992) earlier in this section.

Using concepts similar to Maslow, Herzberg (1966) concluded from his studies that satisfied feelings at work stemmed from a challenging job, extra responsibility, personal accomplishments, recognition from superiors and progress in one's career. These were referred to as real 'motivators'. On the other hand, negative feelings and dissatisfaction could arise from poor relationships with colleagues and superiors, less than satisfactory company policy and administration, poor pay and adverse working conditions. These were referred to as 'hygiene' factors, and if improved could lower the level of 'dissatisfaction' and negativity. Improving the hygiene factors and then building motivators into a job was considered the best way to motivate people. Note the status of pay in the Herzberg

Box 7.5

JOB ENRICHMENT IN ACTION

A job may be enriched by an individual undertaking greater responsibiity – e.g. by organizing and checking his or her own work, or by being involved in decisions about planning the work of his or her unit. The content of the work is changed by extending the opportunities for making decisions and exercising judgement. Job enrichment programmes attempt to build in, over time, scope for the development of an individual's skills to provide a sense of personal achievement. This approach frequently affects the nature of other jobs and therefore careful consideration needs to be given to the whole process of re-allocating responsibilities, re-defining roles, and providing the necessary re-training. Over the years there have been a number of instances where job enrichment led to increased job satisfaction and favourably influenced performance.

(Department of Employment, 1975).

In the 1960s ICI was one of a handful of companies in the UK that seriously experimented with job enrichment. One job enrichment study within ICI examined the role of sales representatives who appeared to be satisfied with their job, but were given very little discretion over the way they operated. The following changes were instituted as part of the job enrichment programme. Sales representatives no longer had to write a report on every customer call. Instead they passed on, or requested, information at their own discretion. They were also given total responsibility for determining the frequency of calls to customers, deciding how to deal with faulty or unwanted stock, requesting service from the technical services department, and making immediate settlements up to a certain sum in case of customer complaint, if they felt this would prejudice further liability of the company. In addition, they were given discretion to adjust prices on a range up to 10% on the price of most of the products sold, the lower limit being often below any price previously quoted by the Sales Office. Following the implementation of the job enrichment scheme both job satisfaction and performance increased.

(Paul and Robertson, 1970).

---

model – a hygiene factor – a position challenged later in the expectancy model of motivation.

There is a strong similarity between Maslow's higher level human needs and Herzberg's motivators. Both would be considered when designing or redesigning jobs by way of job enrichment (see Box 7.5). The notion of job enrichment – attempting to make tasks more intrinsically interesting, involving and rewarding – is updated in the Hackman and Oldham job characteristics model (Hackman, 1977).

This model incorporates the following five core dimensions which are key factors when designing or re-designing jobs:

☐ Skill Variety (scope for the exercise of different skills and abilities).

☐ Task Identity (extent to which the job requires the completion of an identifiable segment of work).

□ Task Significance (extent to which the job has an impact on the life of others).

□ Autonomy (extent to which the job offers freedom and the use of discretion in performing tasks).

□ Feedback (extent to which the job holder receives information on his or her performance).

The five core dimensions are linked with motivation and performance through critical psychological states (i.e. experienced meaningfulness of the work, experienced responsibility for work outcomes, and knowledge of the consequences of work activities). The model recognizes that people differ in their levels of 'growth need'. For example, people with a high need for personal growth are more likely to react favourably in a psychological sense when the five core factors are improved.

The motivational factors discussed above can be classified as intrinsic (e.g. job challenge, skill-based pay) or extrinsic (e.g. pay, performance-related pay, working conditions). Skill-based pay is classified as an intrinsic factor because it refers to the reward an individual receives for the baggage (input) of knowledge and skill the employee takes to the job. The outcome could be the enhancement of competences and personal development. By contrast, basic pay in the form of 'time rates' can be related to the need theories, since they call for fairness and relative security, which in turn can generate social satisfaction at work.

Expectancy theory
Another relevant theory of motivation is expectancy theory (Porter and Lawler, 1968; Vroom, 1964). People bring to work various expectations about the likely consequences of various forms of behaviour reflected in work performance. For example, if people expect that the expenditure of effort will lead to good work performance and generate a satisfactory outcome in terms of intrinsic and extrinsic rewards which are valued, and such expectations are realized in practice, then productive effort is likely to be forthcoming in the future. If this scenario was altered, so that the relationship between effort and reward did not stand, it is possible that the motivational disposition of the employee would change and future effort may be adjusted downwards or discontinued.

In practice it may be difficult to implement expectancy theory. For example, profit-related pay attempts to bring about convergence between individual and organizational goals, in the sense that the individual is motivated to achieve organizational goals, for by so doing he or she is achieving personal goals, particularly with reference to extrinsic rewards. However, with profit-related pay employees may not be sure that specific rewards will be the consequence of particular actions because of the involvement of others. But in the quoted example social needs could be satisfied in the process because the organization is trying to link the interests of employees with those of the organization. Social needs could also be considered relevant in the context of group- or team-based pay.

Goal-setting

The setting of goals is said to have an impact on the motivation of the individual, provided the goals set are clear, realistic and challenging, but not too difficult, and that the person subjected to them is able to participate in their setting. Other considerations are feedback on performance, goal acceptance and commitment to the goal (Latham and Locke, 1979). Management by objectives, which was mentioned as a performance appraisal technique in chapter 6, is an example of a process in which there is an emphasis on participation in the setting of goals. An alternative approach to goal setting as described would be for goals to be set and assigned to the individual, but this approach might not have the motivational impact outlined above.

A reward system anchored in extrinsic rewards, e.g. performance-related pay, utilizes the concepts of expectancy and goal setting when judgements are made about the extent to which performance meets objectives, and the adequacy of rewards.

Equity theory

This theory is concerned with the equitable nature of reward and has significance when the employee perceives the relationship between effort and reward, as would occur in the application of expectancy theory. In an employment situation one considers two important variables: inputs and outputs. Education, skill, experience and effort would be considered inputs, and salary, fringe benefits and career advancement would be viewed as outputs. People compare each other's inputs and outputs and if they perceive unfairness, feelings of inequity can arise (Adams, 1963). The latter could have an adverse effect on production and possibly lead to absenteeism and resignation. Apparently, if after engaging in the comparative exercise the person considers himself or herself over-compensated, there could be a feeling of unease.

HRM and rewards

Systems of pay, such as time rates and payment by results, tend to be associated with the more traditional styles of management, while reward systems, such as performance-related pay and skill-based pay, reflect the spirit of HRM and appear to be growing in popularity. It is claimed that

HRM is associated with a management ethos of self-interest which was legitimized in the era of the 'enterprise culture' and the growth of Thatcherism (Keenoy and Anthony, 1992). Around this time performance-related pay (PRP) became popular and it is clearly linked to the enterprise culture.

In a PRP culture the aim is to make employees more like entrepreneurs, i.e. people who earn a direct return on the value they create (Kanter, 1987). This approach to reward would fit into the category of hard HRM referred to earlier in the book, as it assumes that people are motivated by economic self-interest. However, PRP is more subtle than this; it can also include 'goal setting' referred to in the previous section. As the goals set can be qualitative as well as quantitative, the issue of quality is addressed (Guest, 1989).

Lawler (1991) maintains that traditional reward systems (e.g. time rates) tend to motivate a large number of people to climb the organizational hierarchy. This arises when rewards are given as a result of progressing within salary grades and scales. But given the advent of flatter organizational structures and flexible work designs – developments that receive the HRM seal of approval – skill-based pay would appear to be more appropriate than traditional reward systems. Skill-based pay is a reward system that credits individuals in a way that benefits the organization in terms of goal attainment. It is congruent with the aim of HRM to invest in human assets, and it tries to promote flexibility by ensuring that employees are equipped to carry out a variety of tasks. There is also an element of trust involved: given the acquisition of the right blend of skills there is the expectation that employees will motivate themselves to perform to a high standard, though this may have to be complemented by good management. Overall, it is compatible with soft HRM.

Conclusions

There is evidence to indicate that British companies are continually preoccupied with pay systems. A significant minority of all companies altered their reward system during the past year according to a recent survey of 1,000 companies (Goodhart, 1994). A number of large companies are using a third version of performance-related pay since the early 1980s, with bonus schemes and share options for senior executives in a constant state of overhaul and revision. Now there is a more sober and realistic view of what a reward system can achieve than was the case in the 1980s. The view that a company's success rests principally on adopting state-of-the-art pay systems is now considered too simplistic. This is not surprising, because motivation is a complex phenomenon and designing and managing pay systems is a most difficult task.

There appears to be a tendency to address a number of operational issues, such as the tension between individual performance and group commitment in performance-related pay. The delicate connection between performance appraisal and performance-related pay has given rise to experimentation with appraisal techniques, such as assessment by colleagues. Apparently, some companies justify their attachment to performance-related pay in order to prevent them giving increases in pay to inadequate or poor performers. Progress is being made in developing skill-based pay and gain-sharing. The latter are incentive schemes that give employees who are responsible for initiating specific improvements a return for their contribution. A number of institutional investors would like to see advances in the determination of executive pay, in particular more realistic share option schemes.

The system of 'national rates' for employees is being challenged, and there is a movement away from pay systems that reward managers for loyalty expressed as commitment in terms of length of service, and a movement towards rewarding managers on the basis of individual performance and company performance in order to cultivate loyalty. Linking rewards to the success of the enterprise was considered a sensible way to proceed as it was likely to promote commitment. There is a danger that the commitment of a number of employees could be undermined because of significant income inequality within the company. The weakened state of national bargaining pay systems has resulted in the centralization of greater power in the hands of top management in matters connected with pay determination. Regrettably, it appears that members of top management have been over-generous in awarding themselves pay increases at a time when pay restraint is advocated for most employees.

References

Adams, J. S. (1963) 'Towards an understanding of inequity', *Journal of Abnormal and Social Psychology*, **67**, 422–436.

Applebaum, S. and Shappiro, B. (1991) 'Pay for performance: implementation of individual and group plans', *Journal of Management Development*, **10**, 30–40.

Armstrong, M. (1991) *A Handbook of Personnel Management*, 4th edn. London: Kogan Page.

Cannell, M. and Long, P. (1991) 'What's changed about incentive pay?', *Personnel Management*, **October**, 58–63.

Cowling, A. and James, P. (1994) *The Essence of Personnel Management and Industrial Relations*, Hemel Hempstead: Prentice Hall.

Department of Employment (1975) (Report), 'Making work more satisfying'. London: HMSO.

Donkin, R. (1994) 'An option on perks (flexible remuneration systems)', *Financial Times*, 6 April, p. 16.

Financial Times, (1995) Editorial Comment, 13 February, p. 17.

Goodhart, D. (1994) 'In search of wages that work', *Financial Times*, 27 June, p. 16.

Goss, D. (1994) *Principles of Human Resource Management*. London: Routledge.

Guest, D. (1989) 'Personnel and HRM: Can you tell the difference?', *Personnel Management*, **January**, 48–51.

Hackman, J. R. (1977) 'Work design', in Hackman, J. R. and Suttle, J. L. (eds.), *Improving Life at Work*. Santa Monica: Scott Foresman.

Herzberg, F. (1966) *Work and the Nature of Man*, London: Staples Press.

Huddart, G. (1994) 'Unisys links rises to personal skills', *Personnel Today*, 17 May, 1.

IDS (1991) *DIY Benefits for the 1990s*. IDS Study no. 481, May, London: Incomes Data Services.

IDS (1992) *Skilling Up*. IDS Study no. 500, February, London: Incomes Data Services.

IRS (1991) Employment Trends 495, BT managers hostile to PRP, September.

Kanter, R. M. (1987) 'The attack on pay', *Harvard Business Review*, **March–April**, 111–117.

Kellaway, L. (1993) 'Nice little earner (profit-related pay)', *Financial Times*, 23 April, p. 14.

Keenoy, T. and Anthony, P. (1992) 'Human resource management: metaphor, meaning, and morality', in Blyton, P. and Turnbull, P. (eds.), *Reassessing Human Resource Management*. London: Sage.

Kohn, A. (1993) 'Why incentive plans cannot work', *Harvard Business Review*, **September/October**, 54–63.

Latham, G. P. and Locke, E. (1979) 'Goal setting: a motivational technique that works', *Organizational Dynamics*, **Autumn**, 68–80.

Lawler, E. (1991) 'Paying the person: a better approach to management', *Human Resource Management Review*, **1**, 145–154.

Maslow, A. (1954) *Motivation and Personality*. New York: Harper and Row.

Mayo, E. (1949) *The Social Problems of an Industrial Civilization*. London: Routledge and Kegan Paul.

Murlis, H. (1994) 'The challenge of rewarding teamwork', *Personnel Management*, **February**, p. 8.

North, S. J. (1993) 'IBM trims pay grades in salary shake-up', *Personnel Today*, 9 November, p. 1.

North, S. J. (1994) 'IBM hives off its payroll services', *Personnel Today*, 31 May, p. 2.

Paul, W. J. and Robertson, K. B. (1970) *Job enrichment and employee motivation*. Epping: Gower Press.

Pearce, J. (1991) 'Why merit pay doesn't work', in Steer, R. and Porter, L. (eds.), *Motivation and Work Behaviour*. New York: McGraw-Hill.

Pickard, J. (1993) 'How incentives can drive teamworking', *Personnel Management*, **September**, 26–32.

Porter, L. W. and Lawler, E. E. (1968) *Managerial Attitudes and Performance*. Homewood, IL: R. D. Irwin.

Taylor, F. W. (1947) *Scientific Management*. New York: Harper and Row.

Taylor, R. (1994) 'Must try harder', *Financial Times*, 2 February, p. 9.

Thierry, H. (1992) 'Pay and payment systems', in Hartley, J. and Stephenson, G. (eds.), *Employee Relations*, Oxford: Blackwell.

Thompson, M. (1993) 'Pay and performance 2: the employee's experience', *Personnel Management Plus*, **November**, p. 2.

Trevor, G. (1993) 'Pearl Assurance', *Personnel Management Plus*, **November**, p. 13.

Vroom, V. (1964) *Work and Motivation*. New York: John Wiley.

Wickens, P. (1987) *The Road to Nissan: Flexibility, quality, teamwork*. Basingstoke: Macmillan.

Woodley, C. (1993) 'The benefits of flexibility', *Personnel Management*, **May**, 36–39.

8

Employee development: training and development

Training and development are terms which are sometimes used inter-changeably. Traditionally development was seen as an activity normally associated with managers with the future firmly in mind. By contrast, training has a more immediate concern and has been associated with improving the knowledge and skill of non-managerial employees in their present jobs.

Such a distinction could be considered too simplistic in an era charac-terized by developments in HRM, because nowadays development of all employees is considered crucial. Such development would be reflected in a commitment to multi-skilling and a flexible mode of operation. There is also the recognition that the human resource is valuable and must be developed if the organization is to hold on to staff and retain their commitment whilst at work. One should bear in mind that even managers need to be trained in the here and now, because they need current operational skills or competences quite apart from the qualities (e.g. creativity, synthesis, abstract reasoning, personal development) associated with management development.

From what has been said it would be sensible to regard training and development as interactive, each complementing the other. Finally, the logical step is for the organization to produce a plan for human resource development (i.e. training and development) which will dovetail into the employee resourcing plan (i.e. selection) and the organization's overall strategic plan. As Keep (1992) points out, training and development of employees is not an option, it is an intrinsic part of the practice of HRM and is an investment in people.

Systematic training

In the 1960s training received a fillip with the establishment of the Industrial Training Boards in the United Kingdom. The emphasis was on the acquisition of behavioural skills and what a training programme could achieve. This is referred to as systematic training and it put emphasis on off-the-job training as opposed to the then popular method of 'sitting next to Nellie'. Quite simply a systematic approach would start with a definition of the training needs of employees, that is the attitude, knowledge, skill and behaviour required by the employee in order to do his or her job adequately. Next the required training necessary to satisfy these needs is put in motion using suitable trainers, and finally there is an evaluation of the training undertaken in order to ensure it is effective.

A more comprehensive description of the training process, according to Armstrong (1992), is the concept of planned training. Planned training is a deliberate intervention designed to bring about the necessary learning to improve performance on the job (Kenney and Reid, 1988), and it includes the following points. Apart from the issues raised above with respect to systematic training, there is reference to the importance of setting training objectives (i.e. what the trainee should be capable of doing after the training course has been completed) and the planning of the training programme, using the right combination of training techniques and locations, in order to achieve the training objectives.

Benefits of training

Training, as a vehicle for human resource development, is concerned with improving the skills of employees and enhancing their capacity to cope with the ever-changing demands of the work situation. It could also make a positive contribution to the empowerment of employees. Specific benefits have been identified by Kenney *et al.* (1990) and Armstrong (1992) as follows:

☐ Training facilitates getting to grips with the requirements of a job quickly, and by improving the knowledge and skill of the worker it allows him or her to better the quantity and quality of output with fewer mistakes and a reduction in waste. The enhancement of the skill base of the employee could lead to job enrichment with benefits to both the individual and the organization.

☐ When the outcome of training leads to greater competency in the execution of tasks by subordinates, this relieves the manager from tasks related to remedial or corrective effort.

☐ Training is an invaluable process when the organization wishes to introduce flexible working methods and wants to create appropriate attitudes to equip employees to cope with change. Training could be used as a confidence-builder in a management of change programme when employees are given help in understanding why change is necessary, how they might benefit from it, and when they are given the skills to participate in the implementation of change.

☐ Training has significance in a public relations sense in that it has value in projecting the right image to prospective workers of good calibre.

☐ Where training incorporates safety training as an integral part of the programme, the outcome could be favourable in terms of health and safety at work.

☐ Training could have a favourable impact on the level of staff turnover, and the costs of redundancy schemes and recruitment of staff could be reduced when displaced staff are re-trained.

☐ The motivational impact of training is manifest when staff feel a sense of recognition when sent on a training course, and after been trained they are motivated to acquire new skills, particularly when rewards follow the acquisition and use of skills.

☐ The value of training in a communication context is evident when core values, such as those relating to product quality and customer service, are disseminated to employees, with the hope that they will be adopted and generate commitment.

☐ Identification with the organization could be fostered when a better understanding of mission statements and corporate objectives is achieved through a training programme.

☐ Training aimed at operationalizing certain management techniques (e.g. quality circles) could generate certain desirable side effects, such as analytical, problem-solving and presentational skills.

As a means of complementing the above list of beneficial points associated with training, one should note the following issues related to the success of training programmes (CBI, 1989):

1. Training fosters a common vision throughout the organization.

2. Training enjoys high status when it is seen to satisfy the needs of the organization and produces results.

3. It is important that there are in place organizational structures which facilitate the acquisition and nurturing of skills where employee

development is geared to the meeting of corporate objectives. Likewise, business systems should exist that are flexible enough to cater for the investment in people with agreed budgets, as well as clear targets against which performance is assessed on a regular basis. It is apparent that in this climate training is an integral part of corporate strategy. It is certainly not viewed as a peripheral organizational activity with a narrow remedial brief but is seen as a mechanism for fostering employee motivation with implications for the recruitment and retention of staff.

The success scenario outlined above might, in the eyes of some commentators, err on the side of optimism. But one must recognize the formidable constraints affecting a successful outcome. Factors contributing to the failure of training programmes are as follows (CBI, 1989):

☐ Management fails to consider seriously the existing and future skills needed by the organization. (Often one finds that training budgets are all too easily trimmed when the organization is looking for savings; the belief is that training does not pay off in the short term, and that an investment in training is lost when people leave the organization.)

☐ Management relies too heavily on local or national labour markets to satisfy the needs of the organization for relevant skills at all levels.

☐ Too often a natural response to skill shortages is to poach key employees from other employers even if such action leads to wage inflation.

Competition and change

Competitive conditions facing an organization can lead to changes in working practices, habits, cultures and the redesign of work. To prepare employees for such an eventuality, we can resort to training with the emphasis on development to maintain or enhance the quality of the operations and output. Nowadays words such as flexibility and teamwork enter the organizational vocabulary when talking about change, as we saw in chapter 3. To promote the cause of teamworking requires training of the team and developing multi-skills so that members can do different tasks within the team. Also, the team leader should be trained in leadership skills.

At the Nissan car factory at Sunderland in the United Kingdom there is a commitment to the development of effective teams, with lots of authority delegated to team leaders. Nissan identifies a level of competence for each skill and expects employees to master the operations and eventually be able to train others as well. At Lucas, in the United Kingdom, there has been an elaborate scheme to provide employees with the capacity to handle change. Multi-disciplinary task forces were created and given training to cope with work redesign, product quality and issues connected with marketing the product and how to improve the service received from suppliers. In addition, a cultural shift took place when the central training function moved from a preoccupation with the delivery of training to 'training development' and took an active interest in promoting open learning centres and a variety of courses (Storey, 1992).

Although top management at Lucas backed the above scheme, those further down the hierarchy, such as middle managers and shopfloor workers, did not experience training and development to the extent anticipated. To them what came across was a work environment characterized by pressure and the cutting of costs. This is an example of where employees further down the organizational hierarchy do not share the degree of commitment and enthusiasm held by top management intent on shaping the company's training culture.

In recent years there have been a number of internal and external initiatives in training following developments aimed at improving the competitive advantage of organizations. The major ones that will be examined in this section are training to underpin management processes, such as total quality management, and national schemes to set standards of competences for all industries.

Total quality management (TQM)

This is an approach to management, already considered in chapter 3 in connection with changing culture, which elevates to a position of significant importance a process of improvements in business operations and output. The final judge of its effectiveness will be the customer in the market. Those responsible for TQM will try to ensure that quality pervades all organizational activities. It is the task of every function and every employee to contribute to activities connected with improvements, and quality systems and a quality culture are essential prerequisites (Hill, 1991). Training is at the service of TQM by developing employee skills to cope with change, as well as imparting an understanding of quality monitoring techniques.

At Michelin a training programme was mounted to support a quality improvement initiative and this was aimed at improving existing knowledge and skills, and teaching new skills, as well as knowledge of the inspection process. The company tested the trainees on what they absorbed during the training programme and the outcome of this exercise showed that quality improvements had taken place. As a result, skill-based pay was introduced to reflect the new responsibilities (IRS, 1992). In chapter 7 skill-based pay was discussed as a reward for the acquisition of skills; in effect pay is linked to some extent to the successful completion of authorized training. This is an attempt to underline the importance of training as an aspect of corporate strategy.

National schemes

There have been criticisms over the years about Britain's poor record in education and training. The education system is criticized for not appealing to large numbers of 18-year-olds, who finish their education earlier than many students from some neighbouring countries, and for not providing an educational experience compatible with the needs of industry. Employers have also been criticized for the lack of investment in training. At the national level these criticisms have been taken on board.

The government felt that previous training initiatives (e.g. the Training Boards referred to earlier) failed because they were both too bureaucratic and too centralized. A preferred alternative in the 1990s was to decentralize responsibility for training, making sure that there was participation of industry and commerce in the scheme. Training and Enterprise Councils (TECs) and their Scottish equivalent were set up as the hub of local initiatives. TECs are allocated government funds, which they control, but they are allowed to raise private funds as well. The majority of the membership of a TEC is from commerce and industry; the rest comes from the field of education and training, trade unions and voluntary organizations.

When a TEC makes an assessment of local labour markets it is normally concerned with the potential for economic growth and the level of skill shortages. Business plans, which include overall objectives, targets amenable to measurement and evaluation techniques, are prepared and submitted to the appropriate section of the Department of Employment. Subsequently, the TEC receives funds in relation to the plan and previous levels of performance. The funds are used to provide training opportunities for the unemployed, and on advising employers on the assessment of training needs, training techniques and the resourcing of training. The TEC also encourages employers with a common training need to pool their resources to provide training facilities in circumstances where the provision of an appropriate training facility would be too costly for an individual employer. The TEC encourages enterprise initiatives by allocating pump-priming funds for approved new ventures.

In recent years the government took a particular initiative in the field of training by setting up a national framework – National Vocational Qualifications (NVQs) – that linked the provision of training in a direct way to skills used in jobs. NVQs were designed to set occupationally based standards, to recognize competence in the work-place and to provide a ladder of achievement. On offer are competency-based qualifications applicable to jobs at all levels within organizations across all industries. The qualifications can be acquired by employees whilst engaged in normal job activities at their place of work. The actual training would be monitored by an accredited tester, normally a manager or supervisor, who is qualified to act in this way. The employee should be able to demonstrate performance which can be assessed. If the employee has met the standard required at a particular level in the NVQ hierarchy, a pass grade is given. If the employee does not meet the standards required, this signifies a fail and indicates a training need. The NVQs give employees scope to go on developing their skills and experience and hopefully the overall experience will advance the mobility of labour between employers.

Already reference has been made to 'competency'. This is a term used in preference to knowledge and skills on the understanding that competence, unlike the former, has a better relationship with improved performance. The jury is still out on this one! The Training Agency defined competence as 'the ability to perform the activities within an occupation or function to the standards expected in employment'. This definition would include the ability to transfer knowledge and skills to new situations within employment, and takes on board activities such as organizing and planning, creative and innovative pursuits, tolerance for handling non-programmed situations, and interpersonal skills used in liaising with fellow workers and clients. The case in Box 8.1 illustrates the use of the 'competency' approach in a training and development context.

In this case the company's strategy for training and development is connected to the corporate strategy via HRM, and you will notice that an emphasis is placed on the value of appropriate competences for bringing about organizational success in the future. Also, the competency approach is used at different stages – at the assessment of training needs, the setting of learning objectives and the evaluation of training – and the company values the notion of continuous development.

Reservations have been expressed about the competency approach in the sense that it is considered too restrictive. Doubts have been expressed about whether increasing individual competences enhances organizational performance, that the focus is on discrete areas of a job and not generalized ability in relation to a whole job, and that too little attention is given to the complexity of the process of skill acquisition and the transfer of skills for the benefit of the organization (Holmes, 1990). There is also the view that the competency approach does not consider management style, bureaucratic structure, corporate culture, the environment, career patterns and personal learning abilities. These factors were identified as being

Box 8.1

---

*HUMAN RESOURCE DEVELOPMENT AT MALIN MANUFACTURING
SERVICES (MMS)*

MMS manufactures pharmaceutical products which are sold on prescription. The company's mission statement reveals an intention to produce medicines of the highest quality for the benefit of society. To realize the corporate objectives which flow from such a mission statement would require highly skilled and adaptable employees capable of contributing to the success of the company operating in a rapidly changing technical and market environment.

A number of important changes took place in MMS during the early 1990s. There was a delayering initiative in which the number of layers of organization was reduced, autonomous business units within the organization were established, a team approach to working was introduced, and there was a shift in attitudes and practices in the area of human resources, where now the importance of the 'bottom line' in the thinking of employees, and organizational flexibility, are heavily underlined.

It was felt that that there should be greater objectivity in the employee development process. Hence use was made of assessment centres. The assessments were made with reference to twelve competences, and where a need for development was diagnosed, appropriate development programmes were provided. But in some cases, where there was a failure to meet the criteria, people were made redundant or redeployed.

Competences were also used at the stage of setting learning objectives for employees. These are raised and discussed at the performance appraisal sessions, and training is offered to help correct the deficiency between the current and desired level of competency. Given the importance of flexibility within teams, it is necessary for employees to be multi-skilled. To this end training is provided for new recruits and existing employees. In fact the reward system is mobilized to assist with the acquisition of skills, because pay awards are given to employees who have acquired new skills. Overall there is a firm commitment on the part of the organization to continuous improvement among employees.

(Harrison, 1992).

---

necessary to operate a sound training programme (Training Agency, 1989). The above criticisms are likely to be too harsh when the advanced stages of the NVQ are considered where management training takes place; the earlier stages would focus on operative training and perhaps the criticisms are more valid at this level.

A more recent national UK initiative, administered through the TECs, is the investors in people (IIP) scheme. This attempts to relate training and development to business strategy and provides guidance to companies on how to develop their training programmes to nationally recognized standards. The key issue is the adequacy and relevancy of the company's training requirements in the light of business strategy. The IIP is not too interested in detailed prescriptions on the contents of training programmes, and it is not essential to link training to the NVQ scheme. The IIP national standard embraces the following principles (Goss, 1994):

1. There is a commitment by top management to the development of all employees in order to achieve corporate objectives. This will necessitate the preparation of a written but flexible business plan and there will be an indication of how employees will achieve it.
2. There will be regular reviews of the training and development needs of all employees.
3. There will be a specification of the resources available for training and those responsible for providing training opportunities will be identified.
4. Training and development starts with recruitment and selection and is a live issue throughout the employee's stay in the company. It is necessary to conduct a regular training needs assessment and to act on the outcome of this process.
5. There will be an evaluation of the investment in training and development to see to what extent progress has been made and whether improvements in organizational effectiveness have taken place.

In order to be recognized by IIP an organization is required to engage in systematic planning, to audit its training operations to establish if things are going according to plan and, where necessary, to take appropriate corrective action. Officials from TEC will visit the company to evaluate the progress made and report on whether or not to offer recognition.

It appears that IIP's interpretation of training and development closely coincides with an HRM perspective in this area. There is no distinction between training and development and there is a recognition that all employees have development potential. Also, training is something that permeates the thinking and behaviour of managers at all levels and not something that belongs to the training function in the organization, and it is relevant to the efficient operation of the company. Such a view, if upheld, could be protective of training in adverse economic situations. There have been criticisms of IIP by the Confederation of British Industry (CBI) to the effect that the procedures used are overly bureaucratic and the costs of assessment are too high (Hilton, 1992).

Management development

Management development is an activity that sets out to ensure that the organization has the required managerial talent to face the present and future with confidence. It is concerned with improving the performance of existing managers, giving them the scope for personal growth and development, and makes appropriate provision for the future replacement of managers (i.e. management succession). Among the objectives for a management development scheme are the following:

☐ Identify managers with potential and ensure they receive the right experience, training and development.

☐ Set achievable objectives for the improvement of performance which are amenable to measurement, clearly specifying responsibilities.

☐ Create a climate where serious thought is given to instituting a management succession scheme which would be kept under regular review.

An application of the philosophy of the NVQ scheme to the development of managers is likely to find expression in the Management Charter Initiative (MCI). This initiative was conceived following the publication of various reports in the late 1980s critical of the provision of management education and training in the United Kingdom when compared with other countries. There is an attempt to build on the framework provided by the NVQ, and management qualifications (i.e. Certificate, Diploma, Masters) on four levels are on offer to cater for the needs of supervisors, first-line managers, middle managers and senior managers. A challenge similar to the one levelled at the NVQs is directed at the MCI approach. For example, the practicality of devising a set of standard competences that adequately capture the full complexity of managerial work across different types of organizations and different industries is open to question.

Also, there is the fear that the MCI approach is overly bureaucratic (Goss, 1994). Therefore, it is not surprising that some companies have developed alternative but flexible approaches; an example of such an approach is the capabilities model developed by Brooke Bond. This integrates knowledge and skills with the softer things such as attitudes and qualities. If such a development were to take off in a big way throughout the world of work, it could adversely affect the widespread acceptance of the MCI approach. A number of the approaches to management development are discussed later in the section on approaches to training and development.

Career management

This activity is complementary to management development and it is concerned with planning and shaping the path which people take in their career progression within the organization. It normally applies to managerial staff, but not necessarily so, and follows an assessment of the needs of the organization for managers and the preferences of employees for development. The underlying assumption of career management is that, in the context of management succession, the organization should be alert to providing able people with the training, guidance and encouragement to enable them to fulfil their potential. This view is not shared by all organizations who would take in 'fresh blood' as and when needed and do not subscribe to elaborate internal promotion policies. Another view is to promote competent people who have proved themselves in their current jobs to higher positions when the opportunity arises. But progressive companies are likely to take a considered long-term view when they set in motion sophisticated reviews of employee performance and potential and plan job moves on the basis of the outcome of these processes. Assessment centres, discussed in connection with selection in chapter 5, could be used to identify managerial talent or confirm that it is still in existence.

A sensible line to adopt is to emphasize long-term flexibility (Armstrong, 1992), where an emphasis on good current performance goes hand in hand with some degree of preparedness to groom people for advancement. Finally, even though the notion of a career for life in an organization is becoming more remote, this does not absolve employers from commitment to providing career paths for able employees (Herriot, 1992).

Approaches to training and development

A large number of methods are available to the organization when it is considering the training and development of both managerial and non-managerial staff. The more important ones will be considered in this section.

Sitting by Nellie (demonstration)

The trainee is shown how to do the job by an experienced member of staff and is then allowed to get on with it. The advantage of this method is that learning is directly related to the job. The disadvantages are that the experienced member of staff (who may not be a training expert) may have difficulty explaining things and empathizing with the trainee, and mistakes made by the trainee could be costly. Also, this method does not provide for the creation of structure in the learning process, neither does it provide appropriate feedback which is required to improve effective performance.

Coaching

This could be considered an improved version of demonstration and has the advantage of interaction between the trainer and trainee. It has key ingredients not associated with demonstration, such as structure, feedback and motivation.

Mentoring

This is a method of on-the-job training, particularly for aspiring senior managers, which appears to be growing in importance. The trainee observes the skills displayed by the mentor, usually a senior manager who is not his or her boss, and copies and adopts the senior manager's behaviour. The mentor provides support and help in the various assignments undertaken by the protégé and can provide an invaluable insight into the politics and culture of the organization. The protégé can benefit from the continuous dialogue with the mentor who, if influential within the organization, can exert much influence in securing interesting tasks for the protégé as well as opening windows of opportunities. As a result, the mentor contributes to confidence building and the career development of the protégé and provides him or her with a useful informal network within the organization. Recently the significance of the mentoring system in a corporate culture sense has been underlined. It is said that it provides a channel through which core organizational values and meanings are conveyed and fortified by mentors of the status of senior managers at the twilight of their careers, and absorbed by those who will eventually succeed them (Collin, 1992).

The attractive features of the mentoring system are well stated above, but before leaving it we must be mindful of its negative aspects. According to Goss (1994), these are as follows:

☐ There may be charges of élitism from those who were denied protégé status.
☐ There may be a certain incompatibility between the mentor and the protégé.
☐ The protégé may be over-dependent on the mentor.
☐ The mentor may show an inability to manage the relationship effectively.
☐ Generally, line managers are suspicious of the process and display resistance and lack of cooperation because of its disruptive effect on reporting relationships already established.

Job rotation

This involves moving people around on a systematic basis in order to broaden their experience. The advantages of this method are that links between departments are fostered, and employees develop flexibility because of the range of activities undertaken. However, a disadvantage is that it does not offer people the opportunity to practise the complete range of skills because of the limited time spent on any one job. Also, a problem could arise when errors materialize because of the inexperience of the transferred employee, and when managers nominate poor performers for the job rotation scheme.

Other job-related experiences

Apart from job rotation, job enlargement could be used to broaden the job experience of the employee. Job enlargement expands a job on a horizontal basis, as opposed to a vertical basis found in job enrichment which was discussed in the previous chapter. Diversity is promoted by increasing the number of tasks an employee performs. For example, a word processor operator's job could be enlarged to include tasks such as acting as a receptionist periodically and doing some filing. Job enlargement, along with participating in the work of a project team or task group could be a useful developmental exercise.

Formal training

Among the methods used are lectures and discussions, together with case studies, role playing and simulation, and programmed learning. Case studies make use of predetermined situations to provide opportunities for the analysis of data and the presentation of solutions without the risks of failure associated with real-world situations. Role-playing and simulation offers the trainee the opportunity to perform in situations as if they were real, as in, for example, the training of airline pilots. Programmed learning with the aid of the computer can be used to test knowledge and ability at a basic level to begin with, progressing to more difficult tasks later.

Formal training can take place off-the-job. There could be long college courses which cater for the overall development of the employee, but are not specifically targeted to the job. This gives the employee the opportunity to think afresh and to meet people with different experiences outside the job. Nowadays open learning courses have become popular. The learner proceeds at his or her own pace with the help of a pack of course material, but unless certain measures are taken (e.g. provision of tutorial support) the learner can feel somewhat isolated.

There are also short courses. Although certain short courses are general in nature, others are specifically targeted to satisfy an organizational need. Formal courses can be expensive, and there is no guarantee that learning is transferred to the work situation. Supporters of on-the-job training, by comparison, would argue that learning on-the-job is more likely to find its way into work practices.

Self-development

In self-development control and direction are primarily in the hands of the individual, with a focus on learning from experience. This approach does not have to be unstructured experience tantamount to a process of trial and error, with an intention to steer clear of past mistakes. It can be structured with an agreement between interested parties at the work-place on the best way to make it operational; this could include guided reading and specified work activities.

An influential theorist in the field of self-development is Kolb (1985). The learning cycle he postulated is as follows:

1. The individual has a concrete experience, either planned or un-planned.
2. Next there is reflective observation, and this amounts to thinking about what was responsible for the experience and the implications, etc.
3. Abstract conceptualization and generalization follow where general principles can be drawn from the experience or incident.
4. The final step is experimentation in new situations, and this forms the basis for the development of new experiences.

The application of the learning cycle would necessitate managers diagnosing the work situations they encounter, evaluating the avenues open to them, and finally formulating a strategy to attain their objectives. Ideally a programme of self-development will bear some relationship to career development for managerial staff and both could be linked to organizational needs as gleaned from corporate plans. It would appear that any good system of management development based on self-development must prepare managers to exercise control of events and to take respon-sibility for outcomes within their domain, and particularly control over their own actions and learning (Pedlar et al., 1988).

Action learning
The basic ingredients of self-development are ingrained in action learning, but in addition it has a social dimension. Basically, the trainee relies heavily on experience of what happens at work and adopts questioning and

exploration in a group setting as a mode of operation (Revans, 1971). In action learning the spotlight is on real problems, where the learner or trainee questions the causes of these problems. This is followed by generating solutions that are capable of implementation.

A small group (called a set) is created and 'set' members cooperate in a process which amounts to questioning and testing each other until there is a certain amount of clarity about the nature of the problem and the best way to tackle it. Set members are very supportive as they go about the review of individual projects, and they are keen to provide feedback. A climate of mutual support and mutual constructive criticism can be found in a set that works well. Once the deliberations are completed the set disbands, and trainees are expected to be committed to their chosen action strategies following the various questioning and exploration episodes that took place in the set.

A feature of action learning is the challenge to and the criticism levelled at the *status quo* and traditional practices. In certain organizational cultures such an approach would not be welcome, but it could certainly take root and produce results in organizational conditions where there is a commitment to action learning. It would appear that action learning as part of a management development programme is a useful approach when the organization is interested in increasing the effectiveness of its managers in a behavioural sense (Lawrence, 1986), but it is not necessarily the best approach to develop technical competence or to assimilate new knowledge about managing people.

Outdoor courses

The outdoor training sessions could be on the use of initiative, problem solving and cooperation, and could be used by organizations interested in the development of team-building and leadership skills. Invariably there is a sharing of experience by members of the group in the face of adverse physical conditions, such as a challenging mountain climb, and this can contribute to the development of cooperative modes of operation and psychological closeness.

These training sessions can produce good results if attention is given to a number of issues connected with the planning of the course, the operation of the course and relating the course to conditions in the home organizational environment. For example, does the course have clear objectives? Is the course a natural part of the organization's total training provision? Are the course organizers familiar with the culture and practices in the organization from which the participants are drawn? Have the course organizers taken the necessary action with respect to safety? In addition, the instructor/trainee ratio should below, and where possible what takes place during the training sessions should be related to the participant's work-place.

One should be aware of potential problems. If some or all of the members of the training course originate from the same organization but are of different statuses, superiors might feel uneasy about their image in the eyes of subordinates when they have not performed as well as expected. On the other hand, subordinates might act in a predictable organizational way by adopting a typical behavioural pattern (e.g. submissiveness or compliance) where they perceived superiors to be acting officiously. There might be difficulties in transferring the benefits derived from the training session to the work situation because of constraints with respect to implementation. Certain key people in the organization might feel uncomfortable if those returning were equipped with behavioural skills which enabled them to challenge cherished practices (Lowe, 1991). Finally, there has been a dip in the demand for outdoor courses, according to a recent Industrial Society survey (Hegarty and Dickson, 1995). Critics are likely to point out that it would make greater sense if course participants performed tasks that relate to what they do in their jobs.

Continuous development

It is almost commonplace nowadays to hear the view that training should be a continuing process with the accent on self-development, as mentioned earlier. This is prompted by the suggestion that employees cannot, in a rapidly changing world, rely on the knowledge and skill acquired in gaining their initial qualifications. In 1987 the Institute of Personnel Management (now the Institute of Personnel and Development) produced a code of practice with respect to personal development and the demands posed by jobs. A starting point is the assessment of the organization's present and future training needs; this is done by extracting from the corporate plan the pool of employee knowledge and skill required to implement that plan. Predictably the importance of learning from confronting and solving problems at work is underlined.

The role of top management in cultivating a climate of continuous development is given special mention. The top management are admonished to place high on the corporate agenda the frequent formal review of training activities aimed at the development of employee competences. In the final analysis it should be recognized that it is wise to promote the view that one should make learning a habit and to accept the idea that work problems offer opportunities for learning. Ideally it is hoped that well-conceived continuous development aimed at helping the individual also helps the organization to achieve its objectives.

Learning organization

The arrival on the scene of the learning organization is associated with the need to provide for the internal renewal of the organization in the face of a competitive environment. A learning organization has been defined as an organization which facilitates the learning of all its members and continually transforms itself (Pedlar *et al.*, 1988). It is said that a learning organization has the capacity to learn itself and it creates space and formal mechanisms for people to think, to ask questions, to reflect and to learn, as well as encouraging them to challenge the *status quo* and to suggest improvements (Handy, 1989).

This type of climate should permeate all collective activities (e.g. meetings, conferences) where there is an acute sensitivity to what is going on in the organization and a willingness to experiment in the light of opportunities or threats. The learning organization is keen to assist people in the identification of their learning needs; such needs would be reviewed regularly along with the provision of feedback on performance to date. Also, there would be a commitment to providing new experiences from which people can learn and to mobilizing training resources. Learning from others could be extended to 'benchmarking', which is an ongoing investigation and learning experience that aims to identify, analyse, adopt and implement the best practices in the company's industry (Garvin, 1993).

Evaluation

Eventually the organization will need to know if its training and development activities are achieving the anticipated results. This will be easier to establish in some areas rather than in others. For example, outcomes are more tangible and measurable where there is a change in the way a psycho-motor skill is performed than when a shift in values or attitudes has taken place. How do we go about evaluating training? The following are indicative of the approaches one might adopt.

At the end of a training session trainees are asked to complete a questionnaire stating which parts of the training were most useful, relevant and interesting. The results of this exercise could be useful to the trainer, and could lead to an improvement next time round. However, the following weaknesses are associated with this method:

☐ Positive responses are made because trainees were happy with the training encounter, possibly having been entertained by the instructor.

Such responses would not give any insight into the effectiveness of the training session.

☐ The trainees feel that the training session was useful and relevant to their occupational sphere, but unfortunately this judgement is based on a lack of sufficient awareness of their training needs.

☐ Because of the close proximity of the evaluation exercise to the end of the training session, there is no information on the transfer of learning to the work-place.

As a means to remedy the last weakness, follow-up questionnaires could be sent to respondents after a lapse of time since the training took place (e.g. three months). Questions are asked about the extent to which the learning was used in practice in terms of using knowledge, skills and attitudes acquired during the training session. In the responses there could be an indication of impediments or blocks to the transfer of learning. Of course this may not be the fault of the trainee: it could be due to a lack of suitable equipment or software, or where there is resistance from other employees to the material learnt on the course.

Tests of varying kinds, such as examinations and grading of coursework and projects, can be used to evaluate learning, particularly on the longer courses. These tests are likely to affect the processes and culture of the group engaged in learning as competitive and secretive tendencies develop following a realization that a trainee can be given either a pass or fail mark or grade. A less formal version of tests is that of exercises where trainees engage in role-playing, or tackle a case study or in-tray exercise. Then they are given the opportunity to evaluate their own performance, subsequently receiving feedback from colleagues and the trainer. It is hoped that the feedback expressed as criticism is constructive. Although tests and exercises play a useful part in informing us about what learning has taken place, we are none the wiser about the transfer of learning to the work-place.

Another approach is evaluation at the 'job behavioural level' (Hamblin, 1974). Here the transfer of learning could be evaluated by the trainee's manager or training specialist to establish whether or not behaviour has changed as a result of the training. The following include some of the techniques used for this purpose:

☐ Activity sampling and observer diaries: the trainees are observed to see to what extent they are putting into practice the knowledge, attitudes and skills acquired through training.

☐ Critical incidents: key incidents at work are analysed to establish to what extent 'new patterns of behaviour' are present.

☐ Self-recording: the trainees record how they perform certain activities.

Eventually, the organization will be looking for evidence of how the changed job behaviour influences other employees and the way the company functions. This would mean measuring changes in overall organizational functioning with respect to productivity, output and costs, but such an exercise would be difficult to undertake.

Finally, at the evaluation stage it is worth considering why the training was undertaken in the first place. There could be a number of reasons, such as to rectify a skills deficiency, to project an image as a responsible employer, to convey to employees that the organization is committed to their development, and as a reward to able performers.

Conclusions

If HRM is to fulfil its aim of valuing human 'assets', it is necessary to invest in them. This implies a positive attitude towards training and development. In organizations where there is a core of knowledge-based workers, development is vital to maintain their ability to add value to the enterprise. This is equally true where multi-skilled workers are required to participate in teamwork. On the issue of flexibility, it will be necessary to ask the question, how much investment should be made in temporary workers?

Training and development cannot be seen as a panacea for all organizational ills. However, it is clearly important to equip employees with skills and knowledge and to motivate them to utilize their abilities.

References

Armstrong, M. (1992) *Human Resource Management: Strategy and action*. London: Kogan Page.

CBI (1989) *Managing The Skills Gap*. London: Confederation of British Industry.

Collin, A. (1992) 'The role of the mentor in transforming the organisation'. Paper presented at the Annual Conference, Employment Research Unit, Business School, University of Cardiff, September.

Garvin, D. (1993) 'Building a learning organisation', *Harvard Business Review*, **July–August**, 78–91.

Goss, D. (1994) *Principles of Human Resource Management*. London: Routledge.

Hamblin, A. C. (1974) *Evaluation and Control of Training*. Maidenhead: McGraw-Hill.

Handy, C. (1989) *The Age of Unreason*. London: Business Books.

Harrison, R. (1992) *Employee Development*. London: Institute of Personnel Management.

Hegarty, S. and Dickson, T. (1995) 'Rise and fall of corporate thrills', *Financial Times*, 9 January, p. 7.

Herriot, P. (1992) *The Career Management Challenge: Balancing individual and organisational needs*. London: Sage.

Hill, S. (1991) 'Why quality circles failed but total quality management might succeed', *British Journal of Industrial Relations*, **29**, 541–568.

Hilton, P. (1992) 'Shepherd defends training policy', *Personnel Management*, **December**, p. 11.

Holmes, L. (1990) 'Trainer competences: turning back the clock', *Training and Development*. **April**, 17–20.

IRS (1992) 'Skill-based pay: the new training initiative', *Employee Development Bulletin*, **31**, July, Industrial Relations Review and Report, No. 516, pp. 2–7.

Keep, E. (1992) 'Corporate training strategies', in Salaman, G. (ed.), *Human Resource Strategies*. London: Sage.

Kenney, J. and Reid, M. (1988) *Training Initiatives*. London: Institute of Personnel Management.

Kenney, J., Reid, M. and Donnelly, E. (1990) *Manpower Training and Development*. London: Institute of Personnel Management.

Kolb, D. (1985) *Experiential Learning: Experiences as the source of learning and development*. Englewood Cliffs, NJ: Prentice Hall.

Lawrence, J. (1986) 'Action learning – a questioning approach', in Mumford, A. (ed.), *Handbook of Management Development*. Aldershot: Gower.

Lowe, J. (1991) 'Teambuilding via outdoor training: experiences from a UK automotive plant', *Human Resource Management Journal*, **2**, 42–59.

Pedlar, M., Boydell, R. and Burgoyne, J. (1988) *Learning Company Project*. London: Manpower Services Commission.

Revans, R. (1971) *Developing Effective Managers*. London: Longman.

Storey, J. (1992) *Developments in the Management of Human Resources*. Oxford: Blackwell.

Training Agency (1989) *Training in Britain: Employees perspectives*. Research Report. London: HMSO.

9

Employee relations

Prior to the advent of HRM, employee relations was often called industrial relations and was concerned with the interactions between the employer (represented by management) and the work-force (typically represented by trade unions). It involved the processes of collective bargaining, negotiation and consultation, and occurred at two levels – the organization and the industry. Employee relations differs from industrial relations in so far as there is an emphasis on direct communication with the work-force and liaison with employees at the level of the individual. This creates a scene where there is reduced interaction with trade unions (Bright, 1993).

While traditional collective bargaining concentrated on pay settlements and conditions of work, HRM approaches have sought to broaden the involvement of employees and take a more participative approach to management through increased communication, flexibility and a broader agenda. In some cases this is seen to be a positive development, but in others the rhetoric of HRM has been used to disguise a policy of anti-unionism. The following topics will be discussed in this chapter:

1. Communication.
2. Participation.
3. Trade union representation.
4. Conflict.
5. Health and safety.

Communication

Communication is a process at the disposal of the organization to keep management and employees informed about a variety of relevant matters. For example, it is important for management to let people know about the mission statement, if there is one, and the objectives of the company. Also, people are informed of what is expected of them in terms of performance, and how changes in the strategic direction of the company are likely to affect their jobs. It is also important to give employees the opportunity to communicate with management so that their reaction to proposals put to them is known, as well as having the chance to put forward counter proposals. Good communication, as the lifeblood of the organization, helps to promote the involvement of employees in the decision-making processes, and in so doing can enhance the individual's identification with the organization, which in turn can lead to improved performance.

Effective communication involves the sending and receiving of clearly understood messages between management and subordinates in a two-way process. In this respect one should keep in mind the following steps:

1. Have a clear idea of the message to be put across.
2. Ideas should be put across in a suitable form using, where possible, the language of the receiver.
3. Choose the most appropriate communication medium (e.g. telephone/fax, e-mail, meeting, memo or report). Consider building 'redundancy' (i.e. same information in more than one form) into the process when circumstances justify it.
4. Ensure the message gets to the receiver, but it must be recognized that in the final analysis it is the responsibility of the receiver to tune in to the contents of the message.
5. Ensure that the intended meaning of the transmitted message gets across. This is more likely to be established where two-way communication exists.
6. Monitor the reaction of the receiver if a response is required.
7. Elicit feedback from the receiver not obtained in step 5.

Feedback is a two-way process and for it to be open and constructive requires the establishment of the right climate by management. Managing this climate is seen as a vital activity for success because if employees do not feel they are being dealt with openly and honestly, resentments and conflicts may arise.

The potential for barriers to effective communication to exist within organizations is great, and sensitivity to these impediments is advocated. These barriers consist of the following:

☐ The message is distorted because of the use of unsuitable language.

☐ The message does not get through because of interruptions due to physical noise (e.g. a noisy place of work) or psychological noise (e.g. biases and prejudices harboured by the receiver of the message).

☐ The message is interpreted selectively by the receiver (e.g. the person hears what he or she wants to hear rather than what is said).

☐ The receiver of the message arrives at a conclusion prematurely, or becomes defensive as a result of being insulted by what has been said.

☐ Difficulties arise owing to an overload of information in the message.

☐ The sender of the message is in the dark as to the views of the receiver because the sender misinterprets the feedback or gets no feedback from the receiver.

The size of the organization will influence the style (e.g. formal or informal) of communications. The following internal approaches to communication can be used in different circumstances, but equally they can complement each other.

Noticeboards and memoranda

Written information (e.g. details of vacancies, forthcoming events) is disseminated in a formal sense to employees generally. In the case of the noticeboard, obsolete information should be removed and overcrowding the board with pieces of paper should be avoided; also, censorship, either unintentional or deliberate, whereby only certain types of information gets on the board should be guarded against. A drawback of this medium of communication, which could also apply to magazines and newsletters (examined below), is that it does not provide an immediate reaction where the sender of the message can check that the intended message has been properly received and understood and the receiver can express a point of view. In cases where full attention is not paid to memoranda and noticeboards, the message fails to get through.

Magazines and newsletters

This medium should strive for a balance in its coverage of human interest stories and organizational issues. It is customary for magazines to be produced by management, whereas the newsletter may be subject to more employee control.

Consultative committees

These committees consist of both management and employees and are formally constituted with an agreed procedure. Minutes of the meetings are prepared and could be displayed on a noticeboard. If there is a tradition of industrial relations within a company, such committees could be used.

Presentations

These could be used by top management on a regular basis. In particular a chief executive interested in human relations could periodically visit the various company sites and address the rank and file on such matters as the financial health of the company, present problems and future challenges. This approach was adopted successfully by the previous managing director (Trevor Owen) of Remploy Ltd. This gives the chief executive the chance to meet all employees over time, and provided people do not feel inhibited in such a setting, presentations can be a useful mode of communication. The chief executive of the Body Shop – Anita Roddick – makes presentations to people in the various retail outlets of the company using a video recording.

Team briefings

This is a technique originally conceived and promoted by the Industrial Society in the United Kingdom and has been adopted by organizations seeking to extend face-to-face communications. Briefing sessions take place at various levels within the organization, and observations on important issues discussed further up the organization can cascade down the organization. Team leaders address a group, varying from four to fourteen in size, on a regular basis (monthly or bi-monthly). Information is disseminated on company policy and decisions and the reasons for them can be explained. At any particular level within the organization the greater part of the briefing could be devoted to local issues, but circumstances will dictate the amount of time devoted to important issues originating further up the organization (e.g. the implications of a take-over bid for the company).

Team briefings offer the opportunity for employees to interact in the process of clarifying and understanding decisions and policies and are an example of a more direct form of communication. It is important that part of the session consists of two-way communication so that the organization is aware of the concerns, ideas, and suggestions of the work-force. In such circumstances it would be necessary to have an upward reporting system following the briefing session. Among the problems surrounding the operation of team briefings are not having enough to report on a given occasion, the numbers in the team being either too small or too large, and the system not being uniformly applied in the sense that certain parts of the organization are not taking them seriously.

Team briefings can have a favourable impact in improving the status of the supervisor as a provider of information and can create a positive participative climate for resolving problems. However, in conditions where good industrial relations are absent, team briefing could be viewed by trade unions as a technique used to undermine their influence (Marchington, 1987). Finally, it is important that the 'briefer' receives appropriate training.

Attitude surveys

The organization is keen to feel the morale pulse of its employees and mounts attitude surveys to gauge the attitudes and opinions of employees on a variety of issues. This could highlight areas of concern as perceived by employees. If exercises of this nature are to be taken seriously, it is important that management acts on the results, otherwise employees could consider going through the motions of participating a waste of time.

Suggestion schemes

This is a form of upward communication whereby employees are encouraged to put forward ideas and proposals for the improvement of work practices which in its own right is a worthwhile pursuit. Schemes of this nature normally have a short life.

Communicating with employees is obviously an important process. The results of a recent survey suggest that 90 per cent of organizations sampled used one or more of the methods outlined above (Millward et al., 1992).

Participation

The level of employee participation has a major impact on the way an organization works, and is generally related to two key areas, i.e.

Box 9.1

WORKS COUNCILS

Works councils are committees usually made up of representatives from workers and management, and can be found in a number of European countries. They operate at the organizational level and meet to discuss issues including employee relations and business matters and to engage in joint decision making (Holden, 1994). For example, in Germany regulations governing recruitment and selection, regradings and dismissals require the agreement of the works councils (Sparrow and Hiltrop, 1994).

The Works Councils directive came into existence under the Social Chapter of the Maastricht Treaty in 1991, and Britain used the Social Chapter opt out to avoid its effect. Therefore, technically British companies do not have to comply with the provisions of the directive as far as their UK workers are concerned because of the opt out clause. However, British companies with operations in other EU member states would be subjected to the directive for employees working outside the UK.

Companies to which the directive applies are those with at least 1,000 employees within the 15 EU member states covered by the directive which is due to be implemented by 22 September, 1996. They will be required to set up European Works Councils (EWC) with the express purpose of consulting employees and giving them information about their company's performance and prospects. The alleged advantages of Work Councils are that employees will be better able to understand the pressures business face and appreciate the need to adapt to change in a competitive world. Also, EWCs could be seen as a means to cultivate the commitment of employees to the achievements of their company's objectives.

Although not required to do so, some British companies are setting up or planning to set up EWCs in the UK. Among them are United Biscuits, Coats Viyella and ICI. Electrolux is to include UK employees in its company-wide Works Councils which will cover all its European plants. Interestingly, surprising preliminary evidence from research conducted by the Industrial Relations Research Unit, University of Warwick, suggests that up to 300 British companies could be affected by the directive (Bassett, 1995). Therefore, in the years to come can we expect significant developments in macro participation in the UK?

management style and employee representation, such as the worker director of old. At the macro level, participation with employees as a collective is governed by procedures related to consultation and negotiation with trade unions and workers' representatives. These issues are addressed later in the section on trade union representation. A present-day manifestation of macro participation is the type of works councils used by companies such as United Biscuits and described in Box 9.1. At a micro level, the degree of individual participation will depend on the management styles adopted. Forms of participation in HRM tend to be broadly conceived.

The Harvard model of HRM (Beer *et al.*, 1984) holds that the various stakeholders in an organization should be taken into account when making decisions. The stakeholders include shareholders, customers and employees and unions. It is thought that if employees and unions are involved in the decision-making processes, then they will feel a greater sense of 'ownership' of the decisions made and will be more committed to their implementation. Workers will be more motivated to perform tasks where they have had some input to the determination of work goals and to the way they will be met. Participation can be seen as an important aspect of the way HRM can seek to enhance employee commitment.

Employee participation can be viewed as consultative or delegative. Consultative participation encourages and enables staff to contribute their views, but management retains the right to make the final decision. Delegative participation goes further and allows workers to take on decisions which traditionally had fallen within the managerial prerogative (Geary, 1994). In previous chapters various types of participative practices (e.g. autonomous work groups and quality circles) have been examined. A recent analysis of non-unionized organizations on 'greenfield' sites (Guest and Hoque, 1994) found that nearly half had high involvement/high commitment practices and HRM strategies. Less than a quarter had authoritarian and non-participative management styles.

With regard to authoritarianism in management, in particular where there is a tinge of abusive behaviour, there are some who believe that this style of management is tantamount to firm management and may be particularly appropriate if good commercial results are to be achieved in certain corporate cultures. Others would argue that the dividing line between this type of management and bullying is rather tenuous. A survey undertaken by the University of Stafford on behalf of the British Broadcasting Corporation (BBC) in 1994 showed that 78 per cent of the 1,137 employees sampled had witnessed work-place bullying, which in some cases amounts to a culture of management by fear and intimidation (Fursland, 1995). In Box 9.2 is an example of a management style that many of us would not like to be at the receiving end.

It would appear that the management style referred to in Box 9.2 is unlikely to be popular as we enter the next century. According to an Institute of Management Report (1994), *Management Development to the Millennium*, respondents in a survey of 1,200 managers strongly maintained that 'authoritarian management styles will be increasingly inappropriate'. Respondents also stated that in 29 per cent of organizations there were moves toward a more cooperative, less coercive style of management, and that in a further 39 per cent of organizations such a style of management was partly implemented. The manager, according to the report, will be a team leader who earns the employee's respect, rather than giving orders, by the beginning of the next century. It was felt that 'female attributes' – skills connected with teamworking, consensus management, negotiating, interpersonal skills and the ability to cope with the demands

Box 9.2

FIRM MANAGEMENT OR BULLYING?

Recently a computer analyst with nine years' service resigned from a company in the financial services field called Credit Lyonnais Rouse, London, after being at the receiving end of public abuse from the financial director. Apparently, the financial director swore at him in an open-plan office for allowing an old printer to remain on a filing cabinet in contravention of company rules. The case was brought to the Industrial Tribunal which heard evidence from the financial director that he was unrepentant, claiming that he gave the analyst 'a severe, well-merited and public reprimand'. From this statement one can conclude that the financial director's behaviour was not an unexpected aberration but part of his management style.

The Chairman of the Industrial Tribunal rebuked the financial director, saying that he neither apologized or sought to make amends for his discourteous behaviour. The computer analyst was awarded £11,000 for 'constructive dismissal'.

(Fursland, 1995).

---

of several projects at one time – would be needed by successful managers in the future. It may be helpful for women's prospects if organizations begin to value such skills.

A comparatively recent perspective on managerial leadership, e.g. transformational leadership (Bass, 1990), seems to be compatible with an HRM outlook on organizational life. This type of leadership is executed in a way that empowers and respects people. Leaders are expected to display charisma and influence their followers to share their inspiring visions of future accomplishments. In the process leaders will be supportive and keen to encourage those subjected to their influence to be entrepreneurial in outlook and bold in seizing opportunities to exploit their talent and make innovative contributions (McKenna, 1994).

Cynics might suggest that the rhetoric of progressive management practices belies the reality in today's world characterized by delayering and downsizing or rightsizing, in which job insecurity, occupational stress and poor morale are not difficult to find. Therefore, it is not surprising that at times managers are prone to outbursts that one would not normally associate with a more humane management style.

Trade union representation

Workers are often represented by trade unions in negotiations with management about pay and conditions, in which case both parties enter into collective bargaining. Throughout the 1980s a number of changes

Table 9.1 Relations between the parties

Consultation	Negotiation
The views of the trade union are invited by management	Both sides have a right to make an input to the decision
The decision remains within the managerial prerogative	An agreed outcome has to be reached
The decision may or may not take on board the trade union view	The decision is a bargain between the two positions

occurred in the United Kingdom which affected the nature of the interaction between management and unions, and also we have witnessed the emergence of the new industrial relations.

Relations between the parties can be characterized as either consultation or negotiation as shown in Table 9.1. The union may be involved in joint consultative committees, or negotiation may be conducted through collective bargaining which can only take place where the union has been recognized by management as a legitimate representative of the company's employees. Negotiation can take place in a single organization, or on a wider scale, when, for example, a union can represent workers doing similar jobs in different organizations in the public sector. HRM has been associated with a move towards local level bargaining. This is partly because centralized bargaining (e.g. where pay rates and conditions are centrally determined without reference to local conditions) was seen as time-consuming, but it also reflects the changing relations between management and unions. Collective bargaining can cover a range of issues relating to the terms and conditions of the employment relationship. These include pay levels and systems, gradings, hours, holidays, working conditions and job content.

A series of factors has contributed to changes in the industrial relations scene during the 1980s. There has been a decline in manufacturing industry, high unemployment and an increase in the number of part-time workers. These factors have affected the level of trade union membership which fell from 55.4 per cent of the work-force in 1979 to below 40 per cent in 1992 (Marsh and Cox, 1992). Various pieces of legislation have been enacted which has acted against traditional union activity. A secret ballot is now required before industrial action can take place, and secondary action (in support of other workers not employed by the same employer) is no longer allowed.

'Closed shops', where all employees are required to join a particular union, are no longer enforceable, and the way of handling those who take industrial action has changed. Prior to the new legislation, strikers could be dismissed (as they were considered to have broken the contract to supply their labour in return for remuneration), but everyone striking would have to be dismissed. Individuals could not be singled out; and if one or more strikers were re-employed, the others could lodge a complaint with an industrial tribunal. Under the new legislation it is now permissible to dismiss strikers and to re-employ them selectively after a break of three months. These changes have limited the power of the unions and changed the nature of industrial relations.

In the new industrial relations scene, management has greater power to impose its will without negotiation or the need to enter into joint consultation. Trade unions, which in the past were opposed to management initiatives, such as increased flexibility and reductions in demarcation lines between jobs, have become less confrontational. Recently, the Trades Union Congress (TUC) in the United Kingdom formed the view that properly practised 'soft' HRM is not incompatible with unionism (Monks, 1994). Increasing employee involvement, good communications and treating employees as valued assets rather than factors of production are developments supported by the TUC. An analysis of the 'Workplace Industrial Relations Survey 3' (Monks, 1994) found no correlation between HRM and anti-unionism. It was found that the more anti-union the employer, the less likely the employer was to pursue HRM techniques.

HRM can view unions as a positive factor, assisting in the process of communicating with and involving employees. In some cases this attitude has resulted in single union deals. Single union agreements are those where sole negotiating rights are granted to one union. They are particularly prevalent in companies who set up operations on greenfield sites, and in Japanese-owned organizations. In these situations consultation may be carried out through 'company councils' where the employees' representatives are elected by the work-force rather than appointed by the trade union, although there may be some degree of compromise on this arrangement.

Another feature of the new industrial relations are 'no strike agreements'. Normally these have an automatic referral to an independent arbitrator built into the negotiation procedures where there is a failure to reach an internal agreement. The arbitration is often of the 'pendulum' form, which means that rather than the arbitrator making a compromise decision, a choice is made between the last offer of the employer and the last claim of the union. Because of the normal obligation of the union not to take industrial action while the procedures are in progress, this means that in effect there is an agreement not to strike. However, unconstitutional industrial action may still occur.

Single union and no strike agreements represent a more cooperative approach from unions, and in some cases this is reciprocated by positive

HRM practices. For example, in Lucas Flight Control Systems (United Kingdom), the union (Amalgamated Engineering and Electrical Union (AEEU)) has agreed with management an extensive programme of reorganization, including increases in teamworking and skill flexibility, on the understanding that employment conditions for blue and white collar workers will be harmonized, and that the working week will be shorter, with no loss of pay.

However, with the change in the power relations between management and the trade unions, some organizations have sought to impose the managerial prerogative which has produced a negative effect for workers. For example, in the printing industry there has been a decline in collective bargaining, a de-recognition of unions and the imposition of 'individual' contracts.

Conflict

Conflict in organizations can occur at the collective level (i.e. organized) or the individual level (i.e. unorganized). Collective conflict can lead to industrial action including strikes, go-slows and overtime bans. Individual conflict may manifest itself as absenteeism, a high turnover rate or even sabotage. Any of these actions or outcomes is potentially damaging for the organization, so it is necessary to use methods for resolving conflict at the earliest opportunity.

Collective conflict may occur when there has been a breakdown in collective bargaining, as, for example, in a dispute about pay levels. Disputes can also arise when there is opposition to changes in working patterns and jobs. At one time the trade unions in the United Kingdom were accused of creating the 'British disease', a high level of strike action. However, in recent years the number of days lost due to industrial stoppages in the United Kingdom is not worse than those of its main competitors. In fact the figures have been gradually falling throughout the 1980s with one or two exceptions (such as the miners' strike in the mid-1980s).

The United Kingdom was placed seventh among the twelve EU member states in terms of production days lost due to strikes (Wassell, 1993). Spain, Greece, Italy, Ireland, France and Portugal had a worse record. In a 'militancy ranking' – based on the number of working days lost, the number of reported strikes and the number of workers involved in disputes – the United Kingdom was rated fifth out of twelve EU members (Sparrow and Hiltrop, 1994). While the recent trend with respect to industrial stoppages gives ground for optimism, it would be foolish to conclude that the British are experiencing relatively high levels of work-place harmony. It may be that workers are hesitant to take industrial action for reasons connected with the economic situation and the fear of losing their jobs.

Where it is not possible for management and the representatives of the workers to resolve their conflict, a third party could be invited to intervene. A third party could perform any one of three roles, i.e. conciliator, mediator and arbitrator. A conciliator acts as a facilitator when the main parties are trying to resolve the conflict. A mediator also acts as a facilitator, but in addition puts forward recommendations. An arbitrator actually makes decisions to resolve the conflict.

In cases of individual conflict, as opposed to collective conflict, an employee can make a grievance claim where there is a feeling that he or she has been treated unfairly, or in an unacceptable manner. The UK grievance procedure, which does not have formal legal status and was more prevalent in the pre-enterprise culture, allows the individual to complain to the immediate superior (e.g. the supervisor) in the first instance. If the matter cannot be resolved then, the complaint will be heard by the next level of management (e.g. the departmental manager). A union or other representative of the employee may become involved at this stage. The case will be heard and evidence may also be called, for example, the views of witnesses to an incident which sparked the complaint. The alleged culprit will also be given the chance to submit his or her version of events. The outcome of the process may involve practical ways of dealing with the problem, or alternatively disciplinary procedures may follow. In exceptional cases a third party may be asked to intervene. Normally there is a right of appeal to a higher authority if the complainant is still dissatisfied after exhausting the procedure.

There are occasions where an employer institutes a disciplinary measure because of a belief that the employee is failing to carry out his or her duties adequately, or is behaving in an unacceptable way. Where discipline takes the form of terminating the employment of the individual, one may ask if the dismissal of the employee was fair. The UK Employment Protection (Consolidation) Act (1978) states that the employees (with more than two years' continuous service) cannot be unfairly dismissed. If a complaint relating to unfair dismissal is made, the employer has to show that the dismissal was fair by proving that the principal reason for dismissal was one of the following:

1. Lack of capability or qualification to do the job.
2. Unacceptable conduct of the employee.
3. Redundancy (the job has disappeared).
4. Legal restraint (e.g. an employee works as a truck driver but is disqualified from driving).
5. Another substantial reason (e.g. the employee's spouse sets up a rival company).

In addition, employers must be seen to have acted 'reasonably'. This means that they followed the appropriate set of procedures. The Advisory, Conciliatory and Arbitration Service (ACAS) has a model disciplinary procedure which is adopted by many organizations.

The purpose of the procedure is to provide a breathing space for the employee whose performance or behaviour has fallen short of acceptable standards so that the necessary improvement can be made. Certain principles underlie the procedure. These include that the employee will be given full information, and that careful investigation will take place before any disciplinary action is taken.

Before the formal procedure is invoked, particularly where the fault is a minor one, the option of dealing with the problem informally should be explored. This might take the form of a counselling session. However, where it is necessary to use the formal procedure, the employee (accompanied by a friend or representative where appropriate) should be given the opportunity to put his or her side of the case at a forum which sits at a time to be arranged between each of the stages listed below. The stages of the ACAS procedure are as follows:

1. *Oral warning*. A note of this is kept on the employee's file.
2. *Written warning*. This is activated where there is repetition of the offence following an oral warning, or where the offence is more serious.
3. *Final written warning or disciplinary suspension*. For repeated misconduct where previous warnings have not been effective. A serious alternative is suspension without pay of up to five days.
4. *Dismissal*. Where the employee has failed to comply with the requirements of the final written warning.
   For *gross misconduct*, where the offence is very serious (e.g. theft, fraud, fighting, serious negligence), following an investigation the employee may be dismissed without going through stages 1–3.

The employee will normally have the right to appeal against the decision at each stage of the procedure.

Apart from unfair dismissal which is applicable to cases where the individual has been employed by the company for at least two years, there is wrongful dismissal. An employee with less than two years' service can exercise a 'common law' right to sue the employer for damages if dismissed wrongly. A case of wrongful dismissal arises when, for example, the employer has not given proper notice, or the behaviour of the employee did not justify such treatment. A case of unfair dismissal would be heard before an Industrial Tribunal. However, a case of wrongful dismissal would be referred to an ordinary court where the damages awarded could be higher than the maximum stipulated by the Industrial

Tribunals. Always remember that dismissal has to take place before a tribunal or court can act.

When we reflect on the role of grievance procedures and the use of discipline, our concern should be to solve a problem and make matters better, and not to be totally preoccupied with the administering of punishment. For example, there is a problem where an employee is persistently late for work. Our aim should be to discover the causes of this behaviour (e.g. lack of motivation, difficult domestic circumstances, travel difficulties, a personal problem), and then to help the employee confront and hopefully remove the underlying cause(s), rather than just dealing with the symptom.

Handling conflict in an organization is facilitated by the rules and procedures in place. However, we cannot overlook the part played by management style and organizational culture. An aim of HRM is to create a culture in which employees are committed to the goals of the organization. Where this prevails and is reflected in, for example, increased employee participation, a situation can emerge where employees become more involved in their own 'discipline' (Edwards, 1994). If employees are working in a team, they are not only carrying out the tasks allocated to them but are also interacting with others. In the course of interaction, approved behaviour is likely to be supported, while deviant behaviour could be subjected to sanctions (group discipline). If the team is committed to a goal of achieving high quality work, it is likely to reward team members whose performance meets the requisite standards.

Health and safety at work

Devoting a short section to health and safety is in no way meant to condone its relatively low position in the pecking order of HRM topics. It is recognized that the health, safety and welfare function within the organization has been very much the 'Cinderella' of HRM despite the enormous human and economic benefits that can flow from a well-conceived and properly implemented health and safety policy within a company. Under the UK Health and Safety at Work etc. Act (1974) employers have a duty to ensure (so far as is reasonably practicable) that they provide a safe and healthy environment both for their direct employees and for other people (including contractors) who may be affected by the work activities. This means that employers are responsible for the following:

☐ Providing safe equipment for the job and ensuring that it is used in accordance with correct procedures.

□ Making sure that employees do not undertake dangerous activities.

□ Checking that all the procedures involved in jobs are safe.

□ Providing a safe and healthy environment in which to work (including adequate light, heat and ventilation).

Employees are required to comply with the employer's reasonable instructions with regard to health and safety. So, for example, if instructed to wear safety goggles, or to ensure that a guard is fitted when operating a machine, they are expected to comply.

The Management of Health and Safety at Work Regulations (1992) were enacted to implement the European Commission directive on health and safety. Employers are required to perform the following tasks:

□ To carry out assessment of hazards and risks and surveillance.

□ To plan and monitor preventative measures.

□ To make sure that employees have adequate information.

□ To provide necessary training.

Directives have also been implemented on limiting the manual handling of loads, use of computer (display screen) equipment and the provision of personal protective equipment. A legitimate concern of health and safety practitioners, in association with appropriate HRM specialists, could be the provision of counselling and other services to those who succumb to stressful conditions at work often brought about by a climate of profound change. Such action could lead to people being able to cope better with the demands made on them and could have a beneficial effect on absenteeism and staff turnover.

Traditionally managers have confined their attention to health and safety issues within the workplace, reacting to problems as they arise. Nowadays a number of employers have decided to adopt a more proactive stance in health care. This often takes the form of fitness and health screening schemes designed to change the lifestyle of employees inside and outside the organization (see Box 9.3).

The field of health and safety at work is well provided with regulations and directives with the noble intention to create greater safety awareness and to protect people from hazards in the work-place. Nevertheless, accidents do happen and frequently the cause is human error. Where this is the case, the human element in the man–machine system at work is found to be wanting. Mindful of the prominence given to accidents and mental health in the UK Government White Paper 'Health of the Nation' in 1992, Glendon and McKenna (1995) have attempted to mobilize applied psychology within an HRM framework to shed light on the human factors in safety and risk management.

Box 9.3

HEALTH CARE AT UNIPART

Recently Unipart in the UK spent £1 million on preventative health care for its 2,500 employees, and opened a £500,000 extension to its on-site sports facilities which include squash courts, an aerobotics studio and a centre for alternative health therapies. The facilities, known as the Lean Machine, compare very favourably with the best of the private health clubs.

Unipart's approach to revolutionizing occupational health is seen as a way to combat stress while staying ahead of the competition. According to Unipart's Chief Executive, the rapid pace of change means that employees are facing more and more stress which can have damaging consequences. In the 'Lean Machine' employees have the opportunity to get fit so that they can cope with stress. Also, they receive treatment to deal with some of the problems created by stress, and learn to avoid problems and manage stress through the medium of exercise and therapies.

(Wolfe, 1995).

Conclusions

The emergence of the new industrial relations and HRM is reflected in an increase in the amount of direct communication and an elevation of the status of individualism as seen in the importance given to individually based performance-related pay which tends to replace collectively negotiated pay settlements. These changes, and falling membership, have meant that a response was needed from the trade unions. One type of response which is likely to be on the increase is the merger of unions to form 'super unions' e.g. the creation of Unison in the public sector. The new industrial relations has also seen a more cooperative stance on the part of the trade unions.

The influence of the EU is likely to increase pressure for consultative forums with employees, involving elected members of the work-force rather than trade union-appointed representatives. However, the tradition of management/union relations is not being eradicated. It has been found that although organizations are increasing the amount of direct communication with employees and offering them greater opportunity to engage in participative processes, these developments are taking place within a framework called 'dual arrangements' i.e. alongside existing trade union institutions and procedures (Storey, 1992).

New flexible and delayered structures, coupled with environments of constant change, call for care and sensitivity in the way conflict is managed, and signal the need to create participative forums to elicit mutual benefits for the work-force and the organization.

References

Bass, B. M. (1990) 'From transactional to transformational leadership', *Organizational Dynamics*, **18**, 19–31.

Bassett, P. (1995) 'No escape from the worker councils', *The Times*, (Business News), 2 March, p. 32.

Beer, M., Spector, B., Lawrence, P., Mills, Q. and Walton, R. (1984) *Managing Human Assets*. New York: Free Press.

Bright, D. (1993) 'Industrial relation, employment relations and strategic human resource management' in Harrison, R. (ed.), *Human Resource Management Issues and Strategies*. Wokingham: Addison-Wesley.

Edwards, P. (1994) 'Discipline and the creation of order', in Sisson, K. (ed.), *Personnel Management*, 2nd edn. Oxford: Blackwell.

Fursland, E. (1995) 'No place for the bully', *The Times* (Section 3), 12 January, p. 20.

Geary, J. F. (1994) 'Task participation: employees' participation enabled or constrained?', in Sisson, K. (ed.), *Personnel Management*, 2nd edn. Oxford: Blackwell.

Glendon, A. I. and McKenna, E. F. (1995) *Human Safety and Risk Management*. London: Chapman and Hall.

Guest, D. and Hoque, K. (1994) 'The good, the bad and the ugly: employment relations in new non-union workplaces', *Human Resource Management Journal*, **5**, 1–14.

Holden, L. (1994) 'Employee involvement', in Beardwell, I. and Holden, L. (eds.), *Human Resource Management: A contemporary perspective*. London: Pitman.

Institute of Management (1994) *Management Development to the Millennium*. Institute of Management.

McKenna, E. F. (1994) *Business Psychology and Organizational Behaviour*. Hove: Lawrence Erlbaum Associates, Publishers.

Marchington, M. (1987) 'Employee participation', in Towers, B. (ed.), *A Handbook of Industrial Relations Practice*. London: Kogan Page.

Marsh, A. and Cox, B. (1992) *The Trade Union Movement in the UK 1992*. Oxford: Malthouse.

Millward, N., Stevens, M., Smart, D. and Hawes, W. R. (1992) *Workplace Industrial Relations in Transition*. Aldershot: Dartmouth Press.

Monks, J. (1994) 'The union response to HRM: fraud or opportunity?', *Personnel Management*, **September**, 42–47.

Sparrow, P. and Hiltrop, J. M. (1994) *European Human Resource Management in Transition*. Hemel Hempstead: Prentice Hall.

Storey, J. (1992) *Developments in the Management of Human Resources*. Oxford: Blackwell.

Wassell (1993) 'Job cutters axe chips away at power of labour', *The European* (Business News), 21 October, pp. 40–41.

Wolfe, R. (1995) 'Healthy workers, healthy office', *Financial Times*, 27 January, p. 13.

10

Conclusion: criticisms and developments

We have now reached the stage where it would be productive to examine briefly the criticisms levelled at HRM and to take note of developments likely to shape its future.

Criticisms

HRM has attracted a considerable amount of critical comment and analysis. There has been criticism of both theory and practice.

Criticism of theory

There are inputs to the theoretical basis of HRM from academic disciplines such as sociology and psychology, but there is a view that HRM is not a coherent body of thought with predictive qualities that can be tested in a scientific way (Noon, 1992). In HRM there is no one accepted body of theory. HRM takes on different manifestations in different situations, and some of the aspects of it can contradict each other (Legge, 1989). For example, elements of hard HRM such as performance appraisal linked to performance-related pay do not fit easily with the elements of soft HRM such as developmental and facilitating managerial behaviour. It is not just a matter of the different elements not fitting together in practice; it is that they are driven by different theoretical approaches. The set of assumptions about how people are motivated and managed under hard HRM is opposed to the set of assumptions governing motivation and management embedded in soft HRM. Such contradictions may arise in established subject areas, but they become the subject of intense debate. HRM seems to tolerate their presence, and some would argue that this points to a lack of rigour in the subject.

It has been suggested that HRM is merely a form of rhetoric which does not have a substantial theory behind it (Keenoy and Anthony, 1992). New phrases such as performance-related pay, the enterprise culture and so on do not represent new ideas about practice. It is said that the game plan is not the introduction of rigorously tested concepts, but a ploy to solidify management control in organizations.

Criticisms of practice

Research has indicated that, apart from a few cases, the uptake of HRM practice has been fragmented and partial (Storey and Sisson, 1993). Organizations may increase their efforts to improve communication with the work-force, but will not necessarily increase genuine employee involvement in decision making. Similarly, while there has been uptake of performance-related pay, soft HRM approaches to employee development are yet to be commonplace (Keep, 1992).

It has also been argued that where elements of HRM have been adopted, the result has been negative rather than positive (Fernie et al., 1994). It was reported that the climate of employee relations at the work-place was slightly worse in organizations where HRM had a significant presence. However, this finding has itself been criticized on methodological grounds. (MacLachlan, 1994) For example, it is possible that one group of respondents – HRM specialists – had a more refined understanding of employee relations at the work-place and could see problems more clearly. This perspective would come across in their response whereas the non-specialist HRM person lacking subtlety in perception in matters of this nature reported that relations were good.

Other criticisms have centred around the effects of HRM practice. A difficulty is that while HRM espouses valuing employees, there are aspects of HRM which have the effect of devaluing employees. With regard to the adoption of flexibility, the 'peripheral' work-force suffers instability and uncertain conditions of employment (Pollert, 1988). The management of culture can be seen as an attempt to manipulate the attitudes and activities of employees (Willmott, 1993). Similarly, the adoption of customer-centred quality approaches can be seen as another managerial strategy to control the behaviour of the work-force through imposing new constraints and requirements (du Gay and Salaman, 1992).

Developments in HRM

HRM arose in a set of environmental conditions which included increases in competition, changes in technology and a series of economic recessions. HRM placed an emphasis on flexibility, high standards of performance and the development of employees so that the organization can survive and flourish. As environmental conditions continue to impact on the organization, we can expect to see HRM developing.

The requirement for flexibility and speed of response to market changes is likely to continue to increase. This has implications for the practice of HRM. If increases in flexibility create an increase in the peripheral work-force, the result may be that they are relatively untrained and deskilled, since most organizations are reluctant to invest in peripheral workers. If this is allowed to happen, it will be difficult for flexible workers to be creative and to make a positive contribution to the organization. There is a need, therefore, for HRM to be involved in seeking a way to invest in the flexible work-force and to ensure that its members have sufficient security.

European Union legislation may have an impact on the management of employee relations. In particular, there may be a push to increase employee involvement in decision making, and curbs could be placed on the power of management through health, safety and social legislation. In order to deal with these changes, HRM will need to be proactive and to establish effective systems of communication and employee involvement.

Many organizations have adopted quality approaches, and a customer orientation. This is increasing in the public sector which has been adopting aspects of HRM.

As the 1990s progress, organizations are beginning to seek different ways of working. After the propensity for greed which was in evidence in the 1980s, with the emphasis on self, gain and competition, the 1990s has seen pressures for organizations to act in an ethical way. Pressures have included consumers becoming more environmentally aware and exerting influence on both political parties and companies to think carefully about the effect of their policies and practices on the environment.

Some organizations are entering into network arrangements where they link with others who may be their suppliers or their customers. Agreements are made in which a guarantee of continuing relations between the companies is made, and the emphasis is on a high level of trust. In some cases companies have had an open approach to their accounts so that other members in the network will know the financial details and implications of the deal. This is felt to be an effective way of operating, rather than trying to act competitively and maximize profit at every transaction. It should be pointed out, however, that some companies are not yet ready for this type of cooperation and collaboration.

Increases in trust and a concern for a wider range of stakeholders, such as the local community and those affected by changes in the physical environment, are associated with an ethical approach to the management of people. The concern is to promote employee development, family-friendly organizations and flexibility of conditions which accommodate employees' needs as far as is possible.

References

du Gay, P. and Salaman, G. (1992) 'The culture of the customer', *Journal of Management Studies*, **29**, 615–633.

Fernie, S., Metcalf, D. and Woodland, S. (1994) *Does HRM Boost Employee–Management Relations?* Working Paper no. 548. Centre for Economic Performance and Industrial Relations Department, London School of Economics: London.

Keenoy, T. and Anthony, P. (1992) 'HRM: metaphor, meaning and morality', in Blyton, P. and Turnbull, P. (eds.), *Reassessing Human Resource Management*. London: Sage.

Keep, E. (1992) 'Corporate training strategies: the vital component?', in Salaman, G. (ed.), *Human Resource Strategies*. London: Sage.

Legge, K. (1989) 'Human resource management: a critical analysis', in Storey, J. (ed.), *New Perspectives on Human Resource Management*. London: Routledge.

MacLachlan, R. (1994) 'Robust research – or just headline-seeking analysis?', *Personnel Management Plus*, **June**, 9.

Noon, M. (1992) 'HRM: a map, model or theory?', in Blyton, P. and Turnbull, P. (eds.), *Reassessing Human Resource Management*. London: Sage.

Pollert, A. (1988) 'The flexible firm: fixation or fact?', *Work, Employment and Society*, **2**, 281–316.

Storey, J. and Sisson, K. (1993) *Managing Human Resources and Industrial Relations*. Buckingham: Open University Press.

Willmott, H. (1993) 'Strength is ignorance; slavery is freedom; managing culture in modern organisations', *Journal of Management Studies*, **30**, 515–552.

Author Index

Subject Index

action learning, 169–70
Advisory, Conciliatory and Arbitration
    Service (ACAS), 188
application form, 110
appraisal
    aims, 116–17
    development, 123–4
    evaluative, 120–2
    problems with, 124–6
    self, 119
    techniques, 117–20
assessment centres, 109–10
attitude surveys, 180
authority, 30
autonomous work groups, 43

benchmarking, 172
biodata, 110
Bowey Stability Index, 87–8
bureaucracy, 27–9, 35
Business Process Re-engineering, 66,
    72–4

cafeteria/flexible benefits, 143–7
career management, 165–6
centralization, 34, 39
change
    and competition, 159
    and culture, 62–74
    managing, 58–62
    reactions to, 55–8
coaching, 167
collective bargaining, 179, 187
commitment, 10–11

communication, 7, 16, 177–80
    barriers, 178
    effective, 177
competency, 162–3
conflict
    collective, 186–7
    individual, 187–9
consultation, 187
contingency theories of organization,
    36–41
contractual fringe, 46
core
    activities, 44
    workers, 46
corporate anorexia, 54
critical incidents, 117
culture, 14–17, 59, 187
    change initiatives, 66–74
    changing, 62–74
    and HRM, 74–5
    national, 51
    organizational, 52–4
    societal, 50
    strong, 16, 74–5
culture change
    initiatives, 66–74
    primary mechanisms, 63–4
    secondary mechanisms, 64–6
curriculum vitae, 102, 104, 110

decentralization, 34–5, 39
delayering, 44
demand for human resources, 79–82
demographic factors, 90–1

201